Flipping 2.0

Practical Strategies for Flipping Your Class

THE
Bretzmann
G

NEW B

T 26888

Flipping 2.0—Practical Strategies for Flipping Your Class

The Bretzmann Group, LLC
jbretzmann@bretzmanngroup.com
www.bretzmanngroup.com

Publisher: Jason Bretzmann
Copy and Layout Editor: Cory Peppler
Cover Designer: Kelly M. Kurtz

First Edition
ISBN: 0615824072
ISBN-13: 978-0615824079
Printed in the United States of America

Dedication

To my dad Gary for his love of the idea and content of books. To my mom Marlene who has always been proud of what I do.

To my wife Chris and my sons Jack and Cooper for supporting and encouraging this project, and every other project along the way. I love you all.

To those tireless, energizing, constantly-learning teachers who work hard every day to teach our kids. You hold their hands, push them, support them, challenge them, and encourage their growth in exactly the right proportion, exactly when they need you.

Jason Bretzmann

Contents

Part Two: Can Anybody Flip?

Part Three: Just for Teachers

Foreword

Flipped Learning is a vast ocean that is ripe for exploration and navigation. As the early sea explorers and cartographers explored uncharted waters, they returned with rough, undetailed maps that stood alone outside the broader context of the known world. Although most seafarers would not use these early maps because of their limited scope, others would use the maps to conduct their own exploration and return with an even better map.

I have been active in the Flipped Learning conversation for many years now and, hopefully, through my own exploratory efforts, have provided teachers with a rough map of the seas. Like the apprehensive seafarers, some have looked at my map and have been hesitant to embark because my map was too vague, contained under-developed components, and was designed for other Ed Tech explorers to study in order to modify and develop into their own, more detailed, maps.

Flipping 2.0 is the more detailed guide that many have been waiting for. These authors have taken my map, conducted their own exploration, and have returned with a detailed navigation manual for any teacher ready to embark on the Flipped Learning journey. Teachers who are ready to sail these waters will find detailed accounts of how many of their Flipped Learning predecessors set sail and found their way to a new and exciting world of educating their students. My map was Flipping 1.0, which proved that we can navigate the Flipped Learning seas. These teachers have developed Flipping 2.0, which lays the groundwork for using Flipped Learning as a means to colonize uncharted lands of learning.

I have met each of the contributing authors and have heard their stories of how Flipped Learning changed their own practice as educators. Although each author is different and has a unique story, each reader will be able to glean practical tips for implementation in any classroom from these unique perspectives. Undoubtedly, none of these authors became a better educator because they implemented

Flipped Learning, but rather, they were reflective educators who implemented Flipped Learning because they saw it as being useful to help meet the individual learning needs of their students.

You may dabble with Flipped Learning, you might never try it, and you might jump head first into the deep end of the pool. Regardless of what you ultimately implement in your classroom, I hope you orient your own teaching practice in such a way that learning is at the center of your practice.

Enjoy your journey!

Aaron Sams
August 2013
Pittsburgh, Pennsylvania

Introduction

Jason Bretzmann

Thank you for opening this book and reading this far. Keep reading! Your teaching, your career, and your students' education will change.

Flipclass won't solve every issue in education. No single way of teaching can. But how you think about what we do as educators, and what we want students to do will be transformed. This book seeks to help you and show you how to get to where you want to be. The hard work will be up to you and your students.

While each of us as authors is an expert on our own experiences, we don't claim to be the fount of all wisdom on flipped learning, education, or anything else for that matter. On the contrary, we see this book as a "How To" starting point. A place to get you started flipping your class, and to give you some concrete guidance along the way. A place to start the conversation—notice every author's contact information is included with each chapter so you can connect with all of us—to ask questions, refute assumptions, discuss ideas, think together, learn together, and maybe even debate the finer points of educating our nation's kids.

And this is a place that will hopefully get you moving toward Flipping 2.0.

Why do we call the book *Flipping 2.0*? There is no exact terminology about flipping your class. Even so, a lot of teachers refer to the first steps of flipping as Flipping 101. Putting lectures on video and doing "homework" in class is where a lot of flipping starts. The next step then is Flipping 2.0, described by some as a mastery model, a student-centered model, or even by (accurately) labeling it flipped learning. It is normally characterized by focusing on higher-level thinking as a goal, creating a more student-centered classroom, and determining the best use of face-to-face time with students. Many of the authors of this book include a short description or explanation of how they define flipping in their classrooms.

This book assumes you have decided to flip (although you'll notice that we can't resist trying to convince you here and there anyway). The book reinforces your good decision by adding to the argument. Then it gives you practical tools, strategies, activities, and ideas on how to start flipping. In some cases you might even ask yourself, "How is this flipping? It just sounds like good teaching." We're OK with that. Good teaching and student learning are our goals. Finally, this book shows you how you can move toward Flipping 2.0 as efficiently as possible. The movement is important. Maybe the journey is as important as the destination, and this book will help with both. So please start reading Chapter 1 now. Or read on for information that is not relevant to flipping, but an interesting story, nonetheless.

THE STORY OF THIS BOOK

This book started with smart, courageous people flipping their classes. Some alone. Some with support. Some despite obstacles and opposition.

These people shared their stories of successes and setbacks on Twitter (and other places). Because of their openness on Twitter, I had access to their insight. As I showed up each week at the #flipclass chat, I learned so much from these superstars. As I lurked, asked questions, and eventually shared my own ideas, I began to realize that so many teachers could benefit from their insights. The idea to create this book emerged because I wanted more people to have access to these smart people. I realized that it would have been very helpful to have someone tell me ways to flip my class when I started. So I asked a geographically diverse group of flippers from different disciplines and levels to write about their experiences in order to guide potential flippers on their journeys, and to describe what the destination looks like. The opportunity to give others access to some people who have been there and the opportunity to continue the conversation pushed the process forward.

I asked these educators to tell us what to do by telling us what they did. What follows is our best effort at giving you what you need to start flipping. This is what we did. Please take what you can use, and share the rest.

PART ONE:

Flipping the Core Content Areas

Mastery
Brian Bennett

I am a scientist and romanticist at heart. I love the process of science, but I also love the narrative that is embedded in its history. The process of science allows us to tell a story, which is what I'm going to do for you here.

I first flipped my class in 2010. I was a first-year chemistry teacher, and I was struggling to help my students form deeper connections with the content. They were also having a very hard time with problem solving skills that are necessary in science. I didn't have enough time in class to help *all* of my students, and that was the biggest problem for me.

The language of "flipped classrooms" has evolved since 2010 as a result of more teachers creating their own styles in their classrooms. Rather than talking about "flipped classrooms," I typically talk about Flipped Learning as a process, not as a procedure. Remember, this chapter is simply an explanation of the process that worked best for me and is not prescriptive. As you begin exploring Flipped Learning in your class, you may find that some things work while others fail miserably. Observe your own results. Make changes. Try again. Use this chapter as a guide and then find your own blend of tools and methods to fit your needs.

WHAT ARE YOUR NEEDS?

I needed a way to meet the needs of all of my students. I wanted to get rid of the "bell curve" expectation of teaching. I didn't want winners and losers; I wanted students who were able to think analytically through science. Flipped Learning helped me build a classroom environment which allowed me to accomplish those goals.

I say this because before you read any further, I want you to identify your goal. Why are you reading this book in the first place? By defining your problem at the beginning of the process, you will frame your decisions around *solving* that problem, and your plans will remain coherent. If you begin without having a defined focus, you'll struggle to connect the dots as you put your plans into practice. Go ahead and write your goal(s) into the margins as we start, so you can easily refer back to them.

TRANSITIONING TO MASTERY

Mastery Learning is hard to define. Some would argue that students have proved mastery when they reach a certain score on an assessment. While that works, we're really just changing the performance bar, and not moving the students to internalizing the learning. To me, mastery learning is giving the students an opportunity to both direct and defend their learning. For some, that might mean taking a traditional paper-and-pencil exam. For others, it could mean teaching a peer or giving a presentation to the class. Yet others might want to prove their learning through writing, performance, illustration, or some other medium. The point is that I am no longer *dictating* what learning looks like for my students. I direct and advise, but students are driving the bus.

I am a firm believer that mastery learning is the biggest disruption that can transform the traditional classroom. I watched it happen in my classroom.

Students have been conditioned to take information and regurgitate facts on tests. We all know that learning is much deeper than filling in facts. When I switched to Mastery learning, for the first time, my students were challenged to prove their understanding of the material. It was a major change from business-as-usual.

The first major change was the expectation of "watch videos before you come to school" evolving into "use your time to learn using any resource you want." I had to force myself to accept the fact that my timeline was not always the best one for students. I still set expectations to maintain the overall architecture of the curriculum, but the day-to-day activities of students were self-directed. This presented some interesting challenges.

I had to rethink my expectations about class time.
The biggest barrier to change was my preconception of what "good teaching" looks like. The feeling that I was missing something pushed me to think about how digital content can break down learning barriers that are in place because of the status quo.

Students had to rethink their expectations of class time.
I mentioned earlier that students have been conditioned to follow a particular pattern when in school. Mastery learning breaks that pattern at a fundamental level by requiring students to own their learning in a very real way. Assessment was constant, and they were not able to play the school game.

The teacher-student relationship needs to change.
Again, because of the system of schooling in place, teachers and students rarely have opportunities to experience rich collaboration together. Content becomes the undertone as students are pushed to own their learning and the teacher steps into a supporting role. Building the relationships can feel awkward, but becomes organic and incredibly rewarding as the year progresses.

Second, I had to improve dramatically in individualizing instruction for my students. Rather than approaching this top-down (as I would in direct instruction), I would wait until problems came up, and then differentiate. For one student, it would be procedure-based. For another, they would need an extra explanation about an abstract concept. In short, I adapted on the fly, when students needed me. I was able to meet every need in the room. Students felt empowered and supported, which led to more productive learning.

Finally, students were exposed to real expectations for time management. In the "real world," adults are rarely glued to a particular activity, without breaks, for an hour or even an hour and a half at a time, every day. We take breaks. We prioritize our obligations. We shift schedules to meet needs. Mastery learning allowed my students to get a taste of what responsible time management looks like. So, if they chose to finish a Spanish assignment in chemistry, that was fine. But, they had to allocate other time into their schedule to meet their requirements for my class. This was probably the biggest sticking point for students. Some would consistently procrastinate, but with my support, they developed as the year progressed, and problem spots diminished.

My light bulb moment came in my second year of pushing Mastery Learning. In 2011, I was teaching both Chemistry and Biology, and each group met for 50 minutes every day. I loved it because our time could be focused, and I could build relationships very quickly. I explained to my students what I was hoping to see as the year progressed, and they seemed to appreciate the change in pace.

I had a group of young ladies in my chemistry class that decided to push the envelope without realizing what they were doing. During class, they would often spend a short amount of time on their chemistry before moving to their Spanish work. I took notice pretty quickly that they didn't spend a whole lot of time on chemistry when they were in my room, and my initial reaction (like any teacher worth their salt) was to redirect them to the task at hand. These redirections turned into mini-battles, and I was beginning to think about taking a little more control, and just not allowing other classwork at all.

I'm very glad that I had mentors who taught me to slow down and really think about my decisions. I realized that the girls' decision to not work on chemistry during class wasn't because they didn't care, but because they didn't need the class time to succeed. In other words, their best use of the time they had together in chemistry was to work together on their Spanish, not do practice problems or projects they could do just as easily at home. This was my tipping point.

I quickly began wondering if I needed to dictate time. Now, for that particular group, they continued to meet my expectations and do well on required work. For other students, they needed to spend the time in class on chemistry to be successful. I realized that the best use of class time was to support learning, not dictate their work. If they needed help on chemistry, I was there. I also became a proofreader, math tutor, and support system in addition to my role as the science teacher. It was a major transition in my thinking about the type of environment I wanted to build and support.

Mastery learning is probably the hardest part to develop for any Flipped Learning environment. It took me nearly three years to have a system that worked well, and even then, there are changes I need to make. The important thing is accepting the fact that digital content should disrupt the way you approach teaching and learning. Once you embrace that idea, you can begin to make serious changes.

DETAILED CLASS STRUCTURE

Just like with everything we've talked about so far, class structures evolved as my students and I dealt with obstacles. Similar to the previous sections, I'll outline how things worked during that year, and then list out some of the major points after each section for quick review.

Year One—Quarter One

Use of video: My first year flipping was what you would typically think of: videos at home, homework and practice done during class. I did this because all of my students had internet access outside of school and it seemed like the best way to go. My students were diligent and generally stuck to the expectations of videos being done outside of class. Students were given note packets that they could use while watching the videos which helped to organize notes for the year.

Philosophy: I believed that the time spent outside of class to consume content was very important. That meant they could focus on chemistry the entire time they were in my class.

Grading: Students were graded on note completion as well as my old homework assignments. They were required to complete a list of assignments that I would grade and then return, just like a "traditional" classroom.

Pros:
- Students were familiar with class expectations (aside from video).
- Class time was more productive.

Cons:
- Paperwork increased dramatically.
- Students didn't have choices in their learning...I was still dictating the pace.

Year One—Quarter Two to End

Use of video: Rather than expecting videos would be done before coming to class, I shifted to benchmarks and specific learning objectives. Video could be completed when and where students were ready for the content, including class time. Students would often group together to watch note sections before moving on to labs or other practice and/or assessment materials.

Philosophy: I moved to a Standards-based Grading model at this point. Students would have learning objectives (ex: Explain and apply the appropriate gas laws as you observe a balloon in different environments) that could be met in whatever format they chose. Some would elect a written quiz and others would choose their own assessment method. *Choice* and *autonomy* became more important to me than my prescriptive measures.

Grading: Grading was done based on their performance with objectives. It was a simple "yes" or "no" grade that we could agree on when they came to prove their skill. Students were *always* allowed to re-evaluate any objective they did not pass at the time of assessment up until the chapter test. Once students earned a "yes," they kept it, understanding that they were still responsible for that content.

I still had required assignments, like labs, which all students completed and were graded on. Labs, along with tests, were the only prescribed assignments I gave the rest of the year. Labs were completed on the same day to reduce my prep/cleanup time and to maintain a safe working environment.

Pros:
- Busywork was eliminated. Students would do enough practice until they felt ready for assessment.
- My paperwork/grading load was greatly reduced.
- Students showed ownership of their learning.
- Class time became much more collaborative.

Cons:
- Class time felt less focused to me.
- Procrastination was accentuated.
- Students needed to be taught how to manage time much more effectively.

Year Two

<u>Use of video</u>: Video was a resource this year in the sense that I did not require students to watch the notes for credit. I did this after reading Ramsey Musallam's and Frank Noschese's writings on modeling and inquiry in science instruction. For each unit of study, I worked to either find or develop problems and prompts that would drive the student's learning. Video became a reference and not a requirement. I still provided note pages for the students and many still used the videos for their own learning.

<u>Philosophy</u>: I continued my use of standards-based grading, in which students were scored based on their application of skills and not fact regurgitation. As I worked inquiry and Socratic discussion into class, the students were challenged in new ways. We spent a lot of time discussing ideas and asking questions. I kept this up all year, even though I didn't feel like I was serving their needs at times. In the end, though, I saw higher retention and more positive remarks on feedback forms than I had anticipated.

I also carried the flexible use of class time into Year Two. As long as students could meet expectations and deadlines, class time was a resource. It worked out to about four full days of chemistry for most students, with one "float" day for other learning. Students who didn't use their time well were often left working on their own because their group had moved on without them. I wrestled with this, but I allowed it because it seemed like a natural consequence of their time use. It also led to many valuable discussions about time management throughout the year. These incidents decreased as the year progressed.

<u>Grading</u>: This year, I rolled student self-evaluations into the grading scheme. Each time a student felt like he or she completed a learning objective, I would ask them to score themselves on a 1 (I barely know it) to 4 (I could teach someone else) scale. I would look at their mark, and then ask them to demonstrate their learning. This worked

well, and students, for the most part, were able to prove and evaluate their learning accurately.

As with the year prior, if a student was not satisfied with a mark they received, they would have an opportunity to go back to relearn, practice, and reassess their growth.

Pros:
- Student ownership of learning was high.
- Class time was adaptive to student needs.
- Students felt more confident in their learning because the stress of one-time performance was removed.
- Class time was collaborative and engaging.

Cons:
- Inquiry learning is very difficult for students to do well, especially if you're the only class expecting it.
- Procrastination was accentuated, and some students consistently struggled with time management.
- Grading was "fluffy," and sometimes became distracting to learning.

Year Three

Use of video: For Year Three, I decided to return to explicit reminders that videos would help the students learn. I did note checks for each section, and it helped set the tone for the year. As we progressed through the semester, I began to loosen up on video requirements because it had become part of the learning culture of the class. Videos were introductory and short (no more than six minutes at the longest, most between two and four minutes) and would end with a question or a prompt to be followed-up on in class. This helped strengthen the connection between the content and what we did with it together in the room.

Philosophy: I maintained standards-based grading, but I moved to a simpler format, following the example set forward by Frank Noschese on his blog. The grade they received for each objective also reflected what their next step would be (see below).

Inquiry was still a major part of the class, but it was found mostly in labs at the beginning of the year. I worked hard with my students on content-acquisition skills (how to find and evaluate content) so they were more prepared for harder inquiry activities later in the year.

Class days had specific completion goals, again, to help transition students into a fully autonomous learning environment. As the year progressed, the goals would lengthen into three-day goals, and eventually week-long completion goals. Class time was flexible, free to be used as the students needed. Some would watch videos during this time; others would use it to work in small groups on practice items or assessments.

All of this, of course, was to help students build their independent learning capabilities and move to a fully student-centered learning space.

Grading:
Rather than a four-point scale, I had a 0-1-2 grading scale. A "zero" meant I had not seen the assignment at all. A one-point assignment would be if a student turned in work, but did not demonstrate mastery. This assignment could be corrected and then resubmitted. A "two" meant the assignment was completed and they could move on to the next piece. As with years before, if a student scored a "two," they retained that score, with the understanding that they were still responsible for that content.

Aside from the SBG scale, I also had projects and labs for each chapter we went through. These would be graded based on rubrics or other scales that were communicated to students beforehand. Often, labs were inquiry-based, and they were graded mostly on thoroughness and the thought process the students went through rather than the content or the results of the lab.

Pros:
- The grading scale was easy for students to remember and act within.
- The transition time helped students learn new procedures and expectations.
- Inquiry labs made the content more accessible to students.
- Grading on process rather than content (for labs) helped remove the fear of failure and allowed students to focus on the task.

Cons:
- The transition period (moving from teacher-led to student-led) is difficult and takes a long time.
- Allowing more freedom gradually is frustrating to watch because of failures along the way.
- Time management skills are underdeveloped and often get in the way of learning early on.
- Students initially resist the transition of "power," as it were, recognizing that more responsibility meant higher expectations.

SETTING YOUR STAGE—MATERIALS

Technology Access

Any time you begin thinking about delivering content via the web, make sure your students have adequate access to technology. I have flipped science in Bring Your Own Technology (BYOT) schools, 1:1 schools, and schools that are somewhere in between the two. If your students cannot reliably access content outside of school, you will have to rethink how you use class time.

One way to find out if your students can access the internet outside of school is by being a little sneaky. I would usually ask my students at the beginning of the year how many of them had Facebook or Twitter accounts they checked regularly. If every hand in the room goes up, all of your students will be able to access content somewhere. If there are hands that don't go up, you need to probe a little bit more.

You can still flip if internet access is an issue for a few students. Sometimes, I would send a USB drive home with video files they could watch on a computer. In other cases, we would work out arrangements for DVD's with content, but that wasn't as common. . *The point is you need to make sure your students can access materials if you're asking them to do so.* If they can't, then delivering content outside of class time might not be an option for you.

Just about every device can play videos. Again, depending on your access spectrum, you may need to share content in various places to make sure everyone can get to it in one way or another. I'll outline what I used and why later in the chapter.

Hardware for Creation

To create content, you might need some hardware. The good news is that digital media is extremely easy to create. We do it all the time without even thinking about it. If you're looking at purchasing some new hardware specifically for content creation, here are some things to consider:

Screencasting software can be hardware intensive.

You don't need a professional studio by any means, but in general, older computers will take a longer time to process videos than a newer one will.

Webcams can be handy.

From anecdotal feedback, students preferred videos with my webcam picture included. Think of it this way: you interact with students face-to-face in class. The webcam helps maintain that visual interaction remotely, which in turn translates to better interaction in class (this is also true in reverse).

Consider using apps for creation.

There are plenty of apps that allow for video creation. If you have an iPad, you can run a class from some simple white board apps. If you're on Android, you are a little more limited, but it can still work.

If you want to annotate live, you'll need an input device.

In other words, if you want to write on a PDF or PowerPoint like you would on a whiteboard in class, you'll need something called a "pen tablet." It hooks to your computer and uses a pen interface to help you write on the screen.

It may be useful to invest in a microphone.

Built-in computer microphones can vary from extremely poor to pretty good...unfortunately, it can be hit or miss. Sound is a very important piece of quality content, so you might want to research some kind of microphone to make sure your students understand what you're trying to communicate through speech. Headset microphones also work well for recording.

My hardware was collected over the last four years as I created more complex materials for outside work. I'm currently using a 15" MacBook Pro, an Intuos 5 Pen/Touch tablet, and a high quality USB microphone. However, when I started, I was using a school computer with PowerPoint slides and the built-in microphone.

The point is that you don't need to start with a full studio of equipment. As you're creating content, you may decide that you want to upgrade a portion of your tools. Or, you might be totally happy with what you have because it gets the job done. It depends on your personality and resources, but there is no best way to go about your hardware. The important things to remember are:

1. Your students need to be able to hear you clearly
2. Your students need to be able to see/read the important material.

For name brands, I recommend:
- Wacom pen tablets
- Logitech webcams/headset microphones
- Blue or Audio-Technica USB microphones

Software for Recording
Free Software
If we're honest, budget limitations will probably dictate what you are able to do at the beginning of this process. This section has some free recommendations for you to explore a little bit. However, I will say it is important to remember that "free" does not equal "best." You always get what you pay for with software. Personally, I don't use the free options at all because I've found value in some of the commercial offerings. This is a decision you'll need to make for yourself.

I've only included tools for video creation. There are many others for image or document creation, but you can explore those as you need them in your class.

Screenr.com (Free)—Screenr is a web-based screen recording system that lets you create five-minute videos. I like it because you can sign in with Google, Yahoo, Twitter, or Facebook, which means you have one less password to remember. All of your videos will be hosted under your account on Screenr, but you also have the option to send videos directly to YouTube, or download the files as an mp4.

Educreations (iPad, Free)–While I didn't use Educreations very much, it is nice to have a mobile platform for quick, off-the-cuff recording. I would use this when I gave further explanation to a student on a problem they were having. I could then post the video for the rest of the class to benefit from. Your videos can be saved to the Camera Roll on your iPad as well as shared and viewed on the Educreations website if your students don't have iPads.

Ask3 (iPad, Free)—Another app that I didn't use initially, Ask3 brings a whiteboard as well as collaboration to your quick content. While the content is stuck within the app right now (no sharing, not even to the Camera Roll), if you're 1:1 with your students, this is a must-have in my book. During the video, anyone can ask a text or video question that shows up on the timeline. The point is to get students asking and answering their peers rather than relying on the teacher.

Paid Software
Like I mentioned before, I mainly use programs that are paid. Now, these aren't yearly subscriptions or anything...they're all one-time, you-buy-it-you-keep-it tools. And remember, these are only recording tools at this point. I'll get into other apps/tools I use in the next section. Please also note that all prices are the educator's pricing (if available).

ScreenFlow (Mac, $99.99)—I began my desktop recording on ScreenFlow. As a native Mac app, it was easy to pick up and begin using immediately. You have unlimited recording time, including webcam recording, as well as a lot of editing power. You can save the videos as any file type you could want for uploading to YouTube, Vimeo, or other hosting site.

Camtasia (Mac/PC, varies)—I switched to Camtasia in my first year of flipping because of the interactive functions offered on the platform. You can include quiz overlays on your content as well as clickable hotspots that can jump within the video (i.e. "Click here to skip this example") as well as out of the video to a webpage or document. The software is made by TechSmith and they offer education pricing on their website.

ExplainEverything (iPad, $2.99)—Another iPad app for quick creation, ExplainEverything is the most robust whiteboard app when it comes to creation. You can add images, documents, and other media right to the space as you are recording. You can also share the files in more ways including Facebook and direct email.

Coach's Eye (iOS/Android, $4.99)—Coach's Eye is another TechSmith tool which allows you to take a video on your mobile device and then use drawing tools to analyze that video. Think John Madden's yellow-line instant replay on Sunday afternoon football. It includes side-by-side video analysis and multiple sharing outputs, including YouTube and direct email. This is another great tool for filming demonstrations and then giving the talking points during a slow-mo replay for students to review later.

Recording
If it is a longer, pre-planned recording (i.e. a lesson), I use Camtasia to record, edit, and share. If it is a short, off-the-cuff recording (i.e. how to log into a service), I use Screenr to record and share. If I'm recording on the fly, I typically use ExplainEverything or Coach's Eye.

I don't record much on mobile, just because it wasn't really a large need for me. I would record basic ideas in advance, and then handle specific questions in class with the students who needed the help.

You've also probably noticed that there are no Android apps listed for recording. Unfortunately, due to hardware limitations, Android does not have the capability to record screencasts at this time.

Other Software for Creation
In addition to the software already mentioned, I do use some other applications frequently in my teaching. The following descriptions also include comparable tools, most of which I have *not* used.

Sketchbook Express—This is a free white board app for Mac, PC, and iPad that is more robust than most others. It has multiple drawing tools and colors, and works very well if you have a pen tablet (see Hardware section) for diagramming on blank white spaces. I typically use this for quick Snagit videos or for putting a homework answer key out. There is also a Pro version with even more tools included.
> *Compare with: ScribbleScreen, NotateIt, Open Sankore*

Formulate Pro—FormulatePro is a free PDF editor for Mac. It allows you to open any PDF file and use a pen tool to write on top of it. I use this for fill-in-the-blank style notes during lessons. My students have an exact copy that they fill out for their notes. I can then save the edited version for students who lost their packet or who have a scribe in their IEP.

Compare with: *Jarnal, Foxit Reader*

Audacity—This is a free audio studio for Mac and PC that allows recording and editing of audio only. Very powerful and constantly updated, this is by far one of the best tools for recording mp3 files. I do this when I'm recording discussions or other things happening in class that don't require video.

Compare with: *Soundation, Garage Band*

Prezi—Sometimes PowerPoint or PDF files are too boring. Prezi helps you create more dynamic presentations for your students that can serve as mind maps at the same time. Prezi also now allows you to record presentations right in their website.

Compare with: *Impress.js, SlideRocket, Google Presentations*

Do your homework

There are a *ton* of references you can look to when it comes to Mastery Learning in science. I developed this philosophy and methodology through trial and error and through open discussion with colleagues and friends. I modified and adapted as I came up against my own unique obstacles. Ramsey Musallam is another flipped science educator from whom I took examples, as he focused on inquiry and problem-based learning.

I want to encourage you (if you haven't yet) to do some research on Flipped Learning and Mastery Learning in science, especially focusing on your content area. What should happen in a flipped biology classroom is drastically different than what should happen in a flipped chemistry classroom; I should know, I taught both in the same year at one point. Find examples and learn from teachers through Twitter or reading their blogs. As you do this, begin framing your own philosophy based on their examples and modify as needed.

Brian E. Bennett is a former Chemistry teacher with experience in a variety of educational settings. He is currently the Academic Solutions Engineer at TechSmith, a software company in Okemos, Mich. When Brian isn't working, he likes to write on his blog, Educator, Learner, dabble with new ideas, and read. You can find him on Twitter, @bennettscience, or on his website, www.brianbennett.org.

English
Kate Baker

Up until 2012, I could not define or label my teaching style and classroom. In the fourteen years that I have taught 9-12 English, every day the desk arrangement would change to fit the various activities: students worked in groups, pairs, as individuals to complete tasks centered on the novel studied. Each day the activity would change. I rarely stood at the front of the room and my classroom was always noisy with students completing tasks. But in the spring of 2012, I connected with other teachers on Edmodo and Twitter and could put a name to the structure and design of my classroom. While the term "flipping" seems relatively new, for any teacher who has taught a student-centered, collaborative, inquiry, project-based, constructivist classroom, the principles of flipping are not new.

I apply the theories and philosophies of Bloom, Bandura, Vygotsky, Maslow, Gardner, and many, many others. I'm a proponent of critical thinking, cooperative learning, metacognition, blended learning, flipped learning...see a pattern? I'm a proponent of learning. As Plutarch wrote in *Moralia, On Listening to Lectures* 48C (LCL 1.256-25), "For the mind does not require filling like a bottle, but rather, like wood, it only requires kindling to create in it an impulse to think independently and an ardent desire for the truth," and while my students will attest that I fill up their binders and in-boxes with work, they will state that I do get them fired up when teaching literature.

This is the truth of the flipped classroom: students become stakeholders and active participants rather than passive buckets waiting to be filled. Flipping the English classroom focuses on the promotion of higher-level thinking skills and leveraging technology to facilitate the use of those skills as well as student responsibility and accountability during the class period. The focus is on formative assessment and the process of learning and improving skills, while still meeting summative objectives.

23

WORKING OUT THE WORKSHEET

I teach in a large regional district and for the first 14 years of my career, my students and I relied on worksheets for formative learning and preparation for summative assessments. But, in my defense, I will say that I spent time crafting my worksheets so that the content was organized and the learning scaffolded.

I designed worksheets using Word and was diligent in the use of space. The layout efficiently used one piece of paper two-sided. The worksheets had portability in mind: rather than lug textbooks and overflowing binders around the class, students carried one piece of paper to various locations for group work and stations. Not having class access to computers and prior to the BYOD revolution, the worksheets were a way to organize the lesson structure and give students a location to put information. The worksheets provided guidance and structure for the content. Since students were not allowed to write in school-issued books, having a place to compile information and react to the text was vital, and being able to keep the number of worksheets to a minimum helped students as well. To complement my beautifully designed worksheets, I taught engaging lessons and put on an entertaining show about concepts related to the literature studied, but over the years and with the increase use of technology in the classroom, my worksheets were not being used as I intended.

While I had the best of intentions with my beautifully crafted worksheets, the problem was that, having gone through ten years in a paper-based school system, the students became desensitized and too accustomed to flipping through worksheets as busy work. They were flying through my beautifully crafted worksheets and not dedicating the time to the learning process.

Whether worksheets were used for busy work or organizing information, the result was the same: *Flip flip flip flip flip flip flip, DONE!* Students *were supposed to use* the worksheets for organizing their thoughts about the material studied and then *were supposed to synthesize* the information on the worksheets for summative assessment on tests and projects. What the students *were supposed to be doing* was not being done.

In large classes, using worksheets is one of the easiest methods to keep student learning directed: the teacher (or publisher) has organized the content and all the students have to do is complete the work, but the problem is that the students become conditioned. No matter the intention of the teacher or publisher, the students become more focused on getting through the worksheet as quickly as possible instead of thinking about the process of learning. Now that the digital revolution is in full swing, I am constantly devising means for moving to a paperless and digital classroom that focuses on higher level thinking and collaboration so that the students stop flipping *through* the learning and focus on flipping *in* the learning process with new tools and training.

As an English teacher who has drowned in avalanches of paper and been unsuccessful in cauterizing the flow of red ink, flipping my classes with various digital tools has enabled me to be more efficient and focused on other aspects of the learning process. During class, I do not focus as much on delivery of information. Rather than lecturing in class, I provide other means for students to obtain information. Whether it is via screencasted videos or exploring the topic through guided and collaborative research, the students take ownership of acquiring the information needed to move up Bloom's Taxonomy. I focus on students' analysis and synthesis of information to showcase their understanding and application through tech tools and cooperative learning. As I become more paperless, I do not use the worksheets as much anymore, but instead use the information in my beautifully crafted worksheets and transform them to a digital format. Keep in mind, this involves more than just taking paper-based worksheets and uploading them to the web. While having students fill in answers on an online document can be a transition into the world of technology, the instructional activities need to evolve beyond just typing in responses.

If the instruction and classroom are well-designed, the teacher can just "push play" and let learning happen. Unfortunately, much of the design takes place behind the scenes and is not seen by others. Once the design is created, the teacher can reuse the design and tweak as needed. While I teach English, what I explain below can be adapted for any subject. Teaching skills are universal regardless of the content. Flipping is focused on moving responsibility and workload from the teacher to the student.

*"They walked in single file down the path, and even in the open, one
stayed behind the other..."*

- Of Mice and Men, John Steinbeck

Through literature, we explore themes of personal growth, morality, leadership, and decision-making. By examining the characters' choices in such stories as *Of Mice and Men* and *Romeo and Juliet* and by using a flipped approach, the students use the literature as a lens for their own lives and for mastery of skills.

I've never been satisfied to walk in step, in single file or follow well-manicured paths. On the top file cabinet drawer behind my desk there is taped a quote by Ralph Waldo Emerson: "Do not go where the path may lead, go instead where there is no path and leave a trail." I've always been one to blaze my own trail and strike out for new territory. This has been the mantra of my academic career. Learning is a journey, and not all can walk the same path with the same steps. How we see the path impacts our understanding of the journey.

OVERVIEW OF MY INSTRUCTION DESIGN

My 9th and 12th grade students engage in bursts of asynchronous learning from three days to two weeks depending on the unit. The students in each class are studying the same text, but the daily activities vary and the students control the pace within the framework I design. For example, on Mondays, we go over the objectives for the week and the activities that will enable students to meet those objectives. I organize everything on Edmodo, including links to resources, digital copies of paper handouts, quizzes, and small group discussions.

Once the tasks are organized, my role as the teacher evolves from being a deliverer of information to being a facilitator and mentor for each individual student. Using BYOD and school-provided netbooks, students access Edmodo and work in class completing the tasks. Tasks are scaffolded to align with Bloom's Taxonomy and build student understanding of the text. I circulate around the room monitoring students, guiding groups, answering questions, and providing individual help as needed. Homework is reserved for anything that does not get completed in class. When a student asks,

"Is the rest of this for homework?" My reply is always, "It is 'get it done' work—here, there, anywhere." Students do not need access to technology at home if they budget their time appropriately or go to the computer lab during study hall and after school, and my due dates are designed to account for extra time to access technology. By the end of week, we reconvene as a class and engage in whole-class tests or discussions wrapping up concepts covered that week.

The flip in the English classroom occurs not just in the structure of the class period, but also in how we view the texts studied. Relevancy is paramount. The most important thing in the flipped English classroom is not the book/text; it is the student's connection to the text. Consider: what can students learn about themselves and life from the text? Yes, students should be reading and writing about specifics in the literature studied, but when the approach to studying the literature is flipped, the opportunity for student interest and engagement is increased.

PICTURE THIS...

Prior to reading the novella, students practice visualization skills as I read aloud the opening description of *Of Mice and Men* and have the students draw what they hear. The setting is pastoral, picturesque, and their drawings reflect the description. I then have them listen as I read the description of the same clearing in Chapter 6. This time the language is darker and shows the harsh realities of nature. While the location did not change, the language and author's perspective influences their perception. For a digital assignment out of class and synthesizing the concept taught, students use their smartphones and digital cameras and take pictures of objects or places that demonstrate how a change in perspective influences perception. Students post their pictures to their small group in Edmodo and discuss their findings.

Steinbeck's realistic description of the Salinas Valley provides a frame for the characters, just as the classroom provides a frame and context for learning. The language and tone of the writing influences the reader's perception. Likewise, the context of the classroom influences learning. Are students disaffected or stagnated because they are sitting in single file forced to see one vantage point? Are they successful because they have conformed to the teacher's expectations? And what about the teacher? Is the teacher's instruction stagnated by the same conformity and compliance? I argue that by restructuring the classroom and teaching canonical texts in new ways, both teacher and student performance can be revitalized. The text hasn't changed, but by changing our perspective on the text, our perception of learning is dramatically improved.

The most obvious way to change one's perspective is to change the environment. Student desks aligned in rows with the focus to the front of the room allows only one perspective. Instead, arrange the furniture in the classroom to align with the focus of the activity and allow the classroom layout to be flexible. The setup of the room has to allow collaboration, interaction and ease of movement for teachers and students.

The layout of my classroom is flexible. I move desks into various configurations to align with where I want the students to focus. From standardized front facing rows to concentric circles for fishbowl discussions to long banquet style tables to medium-sized tabletop groups, the formation focuses the students on the task.

Ideally, I'd prefer to create learning zones with multiple configurations and tall lab-type tables with stools, but having to share my room with a non-flipping teacher, we compromised on the daily layout. Wanting a whole class focus with the capability for collaboration among students, the student desks are arranged in a modified horseshoe. The desks on the outside form a horseshoe, and the desks in the middle are close together in lines. This configuration is a successful compromise between having the focus at the front of the room, and still allowing for students to easily and quickly work together.

BEST LAID PLANS

Flipping the reading instruction for *Of Mice and Men* at the beginning of the school year, I use a blended approach with the books, 1:1, and BYOD, using various techniques to ease my students into flipped learning. Using a more traditional approach to start, I read aloud the entire first chapter, complete with my own interpretation of character voices. I want them listening, forming impressions, and getting to know George and Lennie. Once the reading is complete and we discuss George and Lennie's relationship, students complete reading checks and begin the process of close textual analysis by using various tools, including the dreaded worksheet.

Using a hybrid approach and as I phase out the worksheet, students fill out a scavenger hunt style worksheet for them to record their answers: I give them the page number and the item they are to find on the page. For example: "On page 2, locate an example of alliteration." We do this together as a whole class with students volunteering answers. To add a digital element, students use devices and post their answers to small groups in Edmodo or to the Padlet for that chapter.

To review their answers outside of class, students view a ten-minute screencast video I created modeling the process of close textual analysis identifying the answers within the text instead of telling them the answers on the worksheet. If they pay attention and listen, they can fill in the worksheet while viewing, pausing and rewinding as needed. Through the video, I am showing the students the answers without telling them the answers.

For reading the rest of the novella, students are given the following options:
- Read silently in class while wearing headphones and listening to a provided copy of the audiobook.
- Read together in a group, where each person in the group takes turns reading aloud.

Students then work cooperatively or independently following the same process I've modeled to complete the scavenger hunt worksheet for each chapter and again posting their answers online. I'd prefer the students to read a chapter a day and view the corresponding videos or resources, so what they don't accomplish in class is completed at home or study hall. When finished with each chapter, students demonstrate their understanding by taking reading check quizzes on Edmodo and reflecting on their reading using a Google Form.

The Edmodo quizzes can be taken at home, in class on a netbook or chromebook, or in the computer lab during study hall, and the Google Form can be completed on a personal device such as a smartphone prior to taking the quiz. The Google Form promotes reflective practice and metacognition. The quiz questions focus on understanding the plot, themes, and characters, as well as identifying literary devices within the text, and have between a 20-50 point value each. Students are allowed to use their resources, including worksheets and the internet, but students must complete the quiz in the prescribed time constraint: no more than 30 minutes per quiz. Quizzes can also be retaken as needed, but students must speak to me in person and request a retake. The conversation I have with the student is more valuable than a paper or form request for a retake, and I can refer to the student's Google Form reflection for information on why he/she failed the quiz.

Continuing with our theme of perspective influencing perspective, one flipped activity I use to solidify the students' understanding of close textual analysis and to conclude the study of Steinbeck is *CSI: Salinas* (bit.ly/flipping01). This activity can be used for any story where a crime is committed. Students act as crime scene investigators and "interview" characters and collect "physical" evidence found in the text. For *Of Mice and Men*, students role-play as Al Wilts, deputy sheriff of the town of Soledad, and investigate the deaths of Curley's wife and Lennie as depicted in the story. For each step of the investigation, students complete tasks on a Google Site I created to gather evidence from the novella to formulate and support an argument.

This project requires students to examine the story from various viewpoints and use textual evidence to support the perspective. Students begin by collecting witness statements from ALL characters mentioned in the story: The Boss, the various ranch hands and even the quickly-mentioned Girl in the Red Dress. Students need to consider what each character knows and how their viewpoint is different from the reader's perspective.

Students also need to examine the setting in various scenes to collect physical evidence to support their case. The evidence can't be disregarded or changed, but it can be used to support viewpoints. This piece of the project is very important for students to formulate their arguments because there are certain things they cannot get around. For example, (spoiler alert!) the cause of death for Lennie can't be changed. Students can't get around the location of the bullet wound and state that George was attacked by Lennie and shot him in a different spot. The self-defense angle for George will have to account for the ballistics evidence as shown in the story. Lennie never handles the luger so his fingerprints cannot suddenly appear on the gun.

Additionally, students can manipulate the crime scene. For example, Curley's Wife dies in the barn, but the defense team for Lennie could state that she fell from the hayloft and died as a result of her injuries. The prosecution could refute this claim with the physical evidence of hay, fibers, puppy fur, etc. found on Lennie's and Curley's Wife's clothing. We know from Crooks' statements that Curley's Wife is always in the barn, poking around where she shouldn't be and even threatens Crooks in Chapter 4. It is conceivable for the defense team that Curley's Wife was in the barn, wearing her little red mules, and met with an accidental death. The prosecution for Lennie's case should bring up the evidence of Curley's Wife's smeared make-up being on Lennie's hand (which readers know got there when he "reprimanded" her for yelling).

The point of this project is in the process and the ability to support the case. We've watched enough *CSI* and *Law & Order* to know about circumstantial evidence and proving reasonable doubt, and I've done week-long mock trials in class where students are assigned roles, but there are always those few students who don't get into character and invalidate the activity. I've changed this over the years to just a persuasive-argumentative assignment to preserve the integrity and prevent the three-ring circus. The objective is to have the students examine all of the   evidence and witness statements prior to selecting a case, so that students will realize the best argument instead of picking a side and trying to support it and then start over when they realize they don't have enough evidence to support their position.

Students type an outline for their case, and it is an individual grade assessing ability to follow directions, craft a legitimate argument and demonstrate understanding of outline format. Students peer edit each other's outlines using a provided checklist. The checklist includes about 25 items pertaining to outline format, research skills, and writing requirements. For each item, the student receives two points if he/she successfully accomplished the task, one point for an attempt, and no points for not doing the task. Add up the checklist and students receive a score out of 50 points for their typed outline.

For the BYOD component and to make up for not doing an actual mock-trial, students work in groups comprised of people with the same court case and position. Students create a digital portfolio of crime scene photographs, videos of witness' testimonies, and/or scenes from the mock trial. Students write the dialogue, dress in character, and record 1-2 minute clips and snap pictures that can be embedded in a Google Site or all pieced together in one movie using WeVideo. The link to the final group portfolio is posted on Edmodo, and, as part of their online participation grade, students comment on each of the group's portfolios. Students complete self-evaluation forms using a checklist (similar in design to the outline checklist) and OSU rubric. The Outstanding, Satisfactory, Unsatisfactory rubric is a nifty tool for holistic scoring of creative projects. If the group exceeded expectations and "wowed" the reader or audience, then they received 100%, Outstanding. If the group accomplished the task, but did not go above and beyond, they received 88%, B+, Satisfactory. If they did not meet expectations and did not perform satisfactorily or demonstrate proficiency, then the score was 75%, C, Unsatisfactory.

The *CSI: Salinas* project and reading Steinbeck's *Of Mice and Men* introduces students to the skills and process of my flipped classroom. They learn how to analyze a text, work cooperatively in groups, and use digital tools to enhance their learning, all of which will be used throughout the rest of the school year.

REVAMPING ROMEO & JULIET

While a hybrid approach is effective when teaching a novella like *Of Mice and Men*, using digital tools like Gobstopper and Librivox for flipped instruction of longer canonical texts makes my job much easier in managing a more complex text. And whereas Steinbeck begins our journey in the fall in the flipped classroom, Shakespeare concludes it in the spring.

Prior to using Gobstopper, students would read the text of *Romeo and Juliet* on a Word doc I created (bit.ly/flipping02), with arrows and boxes pointing to what I wanted the students to know. Students would pick parts (a.k.a. me coercing students into volunteering).

We'd read together in class; I'd try to get students to act their parts, and stop every page and scene to go over the answers to the questions in the boxes, as well as explain to them the nuances and artistry of the language. While we got through the reading, it wasn't until I would show movie clips that students "got it" and understood the language. WHY? Because Shakespeare is meant to be performed, not read statically sitting in an uncomfortable student desk. Seeing the actors' movements solidified understanding.

While I would encourage students to act their parts out, what that really amounted to was them standing in the front of the room reading monotonously from the text. I was asking them to do too much at once: read, comprehend, and synthesize into a performance. I was cramming all of Bloom's taxonomy into the reading and taking too long to do so. By reading one act per week and with five acts in *R&J*, that amounts to five weeks of reading—in case you didn't know, the play is only two hours long.... five weeks vs. two hours: no wonder students couldn't remember the opening brawl scene when we finally got to end; we were reading slower than Friar John riding a donkey in the Zeffirelli version.

Flipping the reading of *Romeo and Juliet* using Gobstopper and Librivox, students read asynchronously in class similar to the method we used in the fall with *Of Mice and Men*. I signed out the mobile lab with headphones, and assigned students to read and listen to an act a day. Listening to the Librivox recording of actors reciting the lines with feeling and meaning (as well as correct pronunciation) helped students comprehend and understand the text while reading, and watching clips from the Zeffirelli version would further solidify their understanding. If a student had a question in class, I was able to speak to him/her one-on-one and address his/her concerns as needed. What was not finished in class was for homework. I reviewed the Gobstopper class report at the beginning of the next class and clarified any misunderstandings, then let them return to reading independently. This process was much more successful than demanding students to be compliant and pay attention as we read together. No longer did I hear complaints of "you're going too fast!" or "can't we just move on already?!" Now that the reading of the play took only a week, we had time for creative projects.

Allowing students to take creative ownership of the play and create their own context for the language, students chose group members and scenes to act out in front of the class. Having viewed excerpts from the Zeffirelli version of *R&J*, *Shakespeare in Love*, and the Baz Luhrmann adaptation, and having engaged in a class discussion about staging and creative license, students were allowed to stage the scene in any way they chose. Some used Google Translate to change the original Shakespearean language of the scene of the morning Romeo leaves for Mantua into urban slang (*"Yo, homey, that was the nightingale representin', not some lark..."*), others chose to reverse the gender roles of the balcony scene, and one group recast the opening brawl scene with *Sesame Street* characters, while another turned the ending of the play into a zombie apocalypse scenario. Since we separated the synthesis from the reading, students had a better understanding and appreciation of the play.

Paired with our study of *Romeo & Juliet* and providing a culminating project for my flipped class, my students also engage in a sonnet project and practice the skills from the school year. The sonnet project has three parts:

- Analyzing a chosen Elizabethan sonnet
- Memorizing and creative performing of the chosen sonnet
- Writing an original sonnet

The Sonnet Project is a culminating activity that forces students out of their comfort zones as individuals. Whereas we worked in groups through the school year, the sonnet project is completely independent. They may ask for help and feedback from others during the creation process, but the performance is completely independent. Students are assessed using a requirements checklist and the OSU rubric.

Students demonstrate that they can analyze the complex text of the sonnet by typing up an essay or recording a screencast of themselves speaking and working through the text. Students demonstrate memorization, creativity, and speaking skills by either reciting the sonnet live in front of the class or creating a video of themselves acting out the sonnet. To earn an Outstanding for their performance, the student must do more than just stand still and recite the poem. Movement, props, costume, and other special effects show the students' ingenuity and creativity. The original sonnet writing challenges the student to model a structured form and be creative. Students may type up their sonnet and decorate the document with clipart, font, or other textual effects using Google Docs or a template found at BigHugeLabs.com. While the Sonnet Project is complex and multifaceted, it pulls together everything we have done throughout the entire school year and pushes the students to evolve into confident and independent learners.

My flipped classroom is more than just using technology and flipped techniques to teach literature. My flipped classroom takes students on a journey of discovery of literature and themselves that changes their perception on boring books and themselves and evolves them into active and critical thinkers and learners.

ENGLISH TEACHER TECHNOLOGY TOOL BOX:
THE ESSENTIALS

In addition to tools mentioned in other chapters, the following are some of the FREE tools that form the foundation for my students' digital learning.

Voice Comments (also called **121 Writing**): provides students with verbal feedback on assignments typed in Google Docs by just highlighting and speaking. This is the fastest way I have found that replaces the traditional red pen for marking up student writing.

Blogging via **Blogger, Weebly, KidsBlog.org** or **Wordpress** replaces pen and paper journals for more structured writing and reflection and gives students an opportunity for connecting with a wide audience outside of the classroom walls.

Gobstopper, a free interactive reader, has annotations, questions, and quizzes embedded in enhanced versions of canonical texts found on the public domain. Teachers can customize their own "curriculet" in addition to using the already enhanced versions and receive whole class reports on student performance. This tool is a MUST for flipped reading of canonical texts.

Librivox is a website with links to audiobooks of texts found on the public domain. By having students listen as they read along, they can better comprehend the text.

Screencast-O-Matic.com, MoveNote, WeVideo and **Google Hangout** are my choices for free video creation and editing.

BigHugeLabs.com: Replacing posterboard/paper visual projects, this tool provides digital templates for projects such as motivational posters, magazine covers, movie posters, and more. This is a nice digital alternative for students who struggle with artistic projects.

Edcanvas is an easy to use tool for organizing resources. This simple to use and versatile tool allows users to upload personal content and found sources to "canvases". As a visual learner, I really like the layout and display of Edcanvas. In addition, quizzes can also be embedded into the canvas to assess comprehension and understanding.

NoRedInk.com makes flipped grammar instruction a no-brainer. Students join the teacher's class and the teacher selects and assigns review activities and quizzes. Whole class reports are color coded to show student performance.

Kate Baker is entering her 15th year as a 9th grade English teacher at Southern Regional High School in Manahawkin, NJ. Kate describes herself as a "nerdy nerd and voracious reader, but foremost an academic" as she uses Google Apps for Education and Edmodo in the classroom. As a presenter at EdmodoCon 2013, TeachMeet NJ, and EdcampPhilly, Kate focuses on using technology to flip her classroom and promote student learning. You can connect with Kate on Twitter @KtBkr4, and read about her teaching techniques on her blog, Baker's BYOD—Bring Your Own Device, Dog, and Deconstruction of Literature (kbakerbyodlit.blogspot.com), which was recognized as one of Ed-tech's must read K-12 I.T. blogs for 2013.

English

Cheryl Morris and Andrew Thomasson

Note: Although, for clarity's sake, we have referred to our classrooms as separate, we do not consider them to be so. Since we collaboratively plan our classes, and often observe each other through Google+ hangouts, these are truly team-taught classes that happen to have only one instructor in the room. Nothing in this chapter would be possible outside of our collaborative partnership.

INTRODUCTION

For most of its history, flipped English was the white rhino of the flipped learning movement: infrequently spotted, elusive, and once you spotted one, it didn't mean you could figure out what made it different from other species of rhinoceroses. In the past year or so, the number of English teachers embracing the flipped movement has dramatically increased, and the number of resources multiplied exponentially. However, there are still few teachers with the kind of extensive resources available from many of the prominent flipped science or math teachers.

Beyond a scarcity of models, flipping English is fraught with problems. English is not linear, it's not really sequential, and it has as much to do with art of language as the science of grammar and mechanics. Thus, a flipped English class is not going to look the same as a flipped math, or science or even history class. And one flipped English class will vary greatly from another. The most helpful way we know to illustrate those differences is to describe a recent 90 minute block period in our flipped English classroom.

As part of our study of *The Great Gatsby*, Cheryl's students had a Socratic Seminar. They had often done such seminars in other English classes; however the seminars to which they had become accustomed focused more on one-upping classmates and competing for airtime, rather than on promoting inquiry and having an exploratory discussion on a topic. None of that was part of our goal for student discussions of literature. We wanted students to read thoughtfully, and find evidence to answer a question we presented. Most students are taught to start with their opinion, then to proof-text it with evidence from the book; we believe that is backwards.

Students start with a topic, find out what the text says in regards to that topic, and then develop an opinion based on their understanding of the evidence. In that kind of model, there is no room for competition; in fact, it is actually counter-productive. For discussion to work, students need to feel that they are all working towards a single task—understanding the way the text answers the question, in this case—then be given room to argue, and potentially present several wrong ideas before finding an answer that works. That requires a classroom culture to be created prior to the discussion that can support this process. So we deliberately established an environment in which every voice is valued, and all students have a way of contributing. That allows us, despite the limits of class time and student preference and personality types, to create a group dynamic built around collaboration instead of competition.

For this seminar, students had three options for how to participate. This setup was made possible because we were in a computer lab with MacBook Pros, flexible seating, and an LCD projector to display the backchannel. However, we have run seminars like this in our "low-tech" classroom, where students access the backchannel on their own devices, with it projected on the screen in front, and without the collaborative note-taking being in real-time.

So the three options for participating were:
- participate by taking collaborative notes (in a publicly editable document created in Google Drive and posted on the unit playlist on MentorMob)
- participate by using backchannel discussion (todaysmeet.com)
- participate by speaking aloud (contributions recorded as part of the collaborative note-taking document)

Students had the choice to do any of those things at any point in the discussion, as long as they were engaging. The discussion was rich, and explored different topics than I anticipated covering, but it was primarily the students driving it. Andrew joined in on the document and todaysmeet, so it was truly a collaborative effort, both for teachers and students. Here are some examples of the contributions:

Collaborative Notes:

Question #1: What does it mean to be "great"?

Who is speaking?	What did they say?	What do you think? (include your name)
Connor	Gatsby is great bc people want to be him Said Nick doesn't do anything very exciting, he's boring	Robin- I also think this is the main reason that he is great. Everyone looks up to him because he is really successful. Will- I don't think Nick's role in the novel is to be "great" or not. He is a facilitator of many events in the story, and a kind man who stays true to his values and beliefs.
Brady	Gatsby always has hope	
Michael	Self-made man, hopeless romantic, Nick enjoys hanging out with him	
Will	made himself successful, overcame adversity	Michael- I agree- greatness is not given, but earned. The fact that Gatsby overcame war and modest beginnings makes him truly remarkable

Todaysmeet:

@andrew fine. If someone is liked he may not have lots of social or political power, but people who have lots of power but bad morals.. well

Adam at 11:43 AM, 16 Apr 2013

I agree with Nasreen

Kaitlyn at 11:42 AM, 16 Apr 2013

Being nice will support your status in society, which will make you a great person in the eyes of the people around you

Matt at 11:42 AM, 16 Apr 2013

if you are mean and great then people won't like you. And I think one of the reasons for being great is that people like you

Nasreen at 11:42 AM, 16 Apr 2013

At the end of the unit, students said this was their favorite activity because it gave them all a way to contribute, and they got to choose for themselves. They said it helped them understand the book much better than seminars from their previous classes; in fact, for the majority of my students, it was the first time they had contributed to a seminar for which they had actually read the text. Most students learned that using Spark Notes was good enough for most seminars where participation was graded in frequency of response. But the seminar did not just help them understand the book as they read—it also helped them write their analysis essay. The same seminar question we considered (Is Gatsby really great? What makes a person "great"?) was included in the final essay, and students were able to go back to the collaborative notes and find evidence easily, which made constructing their own opinion much easier.

Despite the obvious advantages and successes of this lesson, we remember debriefing the day and asking, "How flipped was that lesson?" All the typical markers of what most people think of as flipped were absent: there was no homework, no video, no practice worksheets in class...and yet, as we will argue in this chapter, this lesson *is* representative of what we believe flipped learning is and should be.

We cannot tell you how to flip your class. But we can tell you how we flipped our class, and take you on the journey on which we embarked, searching for a better way to teach, learn, and live. We can invite you into our classrooms, and show you what has worked for us. Most of all, we can be for you what we wish we had: someone to show that flipping English is possible and can be pretty amazing.

DISCOVERING A BETTER WAY TO TEACH

Before you make the decision to flip your class, you probably had a period of searching for "a better way" to teach. Perhaps that was a function of credential school, perhaps that was a function of a collaborative school culture, or perhaps it was the result of frustration that Things Are The Way They Are and It's Not Good Enough For My Students. Or perhaps, it just fell into your lap and it was the idea you couldn't get out of your head (like both of us probably). You were, at some point, convinced that what you were doing in your classroom wasn't adequately serving students or meeting the goals you have for them.

For us, those goals are that we want to create lifelong learners, people who have a passion for something, and have the reading, listening, speaking and writing skills to be successful in any area of life they choose for their future. We also saw that there existed a massive technology gap in our schools, and our students were the ones suffering. That is where the flipped journey starts: the acceptance that there might be something better out there, and that you're willing to experiment until you can see evidence that it is helping students.

Appropriately enough, both of us found flipped learning through a video published on the internet for free. Andrew found one (bit.ly/flipping03) on a search of new ideas in education, and Cheryl was shown one (bit.ly/flipping04) at a district edtech meeting focused on technology integration. It only took one video for each of us to be convinced that flipped learning had a place in our practice.

We were attracted to flipped learning for many reasons, but one of them was that the core principles—focus on how face-to-face time is used, higher-order thinking, learner-centred pedagogy, emphasis on technology and 21st century skills—seemed to address the problems we found in our own classrooms. So we jumped in, largely on our own, because no one else at our site was interested, and we were.

Flipped learning is difficult to manage alone, but the reason the movement is so successful is that it was started by teachers, spread by teachers, and embraced by teachers, not suggested by consultants, administrators, or district office staff. In fact, it's not the kind of thing you can force on a teacher, because it requires mandates that have to come from intrinsic motivation rather than external pressure. It requires throwing out the worksheets and throwing yourself into an ever-changing world where you don't always see the path clearly. It's easier to know you don't like the path you're on than to find a better way. For us, flipped learning was the better way. But the better way had many roadblocks.

The first roadblock showed up immediately when, independent of each other, we went searching for models in English, only to discover that No One Does This in English. When I [Cheryl] started investigating models, I found a smattering of blog posts about flipping grammar or other direct instruction-type lessons. Those were helpful, but didn't really address the problems I saw in my classroom: covering content in depth, having more time to build reading and writing skills, and incorporating more technology into my practice. So I expanded my search to other flipped teachers and found a few outstanding educators—Crystal Kirch was the first of many—who also shared their work and made me think that I wasn't crazy for wanting to move beyond putting direct instruction on video. On a similar such search, Andrew found Cheryl's blog and resources, and that's one of the main reasons we met: so few people flipped English, blogged about it, AND were active on social media.

After we met, we got to know other teachers who helped us understand flipped learning in a deeper, more complete way. People like Crystal, Karl Lindgren-Streicher and Brian Bennett made us think of teaching differently: we saw what was possible with flipped learning, rather than what had already been done in flipped learning. And that's where we really began flipping our English classes.

NON-FLIPPED ENGLISH, NOW AND THEN

For the vast majority of English teachers who have entered the profession in the last ten years (as both of us have), we have always taught in an educational context that included high-stakes testing and accountability. Because of that, we were training in direct instruction, whole-class engagement strategies, using textbooks and pacing guides, content standards, and structured group work. We weren't trained to teach writing as an art form, or how to get students to collaborate, or how to bring empathy and the ability to imagine others complexly into our English classroom.

Even in our careers, we have seen the five-paragraph essay come to dominate writing instruction, talking-to-the-text strategies dominate reading instruction, and textbooks take over as the dominant literary instruction. By breaking English down into such discrete skills, it allows for standardised curriculum and instruction. It ensures a minimum level of competence in reading, writing, and literary analysis, but, as Wordsworth said, we "murder to dissect" and thus lose what we loved about English in the first place. So we had to go from what we knew English to be now, to what it had been in our own education.

For me [Cheryl], I remember my literature teacher reading everything aloud, doing all the regional accents. I remember going to see Othello at the Oregon Shakespeare Festival after reading and acting out the play. I remember analysing "An Occurrence at Owl Creek Bridge" and "The Fall of the House of Usher" and thinking that literature was so much more deep and complex and beautiful than I had ever known. I remember arguing with my classmates about whether Shakespeare's sonnets or Emily Dickinson's poetry showed a more accurate depiction of romantic love. I remember poems I wrote, books I chose for myself (George Macdonald's "Lilith" and "Phantastes") and wrote about—in fact, one of those essays was an essay for which I received a perfect score for the first time ever.

I loved English because it opened my world up and exposed to the light just how little I knew, and how much I wanted to know. It pushed me into my English major as well—where I had read every selection in the American Literature seminar class already, and where I could take classes that didn't appeal to me at first glance: "Literature and Faith", where I discovered Li-Young Lee and Flannery O'Connor; "World Literature", where I read my favourite book ever, *The Brothers Karamazov*; and "New International Fiction", where I read my second favourite book ever, J. M. Coetzee's *Disgrace*. In that class, I also found that I loved all South African literature, and was inspired to take three trips there and even live in Cape Town. I loved English, but distilling that to an anthology, a five-paragraph essay, and a visualisation strategy made even me hate English class.

For me (Andrew), well, I was a young mathematician and a voracious reader, but reading was what brought me the most joy. The only things I can remember a teacher reprimanding me for in class were all centered around reading books instead of, say, focusing in on Algebra lectures. I have a clear memory of being twelve years old, hiding under the covers with a tiny crack of daylight coming through to read by. I read anything, but at that age, I loved Sherlock Holmes and couldn't put it down, even when the light went.

As a high school student, I focused primarily on writing, rather than reading. Starting from 9th grade, there is only one class for which I read all the assigned books. I thought they were boring, irrelevant and had nothing of value for me. Conversely, writing has always been an area of strength for me; I've been writing poetry and original songs since the age of 15, and there is still work from that period that I can read without cringing. It wasn't great, but it was something I enjoyed and did well. One teacher told me that I was a good enough writer to join the Creative Writing club, and that I even should teach other students a few things.

In that club, and later, when I became a teacher, I realized that even though I've been writing for my entire life, I struggled to explain how to construct writing, or how to read critically, or even what the rules of grammar are. I was a Creative Writing major in college, and focused primarily on twentieth century poetry and writing my own original poetry. There was a magic in poetry for me; it sparked my soul. I try and teach my classes in a way that makes me happy, but also has the potential to spark the souls of my students. I know that for me, my own choice and interest has to drive the selection of texts

We wanted to capture some of what we loved about English, and to bring those things back to our practice. We wanted our students to be creative, and have deep discussions, and do projects they would always remember, and write essays that pushed their analytical abilities deeper than they thought possible, and read and write poems that could spark their souls. And flipped learning was the way we chose to do it. Now, we just had to figure out how to make it work.

THE FLIPPED MINDSET

Normally, flipped learning starts with removing direct instruction from class and putting it on video for viewing at home; the majority of these teachers are high school math and science instructors. Math and science courses are generally sequential with lots of discrete facts and knowledge for the teacher to disseminate. So by removing the information delivery system from their class time, it allows students to get practice (problem sets, difficult equations, etc.) while the teacher is in the room, and they have peers to help teach them. We've all seen kids tutor each other in difficult subjects—in my room, it's usually AP Calculus and AP Chemistry—during our class time, or in the halls/passing period. Kids naturally are social, and are social learners. So by opening class time to allow for social learning of the most difficult subjects for most students, it gives them the time they need and the peer resources to truly master the content. And many flipped teachers stop there, at what many call Flip 101: moving direct instruction out of class time, and moving the practice problems and discussion into class time.

The way that most English teachers envision flipped instruction is usually in the writing or grammar realms, where there is an obvious opportunity for direct instruction. Teachers create videos outlining grammar concepts, or explaining some kind of writing technique, or give instructions for how to construct paragraphs or on what the instructions are for the upcoming essay. Other teachers assign reading as homework and talk about it in class.

But those models have limits. While there is nothing inherently wrong with them, there's also nothing inherently flipped about them, at least as we define flipped. We believe that Flip 101 is excellent as a first step, but that there is so much more to flipped learning than putting direct instruction on video.

Our definition, which we call the Flipped Mindset, has three main parts:

1. Higher-level thinking is of primary importance and should be the majority of thinking tasks
2. Learner-centred pedagogy is the method of delivery
3. Both of those are used to make decisions about the best use of our face-to-face time with students

The real flip is from the teacher making all the decisions and having all the voice and choice, to students taking responsibility for their learning, curriculum driven by their interests, but also designed to meet them where they are skill-wise and help them grow beyond that.

We approached flipped learning hoping that it would make our classroom more learner-centred, with class time used well and with higher-order thinking required. So just moving DI onto video wouldn't do that. The reality of an English classroom, and indeed most classrooms, is that there is far more to the teaching than information delivery and skills practice. That's why most flipped learning teachers didn't really know what to say when asked how to flip English.

So how DO you flip English?

Approaching flipped instruction in the English classroom is a world away from how it looks in science or math at the secondary level. We don't have linear standards, or concepts that build sequentially; English standards (especially the new Common Core Standards) are much more holistic, and are concerned with building literate readers, analytical writers, and critical thinkers. We teach mostly process—reading, writing, thinking, speaking—and so our direct instruction is limited and often as-needed, rather than strictly scheduled. However, the entry point for most teachers is almost always in the Flip 101 realm.

Let's use my [Cheryl's] own entry into flipped learning, etymology instruction (bit.ly/flipping05), as an example. I had five Latin and Greek roots to teach a week, so we would spend about 30 minutes on the delivery of instruction each Monday. Kids would fill out their worksheet in class, and then make flashcards/draw pictures as homework, and I would check it on Tuesday. So I put the instruction on video (which ended up being 8-12 minutes instead of 30) and having students watch the video on Monday night, and come to class with their flashcards. We then used 30 minutes of class time to spend reviewing and playing games to help them apply their knowledge. It worked really well, and students started getting better grades on the weekly tests, too.

Unfortunately, the majority of what we did in class wasn't like that. So while the videos worked really well for that direct instruction, there was far more than direct instruction to flip. Our class time was spent doing DOLs, reading novels, writing essays, practicing skills, having discussions, and working collaboratively. Those are much harder to make "flipped," at least if you consider flipping to be putting content on video and doing worksheet practice in class. So the model had to expand to include all of those things. This is exactly what we discovered when we began our journey in flipped learning—that flipping English is different than all the other subjects. The number of domains we teach—reading, writing, speaking, listening, and even technology—are broad, and there are few examples out there to follow. In the next sections, we will attempt to do just that: provide examples and practical ideas for making those domains flipped.

One point of clarification: in our version of flipped, we don't believe videos are required, but rather, they should be used where it makes sense and brings something you can't have in a traditional class setting. We believe that all of the traditional domains of English class—grammar, writing, reading, discussing, and creating—can be improved by considering the best use of face-to-face time, emphasising higher-order thinking, migrating towards learner-centred pedagogy, and incorporating technology in a way that enhances the content and develops students' skills.

FLIPPED GRAMMAR AND LANGUAGE

This is where most teachers start, because grammar and language tend to be far more sequential and discrete than other aspects of the English curriculum. In this category, we are including vocabulary, etymology, daily oral language, grammar, mechanics, and usage. The common denominator in all of those is that they can be broken down into topics that would make an excellent 2-5 minute videos. These could easily be a routine part of instruction, or part of a self-paced curriculum for students as-needed.

Here is where the experience of most flipped teachers is helpful. You can certainly put these kinds of topics and subjects on video, have students watch as homework, take notes (such as a WSQ—bit.ly/flipping06), then practice the skills and ideas in class when needed. For many teachers on a pacing guide with common curriculum, or curriculum from an anthology, this could make up nearly half your class time. Many English teachers choose to create flipped videos that address these topics and run a Flip 101 model. There is nothing wrong with that—in fact, that's how we both started.

But there are many ways to improve your face-to-face time by moving language and grammar direct instruction onto video and providing it for students as and when needed. This can take many different forms. Instead of just explaining each, we wanted to provide some examples.

The most common way to flip grammar is by creating videos that cover a grammatical term or process (bit.ly/flipping07) using one of these methods:

- An Interactive Whiteboard application for iPad. Cheryl uses and likes ShowMe, but ExplainEverything, Doceri and ScreenChomp all work well. Many science and math teachers, such as San Francisco Chemistry teacher Ramsay Musallam, take their iPad around during class, and as they explain a concept or work out a problem with small groups, they use their chosen app to record and then post that video for all students.
- Screencasting using Camtasia, Snagit, Jing, QuickTime (for Mac, which is freely available on nearly all Macs), iMovie, or one of many other great options.
- A tablet, such as the Wacom Bamboo tablets used by Salman Khan, or a document camera plugged into a computer and captured by any screencasting program
- A video of yourself teaching live during class. This seems odd for many teachers, but if you have a limited amount of time to amass video content, this method is a great way to prepare for the following year. If you teach the same lesson multiple times a day for years, think how much time you could save by recording it live once, then making that available for students,
- A pencast of you explaining the concept, using LiveScribe

We have also used videos to cover questions in the format of state tests. Cheryl often used videos on grammar topics (bit.ly/flipping08) demonstrated in sample questions from the California High School Exit Exam, because it allowed for practice with format, and covered multiple grammar topics in a short time. Andrew has also used video to cover the End of Course Exam practice questions (bit.ly/flipping09). We like the idea of incorporating process into a content video. We'll speak more about content vs. process videos in the section covering flipped writing instruction.

The benefit of putting the lesson on video is multi-faceted. It makes video lecture shorter than it would take to deliver the lecture live in class; when you account for giving directions, frequent distractions, slowing down for some students to take notes while others get bored waiting, and unforeseen interruptions like fire drills, empty Expo markers, and passes, the time can often be cut in half when moved to video. This method also gives all students access to the instruction, even when absent. We all know that athletes in afternoon classes miss class frequently, so having it on video provides them the same instruction their classmates get. Students can also repeat the lesson if they don't understand it, and can learn at his or her own pace.

Beyond your own classroom, these lessons can also be used across classrooms at the same school site, and even in other districts and even other countries. The videos Cheryl posts on ShowMe are shared with over 10,000 followers and have thousands of views—even the ones never assigned to her students.

Grammar videos tend to be the most universally accessible, because most topics tend to be straightforward and don't change much over time. For example, the idea of parallel structure doesn't disappear or change, so a video made by any teacher could work to teach that concept. That's not to say that there isn't a benefit in making your own videos. No one knows what your students need most except for you, and we have found that our students strongly prefer the videos we have made, either separately or jointly. But no teacher has as much time as they need to prepare, and sometimes using a video someone else created is more realistic than creating one of your own in the amount of time you have.

One of the other major benefits of this model is that it also allows for differentiation across a wide variety of ability levels; instead of assigning an advanced learner a video on phrases, the teacher could have a video about appositive phrases, or how to use varied syntax in phrasing. Videos can also be used for remediation, in a way that is easily done quietly, without seeming to single out any particular student. As teachers, we know that our students move at different paces and often need to receive some instruction repeatedly before it sticks.

Starting this way made it possible to find a foothold in a movement dominated by math and science teachers. However, this model treats English almost as if it were a science, which ignores the large part of language that is an art. The traditional model focuses on the concepts that work for direct instruction, and are more linear in nature; it also makes a natural transition from language and mechanics to the writing process.

FLIPPED WRITING

Writing is one of the most important skills students should gain from their high school English education. Yet most English teachers have not been taught how to teach writing. For the last ten years, the instruction commonly found in English classrooms focus on structure far more than content. We have even known some English teachers who think that structure is the only thing that is important, and taught their students how to say nothing in fifteen different ways over the course of five paragraphs. We also recognise that many English departments have standards for how writing is taught; at one of Cheryl's previous schools, a very strict adherence to Jane Shaffer's format, including the specific vocabulary that went with it, were required. Instruction on the structure of writing makes natural subjects for a video. These are some of the videos (bit.ly/flipping10) Cheryl used to teach the structure of an essay.

While we see the benefit in teaching the structure of writing, the distillation of writing to a series of steps or a formula remove what makes writing beautiful, unique, and memorable. So the way we approach writing instruction is to focus first on content, and once students have something to say, we teach them enough structure to say it in a way to which people will pay attention. That does change the form that our flipped writing instruction takes. While we have videos on structure, we focus primarily on the process and the analysis necessary to start the process.

We will cover a lot of writing activities in the section on Flipped Reading, as they are just not discrete skills that can be separated out. However, we do have a few ideas for how to flip the writing process, independent of text. We see two primary types of videos that cover writing instruction: content videos and process videos. Content videos cover structure, instructions for writing a paragraph, discovering the purpose and audience for a specific writing assignment, or even prompt thinking as a pre-writing activity, or as part of the revision assignments.

In contrast, process videos show the construction of writing, and explain the thought process behind each part of the essay or paragraph. There is a lot of great content available for teachers to use on the internet, and this type of video is far more common in flipped learning than process, but we quickly attached to the idea of showing process on video because one of the unique things about collaborative instruction is that you are forced to explain your thinking behind everything you add to the essay. This is the kind of activity we had modeled live in class before meeting each other, but it never was as transparent as we wanted it to be, because our students didn't always get involved enough to ask why we were writing something, or why we started with a particular word, etc. By putting our process on video, not only can our students see what happens when two fairly-smart people discuss writing, but we also had the opportunity to learn a lot about our own writing process.

The first project we embarked on together was a series of videos on the process of writing a research paper (bit.ly/flipping11), from finding a topic to writing the final essay. We also worked through the literary analysis essay process on video (bit.ly/flipping12). We believe that it is important for students to know the make-up of a paragraph, but that it's just as important that they see it crafted, and hear the thought process behind every sentence. We haven't found many other educators who walk through the writing process on video, but we have found it valuable.

We have used these videos in class and as homework, and have even assigned them differently to students based on ability or quality of writing. But either way, we believe in having students compose their essays in class. This allows us to speak into the process of writing, and help them as they are figuring out what to say and how to say it. Because Google Drive allows for real-time collaboration, we have developed a way of doing mini-writing conferences as students begin writing. We have a script that automatically creates and shares a document (bit.ly/flipping13) when students fill out the form for their class; that allows us to keep the files organised in our shared Google Drive in a way that both teachers can access easily.

When we begin the assignment and students have created their documents, we then go into each document and comment on what the student has written so far. Not only does it allow us to check their progress and monitor their time on task, but it gives them feedback and the opportunity to ask questions immediately, rather than turn in something unclear or incomplete. We often project the document in which we are commenting on the main screen of the lab so that all students can see their progress and learn from the comments we're making on the essays written by their peers.

Another variation of that idea is to start with a collaborative evidence gathering activity. For the recent unit on *The Great Gatsby*, students did an evidence analysis on what Nick says that shows prejudice or judgement.

Here is a portion of that document (whole document can be found here: bit.ly/flipping14):

Nick and Judgement

File   Edit   View   Insert   Format   Tools   Table   Help   All changes saved in Drive

Normal text - Arial   -   18   -   B   I   U   A   -   A   -   ∞   ⬛   ▤ ▤ ▤ ▤   ⫶⫶ -   ⬚ ⬚

Nick is a judgemental person

Example (quote from the book, including page/chapter number, and YOUR NAME)	Context (what's happening in the novel - what would you need to understand what this example means?)	Why it shows Nick to be judgemental (in your own words)
Robin: "The undergraduate nodded in a cynical and melancholy way" (page 45, chp.3).	This is when Nick is at one of Gatsby's parties and he is trying to find the host (Gatsby) and along the way meets some other guests there.	I think this shows that nick is judgemental because he is judging the way a person acts and goes into detail about every flaw that they have.
Harrison: Mr. McKee was a pale, feminine man from the flat below. (page 30, chp 2)	This is a scene in the book when Nick first met Mr. McKee when Tom, Nick, and Mrs. Wilson go to a house party and the McKee's so Mrs. Wilson can model and everyone else can enjoy the party.	This shows that nick is judgemental because he is insulting a man and judging a man on how he looks even though he just met him.
Quinn: "There was something pathetic in his concentration, as if his complacency, more acute than of old, was not enough to him anymore."	Tom is sitting with Nick and Daisy and discussing the nordic race.	Nick is more likely to analyze a situation through a negative lens. Even if he is right, he is still judgmental.

Using this table, students immediately had access to dozens of different examples so when they had to write their own essay (which, in part, dealt with the question of whether Nick is judgemental). They had an opinion firmly grounded in fact, rather than their own hastily-drawn conclusion.

One of the main benefits of writing in class is of course the reduction in plagiarism. In the entire time we've been flipped, neither of us have had a problem with plagiarism. At Redwood, where Cheryl teaches, plagiarism is such a major problem that nearly half of the referrals written are for that offence. When students are held accountable during the writing process, as well as having a teacher available to them to answer questions and clear up misconceptions, then plagiarising is far more difficult than just doing the work themselves.

We believe that the most difficult tasks in any subject should be done during face-to-face class time where the teacher is available to help, and peers are available to collaborate. In our estimation, reading complicated texts and writing essays are the most difficult tasks we assign, so we use class time for them. While many teachers would balk at allowing students to collaborate on essays, we have learned that collaboration between students is one of the ways in which their essays are improved substantially. Many students are used to talking through everything, so when they are asked to write without having discussed the ideas, often they end up finishing the essay before knowing exactly what they think. By debating, analysing, and even virulently disagreeing with one another, students are undertaking the process of making meaning for themselves. In our own writing, we have found that it is nearly impossible for us to go back to solitary composition. We are better writers for our collaboration, because it forces us to examine our assumptions, challenge the persuasiveness of our evidence, and clarify the depth of analysis.

More than anything, we want our students to have the same opportunities to collaborate and improve that we have had through working together. That, to us, is an extension of flipped learning. We call that a **metaflip**—deconstructing our process and recreating it so that our students can experience the same benefits for themselves. That value has also forced us to rethink how we approached writing conferences and essay revision.

Writing conferences are one of the most powerful and underutilised tools in the English teacher's toolbox. Most teachers have between 80-150 students, and the logistics of having individual conferences with every single student during class time (or worse, requiring them to come in outside of class time) makes them impossible to implement class-wide even one time a year. And yet those of us who have had a writing conference with a good teacher know how powerful it could be. By flipping the writing conference, we have found a way to make them far more manageable.

We have found that it's helpful to have the student choose their own focus piece for the writing conferences and do a conference preparation activity. While there are occasions where all students choose the same essay, allowing students to choose a piece of writing (even one for another class) gives them ownership and motivation. Here is one preparation form that we used to for the *Gatsby* essay writing conferences:

Directions:
Create a new document called Gatsby Writing Conference Preparation through the tmiclass website.

This is ONLY about Essay Topic #2

Then do the following:
1. Write an abstract. In that abstract, tell me the information in your essay that you think is most important.
2. What is the biggest problem you had writing this essay? I'm not asking about group process. I'm asking about the actual research, preparation and writing of the essay.
3. What do you most want help on?
4. How finished are you with this essay?
5. Is there anything you want me to know about this essay? This is private, between you and me. So say what you want without worrying someone else will see it.

By asking them to identify their main points, the areas in which they need help, and the story behind the essay (in this case, there were many issues with the group process), the conference takes far less time and is far more focused on revision, rather than a status report. As these were group conferences, we were able to have conferences for all seven groups (with 31 students total) in one class period.

Both preparation and working in groups make the conferences shorter and more focused. However, even with individual conferences, they can be fit in over many class periods. To achieve that in our classes, we created a self-paced unit that students could work through while we met with each student for 15-30 minutes. For many of these conferences, both of us were present—one on Google Hangout or in the document itself, and the other in person, and most students who had the option preferred having us both; instead of one writer's opinion, they got two with complementary strengths. This kind of conference took 3-4 weeks of class time in order to meet with all 31 students individually, and we know that many teachers would find that to be a bad use of face-to-face time. However, in the evaluations for the course, every single student named that conference as the most effective and helpful activity we did all semester. Most had never had a personal writing conference before and felt that the personal attention was worth the time it took to finish. It also helped us design the rest of the instruction based on their observed strengths and weaknesses.

For many teachers, individual writing conferences with each student is just not possible. Fortunately, there are ways to have asynchronous writing conferences, where the teacher, on his or her own time, provides feedback to the students for them to view on their own time. This can be accomplished in many ways:

- Using the iPad apps, such as ShowMe, to record the teacher's thoughts as they read the essay and focus on the areas that need revision
- Using LiveScribe, hosted on Evernote or Dropbox
- Recorded in a Google+ Hangout and posted on YouTube, which also allows for more than one person to be involved
- Using comments in a Google Drive document
- Using software like VoiceComments to narrate feedback in Google Drive

We all know that personal feedback is important, but timely feedback is as well. These options all take less time than the traditional method of using red ink to indicate needed revision, and then using class time to discuss the results of the assessment. By giving this personal feedback, it illustrates to students how important revision is to the writing process. We don't even put grades on the first draft because first drafts are not finished products. We only grade finished products, although they do get full credit on the first draft as long as they submit it and it is complete.

We do have students write collaboratively sometimes. We have found that there are certain tasks that work better for groups, such as high level analysis tasks, or an essay that encompasses multiple claims or texts. We gave a final exam for the Gatsby unit that included two high-level analytical tasks with claims too broad to fit into a single overall thesis. Here are the two assignments (one class: bit.ly/flipping15; the other class: bit.ly/flipping16) where a group essay was more reasonable than an individual one. This of course requires students to compose collaboratively, and to accurately assess every student, we use the Revision History feature in Google Drive to see which student did which part. It has eliminated most of the problems where one group member does all the work and another just floats by and takes credit. Even checking mid-way through the process can help alleviate some of the struggles students have before it's too late to change the outcome.

These are just some of the strategies we have used to flip the writing process. This is the area in which we use the most technology, because the power, particularly in the collaborative features, gives us options we never had before. The first time a student realises that the computer crashing does not mean losing all of her work, they understand why we use the new tools...even when the learning curve is high at times. We have published lots of our curriculum through our blogs, and nearly all the curriculum for the writing class we taught this year (bit.ly/flipping17).

Any activity that makes the best use of face-to-face time, emphasises higher-order thinking, and puts the student at the centre of the classroom is flipped, regardless of whether or not video is used, or homework is assigned.

FLIPPED READING

Good writing should be the natural product of thoughtful discussion and critical analysis. So throughout a unit, we have lots of activities that help our students understand the text more deeply and write about it more expertly. Many of those writing tasks are included in this section on flipped reading because in most cases, and in most assignments, reading starts the process, and writing finishes it. So now that we've addressed tasks where writing is less dependent on a text, we want to outline how the writing process goes when the writing product is dependent on a text.

Many teachers believe that reading instruction is already flipped. After all, English teachers have sent students home with reading as part of the traditional model for decades. However, the motivation for moving reading outside of class is more about the time constraint than the intentional choice to use face-to-face time differently. Conversely, for as many teachers who believe that reading instruction is always flipped, there are teachers who believe that reading is unflippable.

But our definition of flipped learning has little to do with what is assigned as homework; instead, it involves making the best use of face-to-face time, emphasising higher-order thinking, and being student-centred, so as long as we are doing those three things, reading is flippable. So we will use our definition as a frame for how we approach flipped reading

Making Best Use of Face-to-Face time

The first question we always ask is what the best use of our face-to-face time is. So the first major decision an English teacher must make is where the reading should happen. We believe that reading communally has a place in face-to-face time. There are many reasons for that choice:

- Reading is an active process, and one with which many students struggle,
- In their previous English classes, most of our students were required to do all the reading outside of class, and almost all students admitted to using internet resources like SparkNotes or CliffNotes instead of reading the assigned chapters, and over half had not ever finished a book assigned to them in English class,
- We believe that ensuring that all students complete and understand the reading is so fundamental to analysis that we need to use class time to read, and
- Our students asked us to allow them to read in class, or that we read aloud to them.

This gets to the "student driven" part of the definition, but it started as giving the students choice as to how we read and whether it would happen inside or outside of class time (you can read more about that process here: bit.ly/flipping18). Every class had a different plan, but all of them included time to read in class. Almost every student read every word of the assigned books, so it seems like that investment of time was worth it.

Now, for our students, reading in class makes sense. But at many other schools, reading in class is not the best use of their face-to-face time. We are not claiming that we know the way you should spend your face-to-face time; however, we think it's important to consider it. We have found that students rarely read and understand as well as we would like them to, and struggle with comprehension even when they have read the whole text in class. Once we asked our students to be truthful with us about their reading history, reading habits, and the way past English classes approached the assigned reading, we discovered that assigning reading as homework only guaranteed that our students would use SparkNotes. So we would encourage you to start asking questions.

One way we used time in class to read was having students listen to me reading, either live or on video (bit.ly/flipping19), and respond in a backchannel. This allowed some students to listen to a proficient reader, while others read on their own. Using a backchannel for reading as a class gives us a way of seeing, in real-time, what students don't understand. Try it with your students, and you may find, as we did, that they really understand far less than we think they do. Even advanced level seniors struggle to understand surface-level information as they read for the first time. By using a backchannel, students can also help each other understand difficult concepts and vocabulary words.

Focus on Higher-Order Thinking Skills

Once it has been established that the students are reading the text in class, we can begin to design activities that make the best use of face-to-face time and that focus on the higher-order thinking tasks like creating, evaluating, synthesising, and analysing. We have found that almost all of these tasks are possible on paper, but we use Google Drive for all of them when we can. You can read about how we make do using little paper in a non-1:1 environment (bit.ly/flipping21).

The first thing we have students do is reading journals. The format of these can vary, but generally starts with what students notice as they read. They have the option of writing them simultaneously while reading, or to do them immediately after they finish the reading.

These reading journals are often what drive the activities and discussions during class time. We help students hone their ability to find important details as well as connections to the text thematically and in plot/character. Connecting personally to the text is important, and often is the primary way we make meaning. Feeling what a character feels and relating to experiences helps us read empathetically. One of our favourite authors, John Green, talks about the process of reading as engaging in the act of imagining other people complexly; in other words, seeing people not as a single story or a stereotype, but as a person with complex, often contradicting actions and motivations, with varying thoughts, feelings, desires, and wishes, and who cannot be neatly summed up in a character analysis paragraph. That is how we want our students to read—as if the text provides a mirror that we hold up to our own lives and that shows us what it means to be human. We want them to read with thoughtfulness and depth, but also with deep empathy. Empathy is what makes us human and should be the centre of the English classroom.

We have a variety of strategies that we use to help students understand and engage with the text as they read, but also to help them engage with each other. Blogging is one new strategy we tried this year, and the majority of the blog posts we required were a variation on reading journals or group discussions. Students have blogged their responses to discussion questions, and have even posted pictures of their paper reading journals (which allows us to grade and check them but also not take them away from our students to do so, and ensures they won't lose the paper). We use Blogger, which allows our students to maintain all their accounts through Google, and allows them to be really excited when they find out what countries blog visitors are from.

Something new we discovered this year was close reading. We had always had students read carefully and thoughtfully, but having them close read is something slightly different. Close reading is about noticing carefully and sharing what you notice. We usually start with a collective close read to model what it looks like to spend a lot of time. This close read (bit.ly/flipping22) started the *Gatsby* Unit. Students began by completing a close read on the first passage in *The Great Gatsby*, on their own, then choosing their two best comments to add to the collaborative one. As the text is open-source, we found a site that had the whole novel, took the first section, and gave students editing access. Not all the comments fit on screen, but here is a screenshot of part of it:

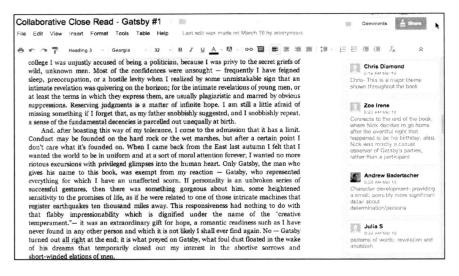

Some students talk about theme, some talk about word patterns, and some just make connections to their own life, to what they've read, and to what we've talked about in class. The second layer is that students go back and respond to each other's comments. We also have had classes respond to another class doing a close read on the same text. Most critically, we go through and reply to many of the best comments in order to show students what kinds of comment leads to the best close reading and analysis. This happens live during class (either in a computer lab or in our classrooms with BYOD), so students are getting instant feedback; if comments are surface-level or incorrect, we can also address those issues instantly. By modeling what good comments look like, we teach them to notice more carefully, and prepare them to do their own close reading.

Another form of collaborative close reading is when a group chooses their own text. In *Gatsby*, our students chose a passage they liked best and did a group close read. They then traded passages with other groups and responded to the other group's comments. It gave students insight on the way other students read, and what parts of the text other students like best. Those group close reads launched some of the best class discussions we've ever had. Students started those discussions by sharing their own analysis of the section, and then responding (or often debating) that analysis with one another.

Creating a Student-Centred Classroom

This is a completely different way of reading from what our students were used to in their other English classes. They are responsible for the success of our class, because so much of it depends on them having ideas then sharing those ideas with their classmates. Generally, they struggle to adjust to a class where they get to be in control of anything. That is hardly surprising, given the fact that their experience in other English classes tended to be similar to the English classes that both of us had in high school and taught in our early years in the profession.

In the more "traditional" model, it often goes something like this:
1. Students are assigned reading to do at home (and as we know, many don't complete the reading)
2. On returning to class the next day, they take a quiz in class to prove that they read it.
3. After the quiz, the teacher talks about the important analytical points in the text—they explain what the symbols mean, what metaphors and similes are important, where there is foreshadowing, and perhaps go over important passages in depth.
4. Students are then either given a worksheet-type analytical assignment, or asked to prepare for a formal discussion about the text.
5. At the end of the period, more reading is assigned.
6. At the end of the unit, students are assigned an essay that is dependent on them agreeing with the analysis provided by the teacher in class.

This model can work, and we have seen examples of it being done extremely well. However, it often creates negative patterns. Students find it difficult to engage deeply with the text, either because of the speed at which they are asked to read it, or because of the difficulty of the text. Some struggle to find the will to do any of the reading, especially if it is not engaging from the start or if they disagree with the interpretation given by the teacher. Breaking all of those patterns is vital to get students to be responsible for their own learning.

Our main goals for a unit built around a novel are to have students read carefully, analyse deeply, and connect empathetically with the text. None of those goals are compatible with the standard fare outlined above from previous English courses. So we have to throw out nearly everything in that cycle. It starts with where reading takes place.

By allowing students to read in class, we gave them more ownership of the process. The end of the year survey showed that with very few exceptions, students actually did the reading for our class. While every student didn't finish every book, we found that students read an average of 80% for some books, and closer to 90% on average for others. Students explained that some books were just more appealing than others, but they also noted that in the final unit (which was the 90% novel), they got to read the majority of the book before doing any analytical tasks. This was a change they requested—instead of reading a few chapters then doing close reading and having discussions, the students wanted to read the entire text and then analyse and discuss it. When students suggested it, we realised that what they were asking for is to read like we read: quickly the first time through, then more carefully re-reading to analyse and form sophisticated opinions.

The other major factor in the success of the final unit was that students chose the text from a short list. The other novels were ones we selected, but giving them a choice where possible allowed for deeper investment. On top of selecting the book, we gave them the choice on what activities we would do together during class time. We provided a list of all the assignments we've completed this semester, and asked them to justify their selections. Here are a few of the activities they chose as their favourites.

Finding Outside Analysis—one of the major surprises from this list came out of the end of the *Gatsby* unit. Students were asked to write a college-level essay, and told that they could use any of the sources they found online. Many of them found professional-quality literary criticism, and used some of those ideas in their essays. They found it so helpful that they asked us to find (or allow them to bring in) similar literary analysis of the final novel, *The Fault in Our Stars*. Because it is a fairly new novel, there weren't many print sources, so we used the author's YouTube channel to find videos of him talking about his own work. We watched these videos and discussed them in class. (Playlist: bit.ly/flipping23)

Theme Analysis Project—while they didn't like theme analysis essays, they found that thinking about theme helped them understand the book. So students suggested that they choose their own genre, like making a video, creating a poster, developing a presentation, or even writing their own alternate chapters, and use that project to analyse the development of the theme. These projects ended up being some of the best work they did all semester.

Reading Journals—we've discussed these already, but here is the assignment options students chose for the final unit:

Reading Journal Sections and Due Dates for 1st period:
- chapter 1-2 (5/17)
- chapter 3-5 (5/20)
- chapters 6-7 (5/21)
- chapters 8-11 (5/22)
- chapters 12-14 (5/24)
- chapters 15-22 (5/28)
- chapters 23-25 (5/29)

So for each of those sections, here are some options for how to complete a reading journal:
- **traditional reading journal** (what you like, notice, think, or are confused by)
- **annotations** (not just underlining, but making notes that substantially show you're engaging with the text. See me for an example and non-example)
- **video responses** (you record, upload to youtube or google drive, and send me a link. Make sure the video is not private or if it's in drive, make sure it's shared with me)
- **blog posts** (you post to your blog and send me a link. These are reflections from what you read and connections to your own life)
- **other option** (anything that shows you are engaging with the book in a meaningful way is okay with me. If you're not sure, check it with me first)

Frequent Informal Writing with Peer Feedback—much like close-reading, students wanted to write short paragraphs that promoted a claim about the novel, and have their peers and teachers give them feedback on them. These short paragraphs allowed us to respond to students' writing much more quickly, as a class set could be started live, during the activity, and took no more than a few minutes per student to give feedback. Surprisingly, they also wanted their peers to help them improve their writing, and we saw informal writing conferences spring up throughout these activities.

Student-Created Video—only one class liked using video as a medium, but there was a vocal minority in the other classes who enjoyed the process as well. Some videos were done informally, where they opened PhotoBooth and recorded themselves talking, while others were done in iMovie or Camtasia, and had far more editing and production.

Many teachers are hesitant to turn over their classroom to their students, but we have found that our students didn't ask for more free time, but rather asked for some of the most deeply analytical tasks. We also didn't completely turn over control until we had shown them what we expected. We always gave them choice, but we slowly released responsibility for the class as they showed they were capable of handling it. We also didn't ask them a broad question, like "What do you want to do?" but rather, we gave them a list of what we had already done and asked them to choose the assignments they liked best, or propose new ones. Our students didn't want us to waste their time, and they want to learn, but that's not how they start out when we get them. We have to engage their curiosity, show them their capabilities, help them learn to trust us that we will be fair in grading and that their voice matters to us. That is not an easy task, especially in a school culture that is openly hostile to our values and methods.

The general rule we have is this: start out by giving students ONE choice (like how they read) and then model everything. Model what assignments help them learn, model how to talk about the texts, model what good discussion looks like, and model what compassionate grading and authentic assessment look like. Each unit, release a little more responsibility, and as they start meeting expectations, raise the standards. Through all of that, we are relentlessly positive and give our students positive feedback where and when possible. For them to trust us, they need to experience success in our class so many times that it erases the negative experiences they've had as much as possible.

FLIPPED CLASS DISCUSSIONS

Discussion is an integral part of the English classroom, and is generally something that happens in face-to-face time. It is one of the oldest methods of instruction, and seems to be one that does not need the improvement of technology. However, there are also ways of pushing discussion outside of class time, and ways of using technology to enhance discussion as well. We will start with in-class options.

We have both informal and formal discussions. Informal discussions tend to be student-led or based on questions students suggest. After time spent reading, we will ask, "Who has something that was confusing, interesting, boring, frustrating, or exciting from the reading?" Then students will volunteer information and we will either answer it ourselves, or more likely, turn it back to the rest of the class to answer. Over the last decade, we have become far less likely to answer student questions ourselves; instead, we ask students to find their own answers, or if they can't, to look them up.

Formal discussions are most likely to be Socratic Seminars, as we described at the start of this chapter. There are many ways to have a Socratic Seminar, and we won't pretend that our way is the best. But it is one way, and it works for us and our students. We've been using a variation of this method for a few years, but have honed it over time to be this basic structure:

Inner Circle: Students self-select into the inner circle if they want to speak in the discussion. We try to have between 10-15 students, but it can run with as few as 4-5 very talkative students.

Outer Circle: Students choose the outer circle if they would prefer to interact on the backchannel discussion. We tend to use Today's Meet for the backchannel, and will project it on the screen in the front of class so that the inner circle can follow the discussion and bring ideas into their discussion. For students without a device (and in the case that we can't provide enough for them), they can either collaborate with a partner to submit their comments, or use paper instead.

We use a small object to monitor who is talking (Cheryl uses a "Kiss Me I'm Irish" frog), and that students can easily and safely pass around. The idea is that students who haven't spoken as much get priority when they want to speak, in the case where there are lots of students with their hands up. If the discussion falters, the teacher can prompt students with new questions, but that was rarely necessary this year.

To prepare for these discussions, we have students complete reading journals and think of questions they want to discuss. This has ranged from having students write mini-essays or reaction papers in preparation for the discussion to spending class time choosing a question in advance. We try to choose questions that are relevant to our own lives, as well as the lives of the characters in the novel we're reading. Some of the best questions have been as simple as, "What is love, and do you think there are any truly loving relationships in the novel?"

In some cases, having a discussion online can be more useful than using class time. Sometimes, we've even had online discussions during class time, or had students make conversation videos and share them with each other, then make responses to the original video. Classes that struggle to have productive discussions in a traditional manner, find online or video options to be easier for giving them the opportunity to speak and think critically in class. (example 1: bit.ly/flipping24; and example 2: bit.ly/flipping25).

Cheryl has used Edmodo as a Learning Management System (LMS), and had discussions between classes on that platform. This is also a good way to give students a choice in which questions they wanted to discuss. She would post five to seven questions and ask students to post a certain number of responses to questions, and a certain number of responses to classmates' posts. She also used these as pre-discussion questions, or to prompt thinking in advance of a Socratic Seminar. It was also a good way for cross-class or cross-country collaborative discussions.

In these examples, it also gives students who are less likely to participate by speaking a chance to be heard. One excellent use for technology is to differentiate so all students can share their thoughts and collaborate in each other's' learning. It also builds digital citizenship by giving students a chance to participate in an online forum with guidance and peer-monitoring. The more practice students can get in a secure, supportive environment for how to operate online with rapidly changing technology, the better.

FLIPPED PROJECTS AND PROJECT-BASED LEARNING

To be completely transparent, we don't do this well. Yet. This is one of the areas in which we are hoping to focus and get better at for next year. There are almost infinite possibilities for what you can do in a Project-Based-Learning (PBL) Flipped English class, and we'd like to share some of the projects that were most successful for us this past school year. We understand that to most people, PBL and flipped learning don't go together; however, using the Flipped Mindset, the two converge nicely. PBL puts students in control, offers them choice and a plethora of higher-level and real-world thinking tasks, and helps students learn how to best manage their own use of class time.

The first, and most substantial project we've used is the Blank White Page Project (originally, the White Blank Page activity, [bit.ly/flipping26] named after the Mumford and Sons song and inspired by the FlipCon 2012 keynote speech). The project starts with students choosing a question or topic that interests them, whether or not it's about English. From there, we've tried a few different options. The one that worked best was having students create a blog for the project. Then they used the blog to compile research, write out their thoughts about final product, and eventually, post the project. Here is a playlist of blogs (bit.ly/flipping27) from the San Francisco Stories class.

The idea for the project was to build time into our classes that would function as the Google concept of "20% Time". Google employees get to spend 20% of their paid time to work on awesome projects unconnected to their job description. There is a proliferation of similar projects with names like Genius Hour, or Passion Project, or just 20% Project, and there is a reason this idea has taken off: in the era of standardised testing and curriculum maps and pacing guides, the idea of turning the curriculum over entirely to our students is appealing.

What we have found through this project is that students haven't had many chances to have authentic choice in their education. It took a lot of help to get them to an idea that would work for the project. A slightly frighteningly large group of students chose some variation of "Top 10 Vacation Spots" for their project, and found that once they had posted their 10 vacation spots, they didn't have much to add. For those students, we had the opportunity to help them figure out what appealed to them about these places and then develop a research project around those ideas.

And while most students did not do a project that was English-y, we got the chance to teach digital citizenship, technological "real-world" skills, copyright and Creative Commons lessons, and research methods. Those are topics that are often not included in English class because we have ALL OF THE STANDARDS to cover, and because they are generally fairly dull topics. But by incorporating a self-selected project, we create an authentic context in which to teach these skills.

Therein lies the entire rationale for creating projects as learning opportunities: projects that incorporate student choice and authentic audience create motivation and facilitate learning more effectively than "traditional" teaching. When we are designing projects, we start with collaboration. There is not a single project that we completed without the help of our PLN and our students. Much of the feedback that went into projects came indirectly. By participating actively on Twitter and by reading the blogs of other flipped learning teachers, we engage in conversation that inevitably influences what we do in our classroom. There are thousands of voices on the internet, just waiting for us to listen, and we have found that both listening and engaging in dialogue can be the most important forces in maintaining passion and enthusiasm for our own practice. Some teachers read blogs to steal ideas or content, but most are looking for ways to change their own classroom practice by finding inspiration in the practice of others. We met through a blog (Cheryl's) and Twitter, and by listening and engaging in dialogue, everything in this chapter and everything we will do in the future has been made possible.

The other major group teachers should consider when designing project is their students. Sometimes, we indirectly use student opinion in project design by surveying them, using their assessment results or clear areas of strength and weakness to choose learning objectives, and sometimes, students are involved in the building of the project. There have even been cases where students are entirely responsible for creating the project.

On that note, even when we set the guidelines for a project, our default rule is that if students can present compelling reasons why they should be allowed to change or bend the rules, that we will consider it. This rule has resulted in students making videos instead of writing an essay, or writing an essay instead of making a video. It has also resulted in students learning to defend their ideas in an adult manner, and being far more clear about what they intend to learn than they had ever needed to be prior to our class. This rule has also resulted in some of the best projects either of us has ever seen.

We want to be clear that just having students make Elizabethan masks while reading Romeo and Juliet doesn't really count as project-based learning. Projects that create learning opportunities have to have not only a "create this" component, but a "find out about this" component. Here are some examples of the types of projects we have used and found to be successful:

Modern Day Crucible—students read *The Crucible* and did some research on the way McCarthyism influenced the writing of the play. Then, they created a scenario in which the same thing could happen again in a more modern context. Most students used sex crimes or terrorism, although we did allow for some flexibility in the rules so that a few students could write science fiction stories with vampires and aliens. The goal was to think about the way society has changed since the 1950's, and to find the situations in which we are most afraid and vulnerable to deindividuation. Here are some of the final projects (bit.ly/flipping28).

Create Your Own SparkNotes—in the San Francisco Stories class, the main novel we studied did not have any online resources, due to it being a local and less-well-known novel. Students struggled with the novel because of its unusual plot structure and abundance of characters with a constantly-changing narrative point-of-view. Because this novel would be used by future classes, students were tasked with creating a resource like SparkNotes that had summary, analysis, and visuals to help students understand and engage more deeply with the text. The final project was built into a website and kept for future classes to use, but it was not finished at the time of publication, so we could not include it in this book.

Character Analysis Video—for the play *Death of a Salesman*, students were shown how to analyse a character in-depth through patterning. Prior to the project, we had read one character's lines in isolation, found patterns, and used those to show personality traits and ways of interacting with other characters. Then students chose a different character and made a video in the style of a video by the Vlogbrothers (bit.ly/flipping29). They started with a very long one-sentence summary, and then they talked about the character in a way that made us understand and empathise with that character.

What they learned from this project is that making video takes a long, long time, and never turns out quite how you want it to turn out. Their final videos are not terribly successful, but they did revise the scripts after we watched and scored the videos in class, and the quality of their analysis was much better in the revised scripts. This project proves that failing is sometimes more instructive than succeeding (bit.ly/flipping30). This was the first time that we had students create the rubric by which they would be scored, and we found it to be incredibly instructive and helpful to have them learn to articulate what the important learning goals should be, and how to judge if they had met those goals. If you have never had students create their own rubric, try it. Cheryl describes this project in her blog (bit.ly/flipping31).

CoFlipBooks Reads The Fault In Our Stars—this is actually cheating a little bit, because students were not involved in the beginning of this project. However, it was the inspiration for videos our students made about the same book, and we included their discussion in the book club as well, so it counts. In January, seven teachers who know each other only through Twitter decided to read a book together and make videos about each of the chapters. All the videos would be collaborative, with changing partnerships throughout the project, and posted to YouTube (bit.ly/flipping32). The idea is to do a reading journal on video that helped other readers notice the things that we noticed as we read, and to see the book and its characters in a more complex and empathetic way.

Those were, by no means, the only projects we completed this year. However, they do give you an idea of how to incorporate new media, reading, writing, research, and technology into the English classroom. Also, notice that all of these projects are available, publicly, on the internet. Many students had only ever experienced posting on social media, where they could limit the number of people who could see their work. Publishing online, especially under their own name, was scary for them, and even more so when their face appeared too. But it also challenged them to think through everything they posted carefully, and put more effort into the project than they normally would have. In the final evaluations for the course, these projects were consistently mentioned as some of the most powerful and impactful projects they had ever completed.

NOW WHAT? OR, WHERE DO WE GO FROM HERE?

As we said earlier in this chapter, we know that we don't have all the answers here. We are just figuring out the role that PBL will play in our classroom; however, there are almost infinite possibilities, and by collaborating with each other, our PLN, and our students, we have created a lot of content of which we are really proud. Like with everything else in our practice, we had to fail a lot in order to succeed at all. So we aren't holding these projects up as the "Be All End All of Flipped English PBL" because that's insane. Instead, we're trying to give examples of project we've used that span a wide range of subjects and skills so that you can be inspired to create projects within your own instructional context. As long as you are: 1) thinking about the learning objectives, 2) giving students multiple ways to demonstrate their understanding of those objectives, 3) creating something for which they will have an authentic audience and 4) creating a pathway for students to get meaningful feedback on the project, it's hard to go wrong.

Our hope is that over the next year, we will develop more projects that promote our students to content creators, rather than passive recipients of information, and give them the tools to be successful in their future education and careers. Project-Based Learning, like Flipped Learning, is really a bridge to a more student-centred classroom, in which students utilise higher-order thinking skills and make the best use of their face-to-face time. We are still trying to figure out what that means for us, and we hope to continue to learn from our PLN and our students how to best do that.

71

Flipping 2.0

The reason we flipped our classes, and the reason we continue to associate with the flipped learning movement is because we wanted our classroom to change and we found a community that made change possible. While our flipped class may look very different from other flipped classes, and even other English flipped classes, we continue to associate and collaborate with the flipped community because we find that we have more in common with a Flip 101 science teacher than we have with traditional English teachers. Our practice is informed by the practices of hundreds of other teachers who started flipping their classes in order to give their students a better teacher and a better learning environment.

That is why there isn't a binder or how-to manual for how to flip your class: it is only a good idea to do something if it works for you and your students. Differentiation is a key component of flipped learning, and it allows you to meet your students individually, and build their skills alongside their responsibility for learning. In our experience, it takes 8-10 weeks of skill-building and transition to get high school students to the point that they are able take on more of the responsibility for learning. We can't tell you that you should aim for PBL, or asynchronous mastery, or whatever other model there is out there. We can only tell you what we've done, how it works, and what we've learned, and hope that you can use that information for your classroom. Flipping inevitably involves failing, and failing forces innovation. That is an evolutionary process we support wholeheartedly.

The final rule with which we will leave you is *you* are the expert on your students. Flipped learning will never replace the teacher because the most important part of a flipped class is the face-to-face time where the teacher can differentiate and build relationships with students. You do not need to be a content-area expert or a flipped pedagogy expert to move your classroom towards a student-centred environment that helps students build higher-order thinking skills. The flipped learning community on Twitter and on the Flipped Learning Network Ning is a great way to find answers to the content-area questions and pedagogy questions you run into as you flip, and we encourage all teachers interested in flipped learning to join the Ning and participate in the Twitter chat (that we moderate) on Monday night at 8 PM EST. It is a great way to meet other educators and get ideas to help you make your class the most effective learning environment possible.

THAT CHAPTER WAS REALLY LONG. CAN YOU DO A TL;DR*?

Yes.

Collaborate. Build meaningful projects with authentic audiences and real-world skills embedded. Use technology to help students experience reading and writing in a more meaningful way. Metaflip your learning process. Consider allowing your students to read and write during class time. Implement the Flipped Mindset as much as possible. Collaborate.

Google it. Okay, fine. It means "too long; didn't read."

Cheryl Morris is an English teacher in the San Francisco Bay Area, who has a decade of experience. Since flipping her class in 2011, she has begun a cross-country collaborative partnership with Andrew Thomasson, and they have embarked on several major projects (other than team-teaching their classes), such as launching the Flipped Learning Journal, moderating the Monday night #flipclass chat on Twitter, and presenting about the power of collaboration and flipped learning at conferences around the country. She blogs at www.morrisflipsenglish.com and can be found on Twitter @guster4lovers, at their shared class website www.tmiclass.com, or their shared email address: cherylandandrew@eduawesome.com.

Andrew Thomasson is a high school English Language Arts teacher and learner in North Carolina. He is the other half of Thomasson-Morris Instruction, a collaborative partnership with Cheryl Morris. Andrew is co-creator of the Flipped Learning Journal and co-moderator of #flipclass chat and #ncedchat. He can be found on twitter @thomasson_engl .

Social Studies

Karl Lindgren-Streicher

I've been tasked with writing about what a flipped history classroom looks like, and this is something I feel eminently comfortable doing: I've been flipping my world history classroom, in various incarnations of flipped learning, for a year and a half. By no means does this make me an expert, but it does make me someone who has made enough mistakes to have a few ideas about flipping a social studies class.

Before we get into the chapter, I'd like to offer a broader definition of flipped learning than is often given. Don't define it by saying that flipping your classroom is putting lecture on video and assigning it as homework. Think about the flip in flipped classroom as the flip from a teacher-centered classroom to a student-centered classroom where students are allowed to make meaningful choices about their learning and are asked to manage their learning while maximizing the opportunity for higher-order thinking.

However, before delving into what a flipped history class looks like, or what any class looks like, it seems like a couple ideas should be marinated upon.

Initially, ask yourself what your ideal classroom looks like—not the physical layout, but what happens in your class. What are you doing? What are the students doing? What materials are being used? Do it. Now. Take five minutes. Or ten.

After conceptualizing your ideal classroom, ask yourself, will a flipped classroom help you get to that ideal classroom? Will aspects of a flipped classroom get you closer to what you want your classroom to look like? In my mind, this should be the starting point: your ideal classroom.

Since you didn't ask, I've got some ideas about the ideal classroom, specifically what I want my history class to look like. I was lucky enough to build my history pedagogical content knowledge with Sam Wineburg[1], a spectacular history education professor who pushed my thinking in this area. History is often presented as a singular glorious narrative of progress that is to be consumed by memorizing a set of old names and dates. Thankfully, I had a couple great history teachers in high school (Mary Schmidt and Jon Friedberg) that presented it quite a bit differently.

The combination of these experiences helped create my ideal history classroom: a classroom presents history not as one story or one set of monolithic facts, but as numerous stories with quite a bit of gray area and numerous points of contestation. The ambiguity about the past, the place where real historians spend their time, are where I want my students using their intellectual energy. To have students spend time in this area, they need access to conflicting primary and secondary sources about events in history. These documents help them confront the sometimes contradictory narratives of history. This requires a literacy-rich approach to a history class. This, then, is my ideal history class—one that lives in the ambiguous gray areas of history, asks students to make judgments about what has happened in the past, and is literacy-rich.

After defining an ideal history class, I also should reveal my bias about what I think school should be. The ninth and tenth graders I teach are No Child Left Behind (NCLB) kids; they have only known the culture of high-stakes testing that has sacrificed critical thinking for content memorization. While this is a travesty of the highest order, this is not the place to make this longer argument. Given the NCLB-influenced push for memorization, I also want school—and my classroom—to be a place where students learn the soft skills that are so important in life: time management, collaboration, and creativity, to name a few. I want school to be a place where students want to come, a place where they enjoy learning because they are offered significant choice about what they will learn and how they will demonstrate that learning. However, I have been contracted by the state of California to teach world history. Because of the requirement

---

[1] For an introduction to Wineburg's ideas, check out *Historical Thinking and Other Unnatural Acts* (Temple University Press, 2001). You can thank me later--it's that good!

that I cover world history content in my classroom, I want my history class to get as close to my definition of both an ideal classroom and school as I can. Flipping my history class has allowed me to do that.

But you aren't reading this chapter to listen to me wax philosophical about history classrooms – this is a book about practical strategies to use in a flipped classroom. Let's get to those!

Unit Setup

For now, I use the California state world history content standards to guide my history planning. I'm not too concerned with the CCSS—in fact, I'm hopeful the Common Core will allow me to move closer to my ideal history classroom: a classroom that is more student interest driven and is less shaped by content standards. I start with a unit question that, in order for students to answer it well, will force me to cover most of the content standards of a given unit.

You'll notice I said most of the content standards; I leave out content standards that don't fit my unit question. Skip them completely. This is a change that I have made while flipping my world history classroom. Flipping my class has come with the choice that I will not teach content standards just to cover them. I won't teach content standards that don't fit my unit question, which is guided by state content standards. This usually means I leave out a couple of the content standards that the state of California says I should teach in each unit.

After creating the unit question, I decide what content absolutely must be taught for students to have a reasonable answer to our unit question. Then, I look for places in the unit I can push students' thinking into those ambiguous gray area of history. Once I find those places, I use a variety of pedagogical strategies. One is opening up the textbook, where bias and misinformation about the past—as well the other inadequacies of textbooks—are vivified by selected primary and secondary sources. I also use inquiries, which start with a multi-sided (not a yes/no) historical question. Then multiple plausible answers to that question are presented to the students in primary and secondary sources forcing students to synthesize disparate arguments and come up with their own interpretations of the past. I also use structured academic controversies, which start with a two-sided historical question. Students then research one assigned side of the question, then combine with experts that researched opposite side of the question and come to a consensus about their own unique right answer to the question. A last favorite pedagogical tool of mine is the Socratic seminar. Socratics are lengthy (entire class period) whole class discussions based around the big ideas in the unit complemented by relevant primary and secondary source enrichment.

Nothing too revolutionary here. However, the more interesting thing—where the flip from teacher-directed learning to student-managed learning occurs—is that for three to four week chunks within a six week unit, students will do this work at their own pace. I design the tasks within a unit so that students can complete them without doing any out of class work. Yes, this means I flipped my class and eliminated homework. A flipped classroom does not necessitate students watching videotaped lectures—or doing any other kind of work—outside of class.

If students don't quite finish the activity they were working on in any given day, they pick it up the next day. If a group of students completed a task early, they are free to work ahead. No more "Finish this off tonight for homework." This anti-homework stance is a personal preference, but one that I believe in strongly. Flipping my class allowed me to eliminate homework. That's a definite win in my mind. And there will be more on self-paced learning later.

I then look into end-of-unit activities. These generally include both a structured academic controversy as well as a Socratic seminar. Students do these end-of-unit activities synchronously, as a whole class. Structured academic controversies aren't nearly as rich when done individually or with one or two other people; there is power in the shared wrestling with a question that structured academic controversies necessitate. Similarly, an entire class is needed to do a Socratic seminar. The more people we have thinking about an idea (or set of ideas), the more information and meaning students are able to create amongst themselves.

So, in short, my units are taught to answer compelling unit questions, make students spend as much time as possible in the gray areas of history, and are structured in such a way to transfer the pace and ownership of learning from the teacher to the student. Each unit also includes about two weeks of whole class activities that work towards students doing evaluation and creation of knowledge.

DAY TO DAY CLASS

This is where, in my classroom, things begin to look a little more interesting. At the beginning of each unit, students receive a list of content and activities they must demonstrate mastery of in order to move on to the summative assessment for the unit. Check out a truncated sample of this below:

Activity	Title	Suggested date of completion	Mastered
Page 1	What caused the Industrial Revolution?	9/1	
Notes 1	IR inventions (use screencast 1, textbook pages 342-345, or your own sources)	9/3	
Page 2	What was the most important invention during the IR?	9/5	

This is an incomplete sample of what the content and activities (classwork) of a unit would look like. I suggest students progress through the unit from the top of this sheet to the bottom. They move through this classwork at their own pace; some students complete in two weeks the work they have three to four weeks of class time to do and head off to work on their twenty percent projects[2]. Others take more time. Yes, this means sometimes students fall way behind the

---

[2] When students finish work for a given unit early, they work on my version of a Google's twenty percent project or do work for other classes. Google has a company policy that twenty percent of an employee's time should be spent on topics that are related to their job but are of their choosing. The innovations that have come out of this time include Gmail.

suggested pace I set for them. A myriad of interventions are available to work through these difficulties: one-on-one discussions, parent emails/phone calls/meetings, or individual contracts for success. The suggested date of completion gives the students a pace at which they can feel comfortable working: if they stay on the suggested pace of the unit, they will complete the classwork before the end of the unit.

When students complete a portion of a unit, we have a discussion about that section. If all is well, I initial the 'Mastered' section of the chart for a given activity and students move on to the next part of the unit. Sometimes, evidence of misconceptions or incomplete understandings arises in these conversations and students go back and revise their work before moving on.

Additionally, at the beginning of each unit my students receive a list of the six to ten short answer questions that will be their unit test. Students earn the right to take this test by demonstrating mastery on the classwork for the unit. They must earn a 75% on this unit test before they move on to the next unit.

In designing units that don't require students to work outside of class and choosing to teach to compelling unit questions (not the bloated California state world history standards), I am able to scale down the amount of content I am asking students to be familiar with, which allows more time to be spent in those ambiguous gray areas that make history so interesting. However, I am still not convinced that in a history class you can do the work of historians—the critical thinking in those unclear sections of history—without some contextual knowledge. This knowledge lives in the lower levels of Bloom's taxonomy. Students gain this contextual knowledge about a historical event in whatever way suits them. As you can see in Notes 1 in the chart above, students may choose to watch a screencasted lecture that I create to get this contextual knowledge. They can use their history textbook. Students are also free to go off and do their own research to gain this context.

These changes in how I teach world history came about in part because of Jon Bergmann and Aaron Sams' now famous question: "What is the best use of my face-to-face time with my students?" I want students with me for all the time they are working for my class.

Wherever they get stuck, wherever they need a question answered, there is an expert in the room ready to help them. This expert might be a classmate that is farther along in the unit than they are. It might be me. But in my opinion, the best use of my face-to-face time is to have students do the work for my class with me, and this work should consist—as much as is humanly possible—of the work that historians do.

Another aspect of my flipped world history classroom I owe to Brian Bennett. Brian has made the point numerous times that by teaching in a self-paced class, we allow students to make judgments about what is the best use of their time in class is. For most students on most days, this means working on world history. However, some students will use my class to study for a math test or to prepare for a Spanish benchmark. In my mind, this is exactly the kind of choice I want my students to make. If the best use of their time in my world history classroom is to do work for another class, that is fine with me. I only ask that when students make this choice that they stay on the suggested pace I set for them—if this means that they will do some work outside of class, that is their choice. By allowing students the freedom to manage their time in my class as they best see fit, I am hopeful that their ability to both prioritize what is most important for them and to manage their time—two soft skills that will never show up on a standardized test—improves.

So what does my world history class look like on a day to day basis? Some students will re-arrange the desks in my room and dig into primary source documents trying to create their own interpretation of a historical controversy. Others will head out into the hall and build historical context with a screencast or a textbook or a computer before launching into some historical inquiry. Still others—those students who are ahead of the suggested pace—might be working on a twenty percent project. A few might be off in a corner studying for a geometry test. Others might have their desks pulled away from their peers while they are taking a unit short answer test.

What's the best part of this? I get to spend my entire class period walking around, talking with students, building relationships, correcting misconceptions, and checking in about a sick family member or their soccer game last night. Thanks to flipping my history classroom, I talk to every student in my room every day.

WHERE I WANT TO GO

Despite all the exciting and innovative learning that goes on in my class, my history class is not where I want it to be. It is closer to my ideal classroom, but there is still a ways to go.

Where am I looking to continue to evolve my world history classroom?

1. I need to learn more about Project-Based Learning; I believe that PBL will inspire in students more of a desire to gain and effectively use content knowledge.
2. I'd love to be able to eliminate tests all together; I worked to make test less high stakes by telling my students the questions for the short answer test, but I'd like to get to a place where I get rid of tests all together.
3. I need to keep bouncing Ramsey Musallam's Explore-Flip-Apply framework around my head and try to more meaningfully integrate it into my world history class. In short, Musallam's framework calls for inquiry (Explore) to learn material and surface misconceptions before instruction (Flip) fills in gaps in knowledge and corrects those misconceptions. Then, students are asked to Apply their knowledge in a novel environment.
4. I need to free up more time for my students to work on their twenty percent projects. There has been time for this in my class, but it has not been twenty percent of the class time. I'd like to get to a place where twenty percent of my class is spent on this project.
5. I have also had a couple of failed attempts at student blogging. I'd love to get to a place where students have the space, desire, and authentic audience to blog regularly.
6. Additionally, I'm sure there are fifteen other things I've forgotten.

FROM THE MOUTHS OF BABES: MY STUDENTS' WORDS

Since my students have spent a year in the environment I've already described, I asked them for some advice for teachers and students who move into a self-paced environment.

My students' advice for teachers

- Think about how long it would take students to complete the work, not adults. *Aiden H*
- Teachers should make sure every student knows the suggested due dates. It is easy to get behind or procrastinate, but a constant reminder of the dates coming up helps keep people on task. It will also make sure that people are at a good pace. *Matt K*
- Kids will be off task, and it'll be annoying, but if you structure your class with self-pace, they are going to make that choice. *Kaylie S*

My students' advice for students

- Don't talk or sit next to your friends you talk to a lot. Sit next to people who will motivate you to work. *Nancy S*
- Do your work, try to fulfill the due dates, your life will be so much easier. *Kevin O*
- Students should know that just because it is unstructured, doesn't mean you can slack off. All the unstructured part means is that you can relatively go at your own pace, but there is a point where you have to do the work you are supposed to. *Aidan S*
- Respect their teacher who is doing this because not many students have this much freedom with their work. Be constant with working or you may fall behind without knowing. *Josh B*
- You need to get work done during class and if you slack off you will have to catch up later and do a lot of work then. *Parker A*

SUMMATION

So, why flip your history class? Several reasons:

- Move closer to your ideal classroom.
- Personalization: I build relationships with students pretty easily, but since I flipped my class these relationships have been created much more quickly.

- Knowledge of the strengths and weaknesses of your students. Similar to personalization, I learn my students' strengths and weaknesses so much more quickly now because I spend all class walking around talking to students.
- Opportunity to emphasize soft skills: the never tested at school—but oh-so-important-in-real-life!—things like collaboration, resolving conflict, and creatively solving problems.
- Student choice and differentiation. In my experience, differentiation and student choice have been more easily and more commonly integrated into my classroom after I flipped it.
- Finally, the numbers. My failure rate decreased by seventy five percent after I flipped my class. The percent of students receiving a C or higher[3] in my class increased as well.

LET'S TALK

So get out there. Talk to people- me, the other (way smarter than I am) authors of this book. Find us on Twitter--use the #flipclass hashtag and check out what gets posted to that throughout the week. Join us on Monday nights at 8 EST for the weekly #flipclass Twitter chat.

Join the conversation. Let's make education better. You know you want to!

Karl Lindgren-Streicher learns and teaches with 9th and 10th graders, mostly about world history. He has been teaching at Hillsdale High School in San Mateo, CA since 2008. He believes that school should focus on critical thinking and literacy, and his classroom reflects that. Find him on Twitter at @LS_Karl or email him at karl@eduawesome.com. Links to his blog, class website (with all sorts of world history content), and various other things can be found at about.me/LS_Karl.

---

[3] In California, classes where students receive a C or higher allow them to receive credit for the entrance requirements for all University of California and California State University schools.

Social Studies
Jason Bretzmann

In 2006 I was cutting edge. Unlike my predecessor who used write-on transparencies, I had a PowerPoint presentation for every chapter.

Half a dozen years later I noticed changes in my students. They were no longer able, or willing to engage with me on what I considered to be pretty engaging lectures. Every other day I was frustrated. Why weren't they the same as last year's students? Or the students from six years ago? Or when I first started teaching full-time in 1997? Apparently things had changed, and I was ready for a change to something better, too.

Perhaps I knew it was necessary before a high school senior commented on her end-of-the-year evaluation that "PowerPoint is a terrible way to learn," but it wasn't until I woke up early on a Sunday morning in August that I determined what I needed to do. I needed to flip my instruction, and I needed to figure out how to do it. Before I got there, I asked myself questions as I went through a step-by-step process to arrive at the first day of school as the lead learner in a flipped AP Government and Politics course. Teachers should take themselves through a similar process when flipping.

WHAT MORE DO I NEED TO LEARN?

My first step was to find out more information. I read *Flip Your Classroom* by Jonathan Bergmann and Aaron Sams. It's an excellent starting point that everyone thinking about flipping should read. I think their book outlines what flipping is, why to do it, and gives some ideas on how to start. I also participated in a flipping support group that was facilitated by the technology integrators in the Muskego-Norway school district where I teach. It's important to have a network of people to bounce ideas off of, ask for ideas, and commiserate with when necessary. This group turned out to be another starting point for me, and my more powerful learning network became the flipclass chat on Twitter that I started attending on Monday nights at 7p.m. (CST) using #flipclass.

We all have different needs in this regard. I liked the ability to be anonymous and lurk in the beginning. I was brand new to all of this, and I didn't want to discover the many things I didn't know while also broadcasting them in a world-wide forum. Many would say that putting our ignorance and vulnerabilities out there for all to see is a better process, but in the beginning it wasn't for me. Either way, eventually I asked a question, and then made a few comments. Now I feel comfortable chatting, sharing links, giving suggestions, and of course I still ask questions. It's an on-going process that I hope never stops helping me improve. Another online group that helped was a great online flipping forum that I joined www.flippedclassroom.org. There are a lot of smart flippers there sharing content specific ideas and questions. My bottom line was that I read as much as my research abilities and time would allow.

HOW COMFORTABLE AM I?

I did an informal self-inventory to determine my level of comfort with flipping. How comfortable was I with something new and different? Could flipping be successful in a social studies class when most of the current flippers were in math and science? How would students, parents, and colleagues respond? How could I give up lecturing (especially since I thought I was pretty good at it)?

I've always been open to what's new and different *if* I could see the benefits for my students and move forward on my own terms (i.e. with my students' learning in mind and without someone telling me I had to do it, or had to do it their way). Because I have always been an early-adopter of educational technology, I liked the opportunity flipping afforded to leverage the new technologies I was using and researching.

(If you're not an early-adopter and someone who tries different technology tools to engage students, flipping will be a little more challenging in the beginning, but it is still possible. When you start flipping, you'll probably need to use some technology so be aware of that. Don't let it discourage you from trying. You will probably learn as you go with the technology you need and with your overall flipclass experience. Forge ahead anyway.)

While I felt comfortable with some aspects of flipping, I had not figured out yet how this would work in social studies, but I determined that if I could work that out, the potential for in-class discussions and the higher level thinking that would happen would be so powerful that I couldn't walk away. I figured students would respond with skepticism at first, followed by the excitement associated with having their voices heard, and then real learning could occur because of the collaborative nature of the work, and the guidance I could provide. Students are resilient. You can't break 'em. I was less concerned with the response from parents and colleagues because after the reading I had done, and the networks I was a part of, I felt I could explain the extensive benefits of flipping and could therefore assuage any fears or concerns that might be brought up.

Not to mention, I had a very supportive administration that not only supported innovation and experimentation, but encouraged it. Principal Ryan Oertel and Associate Principal Ken Dunbar emboldened my efforts by indicating in various ways and at various times that they wanted teachers to feel like it was acceptable to try new things (and sometimes fail). Associate Principal John LaFleur even suggested I talk about what I was doing at a statewide conference. When I declined, he kept asking and gently suggesting that I should do it. I relented, loved it, and I received entirely positive feedback—now my group and I are available for various educational technology and flipclass professional development sessions. We can also keynote your conference or opening sessions at your school or district. We inspire, educate, and entertain. Contact us through www.bretzmanngroup.com and we'll tailor a presentation for you. Shameless self-promotion complete.

Finally, after convincing myself I could succeed without all my engaging lectures full of silly walking styles, strange voice intonations, and terribly drawn illustrations, I decided that I could work my way toward being more comfortable with the answers to each of these "level-of-comfort" questions because flipping had the potential to have a powerful and substantive impact on the depth of learning that my students would do. I pledged to go forward. That commitment only raised more questions.

WHAT DO STUDENTS DO AT HOME
(OR ANYWHERE IN THE WORLD)?

My initial thought process was that it didn't make sense to have a bunch of explanatory videos to replace book reading. My students need to read. Bergmann and Sams said that it was acceptable to flip your class in a way that works for you. Students reading the book works for me. I decided that at home students would need to read the textbook as they had done in the past.

In addition to the reading, students would need to watch videos of me explaining the learning objectives for each chapter in our text book. The video lectures would replace my in-class lectures. While video lectures are important for my class right now, most people who flip would tell you that flipping is not just about videos. Some teachers don't use videos, and some who do don't make their own. What I decided was most important was that I was working my way up Bloom's Taxonomy. The lower level thinking would be done at home (reading and watching), and the higher level thinking would be done in class (everything else).

I believe it is best to make your own videos because you know exactly what your students need, exactly how you want the content explained, and you have a relationship with and connection to your students (they want to hear from you, and not somebody on the internet that they don't know). At the same time, I fully recognize the limitations and numerous obligations that teachers have in their professional and personal lives. A video created by someone else is a great substitute when time constraints create no other option.

Eventually, I tried one chapter without videos because it made sense for that chapter. Instead of me telling students on video about the chapter's concepts, students researched to find their own examples in order to show their mastery and ability to apply the concepts. I was happy that through the whole chapter only one student asked when the videos were going to be posted. The other students were learning from the book, from each other, from the world, and from me in class. They either didn't notice or didn't care, but they didn't ask. After all, they had the textbook from the experts and the whole world to learn from. They were learning on their own.

This was good for the particular chapter I tried it with, but it was not good for every chapter. I thought that students were ready to be on their own without my video guidance, and with control of their own learning, but that was not the case. I think the lack of videos in some successive chapters gave students a license to let up and slack off a bit. It gave tacit approval in some cases to not work hard outside of class, and that led to less intense discussion in some cases in class.

For now videos continue to be an important part of the introductory, lower-level thinking part of my flipclass. It took me about a month to figure out which video-creation tools worked best for me. I tried a lot of them. Some of them worked, but didn't do everything I wanted. Some of them shut down my computer, or didn't do anything at all. For me the Camtasia screen-capture and editing program by TechSmith is the most useful. It comes with a 30-day free trial, but then it costs money. I was willing to buy it because it allows me to make videos that can not only include what is on my screen with my voice, but it can also include a picture-in-picture option so I can appear sparingly in the videos. My students seem to like it that I'm in the videos instead of being some disembodied voice talking to them.

Camtasia also allows me to edit like an expert, and add call-outs when I want to add text to the videos. Inserting extra explanations as callouts is particularly useful for when I forget to mention something in the video or realize later that something I said needs additional explanation. Camtasia also allows me to include pictures, music, and intro or outro screens to further engage students. As I advanced more with the program I was able to highlight, zoom in, and add other interesting features to my videos. My next step is to figure out how to incorporate the "Green Screen" option that was added.

To a lesser extent I have used the free and useful video creation tool called Educreations. Although it also has a website at www.educreations.com that works with the same login information as the iPad app, I find the iPad app to be more useful and user-friendly because I can use my finger or a stylus to draw and write. I've used Educreations more for short vocabulary videos because I can include a picture on the background and write on it to further explain a term. Because these are usually short, easy videos I'm not too concerned about the lack of editing capability since I can simply start over if I have a major mistake, outtake, or screaming three-year-old. There are other free apps and websites, but these are my favorites.

Let me reinforce the idea that flipped learning is not a way of replacing "real" teaching and learning with videos by sharing two examples.

When studying Congress, I determined that there was a better way to learn the content than me telling students via video or other means about the intricacies of that body. I told students that everyone in politics has written a book and asked, "Why not you?" Instead of me presenting the information, students wrote their own book on Congress.

I gave students three big ideas that served as the focus of the three chapters they were required to write. They were responsible for researching, selecting, and including information that fit within their chapters and was relevant and meaningful to them. Students explained their content and then curated it in a published print book using the online tool createspace.com (to create a free e-book, use www.yudu.com). Outside of class, students did their preliminary research. They brought it to class and we worked together to make sense of it and organize it into meaningful prose. To aid that process, we used a Google Form for self-assessment and to monitor their progress, and we had constant conversations in class. Because they owned the process and the outcome, and they were producing something for an authentic audience, students created exceptional work that had depth, insight, and an exhaustive explanation of the concepts and vocabulary. Some even added chapters so they could include a more thorough explanation.

Another example occurred during our exploration of the campaign process. We called it "Curate the Campaign." Instead of telling students about the campaign process, students were required to sift, select, and store the information that showed they had mastered the content. Instead of me explaining on video what retail politics is, for example, students found videos or articles of retail politics and applied their definition to these real-world examples. They curated their examples using tools like Symbaloo, Diigo, or MentorMob. They then shared the information by presenting it in class and disseminating a link to their classmates. The flipped mentality that includes the idea that students are responsible for their own learning helped with the success of this process. Students worked hard to showcase their mastery of the content and made good decisions to include the most relevant, meaningful, and accurate information and examples.

HOW DO I KNOW THEY DID IT?

As teachers we need proof. While I had never done it before in this college-level class, I required students to take notes related to each learning objective for both the book and the videos. I decided that students would have to show me the notes to prove they had done the reading and watching. This seemed to be a way of ensuring that students would be prepared for the in-class activities.

To show they did it, and to organize the information, I suggested students take Cornell notes. If students had their own note-taking system that worked for them I allowed them to use it, but I insisted that they include two things: 1) Cues, questions, or labels that identified the "traditional" narrative of the main body of notes, and 2) A summary of each topic, or page of notes so students had to synthesize and connect the information.

In the beginning I checked the notes student-by-student in class. I spent so much time checking the notes that I never got to talk about the social studies content with my students. That bothered me. Flipping was supposed to be about all of us talking about the content in class. I did not want to be the lead note-taking specialist. I wanted to talk government and politics with my students.

I reflected on and changed this after I had an associate principal come in to teach my class. I had gone to watch another teacher teach, and when I returned I asked my students how it went with the principal teaching. They said it went well, and they worked on learning and collaborating like every other day. He asked them to explain what they knew about the learning objectives. They were proud that they could answer his questions and discuss the content, but they said all he did was walk around and ask questions about what they were learning. Almost immediately I said, "That's what I should be doing." So that's what I started doing.

In order to make it happen, I had to solve two problems. How do I continue to check notes to make sure students did what they were supposed to do (without taking up class time)? What do I ask students in class to keep the questions and answers fresh and focused?

To solve the first problem, I turned to technology. I had students use my iPad to document what their notes looked like so that I could check them outside of class. We started by having students take videos and explain what I was looking at, but that turned out to take up too much space on my iPad and we kept running out of room by the third hour of the day. So we switched to taking pictures of the notes. The students added an index card with their name and e-mail address to each photo. This allowed me to clearly see who did the notes, and e-mail the picture back to the student with comments if necessary (it was also a great use for all those old index cards I had in my desk from a by-gone era).

To solve the other problem, I developed a list of standard questions that resulted from research on Socratic questioning. For each chapter, I printed a one-page sheet of possible questions to ask, and then added the learning objectives for each chapter to it. I carried that around with me to each group and used it as my personal assistant for asking good questions each day. When I felt like I ran out of questions, or like I was asking the same questions over and over, I consulted my list and asked something new and challenging.

WILL I USE A MASTERY MODEL?

My next thought was about what students would do in class, but before I could answer that I had to decide if the class would work off of a mastery model or something like it. Once again I was liberated by the approach outlined by Bergmann and Sams to do what would work. I determined that a modified mastery model would work best. Students would work their way through mastering predetermined learning objectives. They would all proceed at different paces and go to different depths as true differentiation occurred. Students would have choices on how they would show mastery. Nevertheless, all students in the class would have to arrive at the same point on certain dates that were determined by the class. I believe it is important for social studies students to have full-class discussions so it was important to me that the whole class was available and knowledgeable for a discussion. In addition, since it is an AP class, I determined that while they could show mastery in any way they wanted, all students would still have to take the high-stakes test at the end of every chapter's activities. They had to practice for the important AP test in May.

In the middle of the year when students started to wander off in their focus and intensity, I introduced the "10 Minute Tune-up" to help students prepare to show their mastery. To introduce it, I made a short video using another TechSmith tool called Jing. At the end of the video, students had ten minutes to make sure that each member of their group understood and could explain each of the learning objectives that I chose. After ten minutes I randomly chose one of the group members to go to another group to present their knowledge (e.g. oldest in the group, alphabetical by middle name, etc.). The new group would determine whether the student was proficient in the assigned learning objective.

I usually instructed students to prepare for two learning objectives during the ten minutes and then I would assign them alternatively to every other group—i.e. group one gets learning objective #1, group two gets learning objective #2, and group three gets learning objective #1. This was billed as "Pass/Fail." If the member from your original group passes, your whole group passes. If she fails, the whole group fails. It gave an incentive for all group members to make sure everyone in their group was proficient. A lot of focus was placed on the sometimes-struggling-learners for that ten minute period. There was intense discussion for ten minutes and then real sharing of learning as the chosen student went to the new group. All groups passed each time.

Another way I added to the process of mastery was by using Google Forms and the Flubaroo script to offer formative and summative assessments. This allowed me to show students what they need to know, discuss immediately in class the questions students had trouble with, and gave students almost immediate feedback via e-mail.

WHAT WILL STUDENTS DO IN CLASS?
In math classes students could do the odd or even numbered problems. In science classes students could do lab experiments.

Since those types of activities don't usually exist in a social studies class, I had to figure out what students would do with all of the time that was now available in class. I wanted students to engage in higher level thinking, and I wanted to be there to guide them through it and challenge them to go farther and deeper. In addition, I wanted to try to talk to each student in each class every day to help eliminate misconceptions in their thinking about the content, and to build a relationship with each student.

I decided that after reading the book and watching the videos at home, students would come to class and discuss each of the learning objectives using ten prompts as a guide. The discussion starter for these 2-4 person collaborative groups was students' Interesting Questions (IQ). Their IQs were student-created, content-related questions that that they didn't know the answer to. Students attempted to answer the questions in class, and did additional research to create an answer. The intermittent availability of technology limited the exploration that students could do in the beginning, but this improved when the Bring Your Own Device infrastructure was improved and even more when we were able to use nine Chromebooks after spring break.

Students also created multiple choice and free response test questions to connect their learning to how the learning objectives would show up on a test. Later, students evaluated whether the questions they wrote were good or bad test questions. Students applied their knowledge by connecting the learning objectives to recent news stories and to other chapters in their textbooks. Students clarified the meanings of all the vocabulary terms, shared their mastery product ideas, and gave feedback to each other on their mastery products. In addition, students explained their notes summaries and the learning objectives to me as I went from group to group asking questions, clarifying meanings and tweaking discussion topics.

Initially I thought that we wouldn't have enough to do in class. It turned out that discussing, exploring, and understanding take a long time. I have found that when my students have a lot of control over their learning, they take a lot of responsibility for it. Their discussions have been focused, meaningful, and they have led to a deeper knowledge of the content.

With student feedback added to my own observations and reflections, I scaled back the in-class activities because they were taking too long, and they weren't producing any meaningful additional results. We repositioned the creation of test questions, and the discussion of mastery products, and refocused our efforts on the following:

1. Constructing a shared meaning of the learning objectives in a collaborative effort,
2. Sharing and understanding the significant vocabulary,
3. Connecting the chapter's content to other chapters, and
4. Connecting the chapter's content to examples in the news (current events).

We made the other topics into additional topics to discuss if students had time.

Overall, one of the major problems that we ran into was pacing. With student choice and student voice as an important component in the class, I included students in the decision-making process for due dates and timelines. Unfortunately, we didn't realize how long the learning would take, and how the presentation of products would add even more time to the learning of the content for each chapter.

Students created wonderfully meaningful ways to present their knowledge, but the products took a long time to share with the rest of the class. As I reorganized for the following year, I decided to require that all products to show mastery are recorded as a video, or are able to be turned in in some other way. We'll choose which products we'll have presented during class time with an opportunity for each student to share his or her knowledge at some point throughout the quarter or semester.

In addition, I created a suggested calendar so that each chapter gets the necessary time allotment during the year. Students have some negotiating ability within that framework to maintain the student choice and student voice that I think is important, but the framework will help us get to where we need to get to in this AP class. I also added more chapters that should be read simultaneously. For example, when we are intensely studying the chapter on Federalism, it makes sense to also have students read the chapter on economic policy. They go well together, can create connections for students, and will allow students to get the information from that chapter without having to go more deeply into a chapter that doesn't necessarily require it.

My next steps also included the introduction of additional short, explanatory, teacher-led activities, and more directed project-based learning for my students (these are short, engaging, rigorous and relevant). But let me emphasize that while I will include more mini-lessons in class, I'll never go back to "all lecture all the time.'" I tried going back to lecture for one chapter (mainly because I had determined at the beginning of the year that I would do that to compare). I did it and I thought that students would respond by carrying their previous experiences forward and continuing to be engaged learners. Nevertheless, the majority of my students fell back quickly into last year's style of not responding. They were mentally back in the big lecture hall where nobody spoke, or answered questions. I was broadcasting, and they were in the audience. They were non-responsive, and in some cases they might have fallen asleep.

The bottom line was that they were not learning at deep levels, they were not actively engaged, and I wanted to go back to the small groups where I knew students had learned and were engaged on a daily basis. I raced through the lectures so that I could move on to the next chapter and let the real learning happen again. The chapter was good for that anyway because it had large theoretical ideas and not a lot of specifics. I hit the high points of that chapter then we moved on. It was a relief to go back to real learning and engaged students showing deep mastery of the content.

HOW WILL STUDENTS SHOW MASTERY?

After their intense discussions in their collaborative groups, in class students created their products to show mastery. In the beginning of the year, I told one group of students that they should work on completing their discussions by that Friday so they could work on their products over the weekend. I came back the next day and corrected myself. I told them I didn't want them at home alone banging their heads on their desks because they couldn't figure out what to do. I said I wanted them to come to class and bang their heads on the desk there. After some initial chuckles, they understood that I wanted them to work on the higher level thinking at school so I could help and guide them along the way.

Students are required to present their product or make it available to other students because their products are one more learning opportunity before the high-stakes test. The products they have chosen to show mastery have included well-constructed essays, competitive test-question games, detailed PowerPoint and Prezi presentations, student-created videos, and scavenger hunts of test questions using QR codes and smart phones.

Some of my favorite flipclass experiences have been the creative and engaging products that I got to see my students present. They spent a lot of time creating them, and they were proud of the work they did. They were experts on their topic and they were able to show that they had mastered each of the learning objectives. One student, Brittany, even asked a half-rhetorical question. "What if every teacher flipped? I wouldn't have time to create all the products. I worked really, really hard on this!"

HOW DO I KNOW IT'S WORKING?

My students come to class with knowledge and are ready to apply it, evaluate their understanding, and create something new. They have detailed and organized notes. They discuss the content and challenge each other on different topics. They use Google Forms for self-evaluations in order to assess their learning and ask for help when they need it. They have developed positive relationships with their classmates and me.

When I show up at a group and ask one of the students to explain a learning objective to me, the student can do it. Students are striving to construct meaning, and connect vocabulary terms to other concepts instead of memorizing words next to other words. My students are internalizing and connecting the concepts instead of remembering random facts for a test. Even so, students are taking the tests, and test scores are improving.

For now I'm going to side with my former student who has a noticeable contempt for PowerPoint and continue to move forward with the flipped classroom. She's onboard, too, as evidenced by her recent e-mail. "It's really awesome that you changed the class to be more engaging..."

Jason Bretzmann *is a respected teacher who has been a leader in bringing technology to his students in the traditional and flipped classroom. He is the lead learner in his AP Government and civics classes at Muskego High School in Muskego, WI where he has taught full-time since 1997. A national presenter and consultant on educational technology and flipclass strategies, he is the founder of the Bretzmann Group of edtech consultants who provide engaging, inspiring, and practical professional development. Jason also authored "Using Todaysmeet to Engage Students" in the book Instructional Strategies that Work. Find him on Twitter @jbretzmann or email him at jbretzmann@bretzmanngroup.com.*

Math
Audrey McLaren

This chapter is about my flipped math class. Like every other flipped class, it's a work in progress, with the accent on progress. It's also a composite of ideas I got from many other people, some math teachers, some not, some of whom are flipping, some not. I am an equal-opportunity ideas user. One of the best things about the journey I began three years ago has been the constant renewal through the people I have met, and the collaboration that has resulted. Which is kind of what I want my students to experience!

Looking back on the three years since I started the flip, I see three distinct "Flip-ages", which is why the chapter is split into three sections: Flip-age 1, 2, and 3, which correspond roughly to beginner, intermediate, and my current stage of math-class-flipping, which I am extremely hesitant to label expert. I have given Flip-ages 1 and 2 the subtitles Lessons and Class time/Help, respectively, because those periods, for me, were characterized by my focus on those particular aspects of the flip. Please feel free to jump to whichever section you feel is the one you need.

A WORD ABOUT THE WORD "FLIP"

Like most teachers who flip their classes, I began by recording my lessons and having my students complete work during class. But those lessons, and the class work, were at first very much the same ones I had been using pre-flip, because my way of teaching, and I suspect yours too, was never pure lecture anyway. I had always woven into each lesson lots of opportunities for students to participate, such as diagrams to label, notes to fill in, and examples to work out first with me, then on their own. Good math teachers have always been aware that to learn math, you have to do it, not just watch it.

So the biggest change that flipping represented for me, initially, was not so much about *what* I did, but *when* I did it. You can see a visual representation of this on my blog (bit.ly/flipping33). For that reason, I prefer to call it the shifted class, but since I'm terribly outnumbered in this regard, I'll keep calling it the flip here!

FLIP-AGE 1: THE LESSONS

Flipping my class, at first, didn't mean starting over from scratch, or changing everything about how I teach. Mind you, that is what eventually happened as a result of flipping, but it's not how it all started. I happened to be lucky enough to have already taught the courses I first flipped, and I had also made PowerPoint versions of all my lessons, so it was relatively easy for me to go full-flip right away. All I needed was a way to record my "teaching" to accompany the slides, and to make the resulting lesson available for my students.

I had heard of a tool called VoiceThread sometime before this, and it turned out to be a perfect fit. (Funny how the tool only became useful to me once I had a pedagogical need for it!) VoiceThread is an online tool that allows exactly what I had been looking for, plus the bonus that my students could then add their own questions or comments wherever they needed to right in the lesson. After a few views, a conversation around the content begins to take form entirely outside of class time. You can see an example of that here: bit.ly/flipping34.

I make my VoiceThread's by uploading something to VoiceThread. That "something" is either a PowerPoint, or a Camtasia-recorded version of the PowerPoint. Initially, I stuck to the PowerPoint-to-VoiceThread formula but eventually, and as time permitted, I used the Camtasia-recorded version of the PowerPoint. The Camtasia version takes much longer, but is much more fun! I'm still learning how to use all these tools, even though I've been using them for years now. Note that everything ends up on VoiceThread, so that my students' voices are always part of the lesson. In this way, that part of the cycle is less static, and less passive for the students. In fact, I find that their questions and comments feed into the face-to-face time in an invaluable way, as I'll explain later.

Making of recorded lessons

I have two suggestions about the making of the recorded lessons for anyone who is at square one, that is, anyone who has never flipped a class before:

Suggestion 1: Watch other people's lessons (Khan Academy, Mathis power4u, mine) to get ideas. If you like them enough, then instead of trying to make your own right away, use them for your own students.

Suggestion 2: (Me neither! I felt uneasy about my students learning from someone else, but it was worth a shot.) Then I suggest you make your own *using lessons or skills you already have.*

If you *haven't* already taught the course you're planning to flip, at least use a medium or tool that you already know:
- If you use a regular chalkboard, get someone to record you doing a lesson that way.
- If you have access to an interactive whiteboard, use the recording tool that comes with it.
- If you have an iPad, there are many apps, for example, Explain Everything that many teachers recommend for creating recorded lessons.

If you *have* already taught the course you're flipping, record the lessons you already have. Don't try to redesign them just yet, just record them, put them somewhere your students can get at them, and that'll do just fine for now. The inevitable tweaking and refining will happen later, I guarantee.

If you decide to use VoiceThread, here are a few tips:
- I make students' comments a requirement, as proof of watching and participating.
- Their comments can be:
  - their answers to question prompts in the VoiceThread
  - their questions about whatever the lesson is
  - a response to another student's question or comment
  - an observation about something in the slide or VoiceThread
  - anything else that demonstrates their participation

- I show them examples of good comments and "H.O.T." (coined by Crystal Kirch) questions made by students

- I often begin the next day using those comments, so that the "lesson" is not isolated from the face-to-face (face-to-face) time:
  - to address a common mistake they have all made
  - to address a particularly good question asked by a student:
    - see if anyone else was wondering the same thing
    - see if anyone knows the answer
  - to address an important question I posed in the VoiceThread (which I sometimes put there for that very reason)

Whatever you decide as your lesson-creation-and-delivery tool, you'll find right away that moving the lesson outside of class makes a difference to many of your students. Suddenly, there is elasticity exactly where your students need it, in the amount of time needed to absorb the math.

On pacing

I recommend no more than three lessons per week. If you are making video lessons, the total play time should be around ten minutes. This doesn't necessarily mean that it will take your students only ten minutes to watch it, however. It will take longer than that if you require, as I do, that your students take notes or do examples as they watch, just as used to happen during my pre-flip class. My students tell me that it takes them between 30 and 45 minutes to complete everything.

My examples:

You can see an example of a VoiceThread made from a PowerPoint (bit.ly/flipping35), and one made from a Camtasia recording (bit.ly/flipping36). You can find examples of all my lessons on the VoiceThread page of my blog (bit.ly/flipping37).

FLIP-AGE 2: THE CLASS TIME

The reason I recommend you not tinker too much with your lessons at first is so that you can arrive here, in the face-to-face, as quickly as possible. This is where the real transformation started, for me. This phase began about two weeks after I started flipping. I don't mean that I was done creating my lessons—I was still spending all kinds of time making the VoiceThreads at this point—but what really kept me awake at nights was the face-to-face time. A few students would ask questions during class, but they were the same students I'd had at "hello". Other than that, it was disturbingly quiet in my class, and I knew it wasn't because everyone was suddenly getting everything. Things have evolved considerably since then, and now I use my class time in two ways: for activities (whole group and/or individual), and for individual help.

On creating activities

First of all, my advice is the same as it was for the lessons: use the ones you already have! We all have some in our toolkit, and they're good right now, flip or no. One teacher who came to see a presentation of mine explained to me afterward why he was thinking of flipping. His favourite part of teaching math happened at the very end of a unit, when he would assign challenging problems, walk around his classroom talking to his students, helping them as they needed it, and getting to know them better by interacting over the math. But until then, he felt like he was just powering through the content so he could get there. He already knew, as I'm sure you do too, at least one way he would use that face-to-face time.

Whole group activities

A few guidelines for whole-group activities: I try to fit at least one of the following aspects into the activity:

- *Take advantage of the group*: The activity is best done in a group, something for which they are at an advantage doing in a group as opposed to alone.
  - A large task that would be too much for one person to handle but which can easily be divided up in a group.
  - A problem that can be solved in more than one way.
  - An open-ended problem with more than one possible solution (in Quebec, we call these situational problems).
  - A task where you want collaboration and brainstorming.
  - A task that involves students' opinions.

- **Zooming in and out:** The activity allows different zooms, or perspectives:
  o **Social zoom**: As humans, we all like to know what others are thinking. The sharing moves from the individual work (at home or during class) to small groups (2-3 people during class) to a larger audience (whole class, Google Doc, or blog.) For many students, this order is the most comfortable way to get real collaboration happening. I compare it to navigating a neighbourhood using street view, then map view, then Google earth view. It exposes students to other working methods, reinforces a sense of belonging, and validates their own intuitions.
  o **Content zoom**: The activities give the perspective of details, where those details fit into the big picture and some other layer over that big picture. I'm not suggesting that this be in any particular order; whether to start with the big picture or end with it probably depends on the unit you're teaching.
- **Differentiation** of the level of difficulty so that everyone can jump in somewhere—those who are struggling as well as those who are ready to move ahead.

My examples fall more or less into the categories below. They don't all hit all three of the above guidelines, but they're a good start:
1. **Organizing** large amounts of information
2. **Summarizing** a skill or a concept
3. Doing one of the types of activities outlined by Malcolm Swan in "Improving Learning in Mathematics" (bit.ly/flipping38)
   a. **classifying** mathematical objects
   b. **interpreting** multiple representations
   c. **evaluating** mathematical statements
   d. **creating** problems
4. **Investigating** a new topic

Example #1

Organizing exact values on the unit circle—Unit Circle Palooza Students move the information to their appropriate locations on the blank unit circle. I created several copies of a PowerPoint in Google drive (bit.ly/flipping39) so that they could work on it in groups. Since students could simply move the values around, and hence didn't have to do any writing, their time was free to discuss, debate, explain etc.:

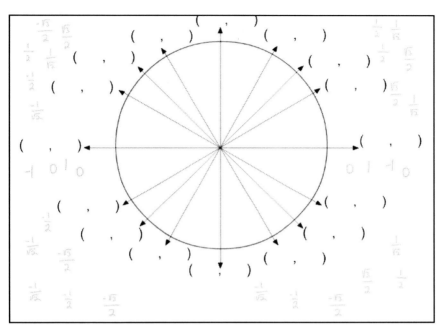

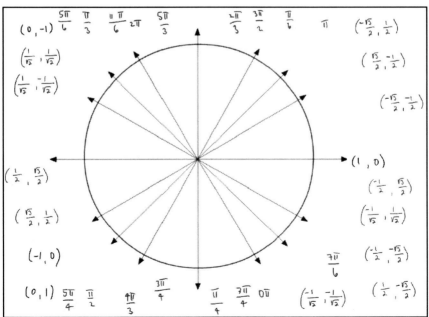

Group advantage: The sheer quantity of information that they have to absorb makes this a task that naturally gets spread out over the whole group

Zoom: Each group later had their own group's finished product to see and compare with their own notes, as well as other groups' to compare with on a larger scale. This is great validation. Content zoom went from ordered pair to individual numbers in the ordered pair—in other words, the detail came after the bigger picture. This lead to a third viewpoint—a discussion about the patterns that exist due to symmetry.

Differentiation:
- Those who were least confident were able to place the simplest ordered pairs, and give input as to which quadrant other ordered pairs belonged. This activity also gave them a good visual cue to the fact that the values with pi in them were angles, and the ones with square roots in them were coordinates.
- Those who had watched the VoiceThread's but not fully absorbed now had the opportunity to straighten out details that often trip up students, like the difference between $1/2$ and $1/\sqrt{2}$, or the fact that $\sqrt{3}/2$ is always paired with $1/2$.
- The strongest students had no problem arranging the info, corrected mistakes, had it all memorized as a result, and explained to their peers how they remembered when the $\sqrt{3}/2$ comes first or second in the ordered pair.

Example #2
Interpreting multiple representations of vectors:
Students are given what appear to be many different vectors, but in reality, there are only three different vectors represented. They must sort the identical vectors by shading with identical colours.

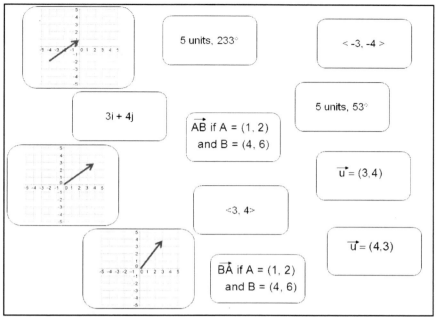

Example #2 figure

Group advantage: Quantity of information, more people involved increases the likelihood of someone noticing the subtleties that are easy to miss

Zoom: This activity is awash with content zoom: recognition of basic notation, skills involved in comparing two vectors by magnitude and direction, comprehension that there are in fact only three vectors on this page

Differentiation: The discussions that revolved around this activity were rich in learning and in math. Some of the matchings required only recognition of the various notations, while others needed some calculation. Everyone had the opportunity to find out that that there are many different ways to represent the same vector, and those who were very strong saw the subtleties like the effect of changing the order of the components.

Example #3

With sohcahtoa: the task: Students worked in pairs to make up trig problems, solve them, exchange with their partner to solve theirs, compare answers and methods:

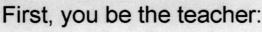

First, you be the teacher:

- Give this triangle an angle, a side length, and an x.
- Find x using sin, and write your answer on your notes slide.
- In your BOR, ask your partner to find x for your triangle, and check if it agrees with your answer.
- Once you both agree, you do your partner's triangle.

At this point, they were only familiar with the sine ratio, so before we moved on to cos and tan I wanted them to be very conscious of which sides are involved with sine Θ. As they made up their problems, they had to be very intentional about where they put their "x" and their known side, once they had placed their angle measurement. If they hadn't put them in the right place relative to their angle, it was revealed when they tried to use sine in solving their own problem.

With logarithms—The task: Identical to the above except they were making up questions like $\log_4 64$. They had just been introduced to logarithms, and again, before moving on to examples involving negative or rational answers, I wanted to be sure they saw the relation between base and argument. Again, having to make up a question that made sense (argument should be a power of the base) helped the idea of logarithms make sense.

Group advantage:

- Students get to enjoy the same satisfaction teachers do when they watch someone else solve a problem that they made up. The sense of ownership is a big motivator.
- It's also a really safe group size to make a mistake in. I made an effort to pair students by matching their abilities, to minimize the risk of anyone feeling saddled with the task of tutoring, or anyone feeling outclassed by their partner.
- It's way more fun in pairs!

Zoom: I have to admit I didn't do this last time, but next time, I will get them to upload their problems and solutions to a Google doc, their blogs, and/or our class blog. Not just for the extra practice examples, but so that they can see that the given information can look different even when it's all the same type of problem.

Differentiation: This worked really well with the medium-to-high level student pairs, but I spent a lot of time working with those who were struggling. Fortunately, I was free do so, seeing as the others were off and running.

Example #4
Investigating the log function:

Students were to find out everything they could about a new function: $y = \log_2 x$. They were pretty familiar with the log operation, but had never seen the function before. I blogged about this activity, in which I used something I call a "hintroduction" (bit.ly/flipping40).

Group advantage: This is a huge task, to be sure. It took an entire period of 50 minutes. This was definitely a case of the rising tide lifting all boats!

Zoom: Content zoom between the hintroduction and the task. One was about the operation, and the other was fitting it into a bigger picture.

Flipping 2.0

Individual activities

When it came to "cooperative learning", I was, as a student at least, a decidedly uncooperative learner. I did not enjoy group activities! Now I feel very strongly that well-designed and organized ones are essential, but individual work is just as important. Not only for variety's sake, but to acknowledge that there are different personalities in my classroom, as well as times when everyone needs to work alone. This section is about tasks that I leave up to my students to decide whether they want to do it alone or with someone.

I do assign the usual practice examples from our text book, or worksheets that I have made up. More and more, I like to use tools of a more interactive, creative nature. It's much more interesting, for them and for me! My hope is that in doing the task I've made up for them, they will inadvertently discover something unexpected, or something that I don't know. I don't want anybody to be limited by me or by the curriculum! This is much more likely to happen in a one-on-one setting, where kids are more free to follow their own interests rather than a group consensus. It's also more likely that they will happen upon something that they can teach me if they're using a tool with which I am only slightly more familiar than they are. Which is pretty much everything I use. This way I get to be an authentic model of lifelong learning, and as a bonus, maybe one of my students gets to take on the role of teacher once in a while.

My current favourite for this kind of individual discovery is Geogebra, a free Dynamic Geometry Software. I have created some very simple interactive worksheets with it, (see *Figure 1*), which was all about finding the rule of a square root function:

They type in a function rule at the bottom of the screen so that the curve has the given vertex and passes through the point with a matching colour, so that it looks like *Figure 2*.

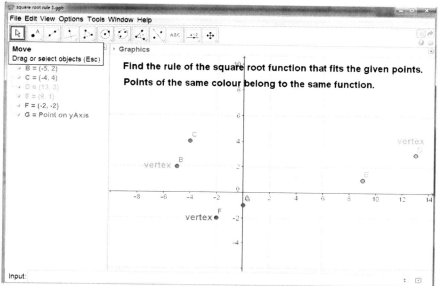

Fig. 1

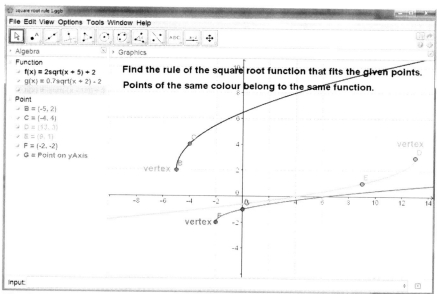

Fig. 2

Note that they know right away, by looking at the graph, whether or not their rule was right. This is another thing I love about this software—not only that it saves me correcting time, but the instant visual feedback makes students more motivated to keep trying till they get it right. The example with vertex D, in particular, finally convinced them of something I had been unable to—the impact of the negative multiplicative parameter in the square root rule. I gave myself an inner high-five every time one of them informed me that Geogebra "wasn't working", because their curve was going off to the right instead of through E. Good times!

Geogebra can be used for more inquiry-based learning. Here is an example of what I call an explorer, in which students can type in any function (*Figure 3*), then move the sliders and watch the effects of the parameters (*Figure 4*):

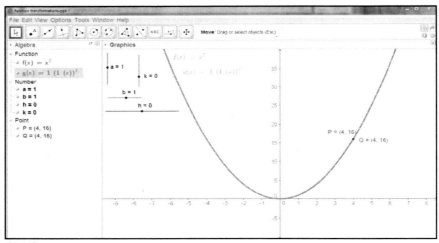

Fig. 3

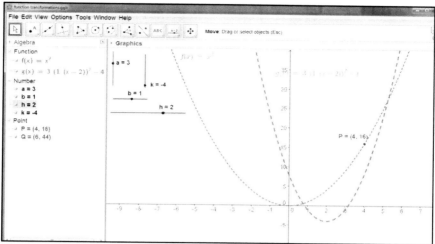

Fig. 4

If you would rather use ready-made interactive worksheets instead of creating your own, you can find many at geogebratube.org. There is a large world-wide community of talented teachers who create these worksheets and share them via this website. In fact, the last example was created by math teacher John Herbert, who very kindly shared it with me.

Individual Help

Of course, what's nice about the flip class is that I'm not the only one for students to turn to for help. Their peers are also available, usually much more so than I am. But, as a teacher, I still want to have regular conversations with my students, even if they don't need or want help.

Many teachers say that they get to talk to every student every day in the flipped class. This has not always been the case for me. For one thing, not every student will initiate a conversation with the teacher. We all have a handful of those students who always do, and who, more importantly, know when they need to do that. But then there are the other kids—those who either lack the confidence to talk to the teacher, or don't have a clue what to ask. I remember one student saying to me "I know that I don't know, but I don't know what I don't know."

This is our chance to have those conversations with the other kids—the ones who won't or can't get the help they need. But if you open with "How's it going?", it won't go very far.

Ideally, by the time you sit down with them, you need to have a lot of info already at your fingertips so that the conversation will be based on reality, and so that you can both hit the ground running. For example, what have you done, when did you do it, how did you do it, did you watch the lesson, what assignments did you do, did you have trouble with any of the questions, when did you do stuff, all in one shot or spread out, did you check your answers, did you have the TV on while you were working.....obviously it would take an awfully long time to ask all these questions, so I provide my students with plenty of ways to communicate this kind of information to me not only during class but between classes.

In addition to VoiceThread, I use checklists, a class blog, and student blogs. Other teachers use handwritten notes or interactive notebooks (and I mean real paper ones), but the point is, to some extent, the gathering of that info needs to happen outside of class time. Since it's a huge amount of data, it's simply too much work for the teacher to collect, so *I let the students and technology take care of that.* In effect, *they* begin the conversation with this information.

Checklists:
Most of the students' information comes from checklists that I create using Google Forms. I make an online checklist each week that they must update as the week progresses. Here's what a typical week's checklist might look like (*Figure 5*):

Weekly Progress Checklist:

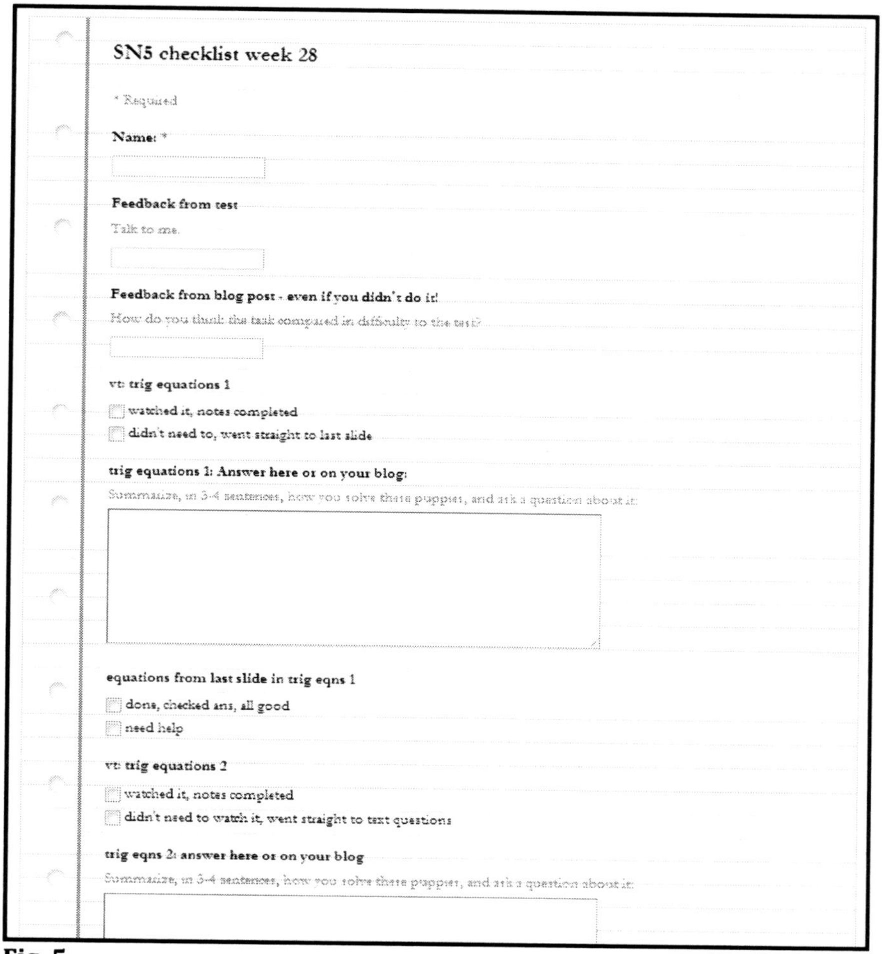

SN5 checklist week 28

* Required

Name: *

Feedback from test

Talk to me.

Feedback from blog post - even if you didn't do it!

How do you think the task compared in difficulty to the test?

vt: trig equations 1

- [ ] watched it, notes completed
- [ ] didn't need to, went straight to last slide

trig equations 1: Answer here or on your blog:

Summarize, in 3-4 sentences, how you solve these puppies, and ask a question about it:

equations from last slide in trig eqns 1

- [ ] done, checked ans, all good
- [ ] need help

vt: trig equations 2

- [ ] watched it, notes completed
- [ ] didn't need to watch it, went straight to text questions

trig eqns 2: answer here or on your blog

Summarize, in 3-4 sentences, how you solve these puppies, and ask a question about it:

Fig. 5

As you can see, some of the items require a simple check, and others require a text answer. Since I create the checklist using a Google Form, Google takes care of organizing all the data into a spreadsheet for me, and I can view it by student, by day, or by any other field I choose. Only I see this information, so that they can be perfectly candid. Here is what I see, for one student after two days into the week (*Figure 6*):

Timestamp	Name:	Feedback from test	Feedback from blog post even if you didn't do it!	vt: trig equations 1	trig equations 1: Answer here or on your blog:
(All)	C	(All)	(All)	(All)	(All)
3/25/2013 7:52:19	C	I did not have time to finish but overall it wasnt too hard)	I definetley think the blog post was a lot harder than the test but I hope I got a better mark on the blog post because I am not sure if I passed the test S [1]	watched it, notes completed	
3/26/2013 15:48:05	C				see blog)

Fig. 6

A colour indicates on which day of the week the student updated their checklist, so that a quick glance tells me what they did and when they did it. When it's time for individual help during class, I have my Google spreadsheets open, so that I already know how each student's week has been going. Of course, if they haven't updated the checklist yet, that's the first thing we'll talk about. If they have, I'll respond to whatever needs to be seen to. For example, if "Need help" has been checked off, or if I need to follow up on a test result, that's where we start.

These checklists have become crucial way for me to track and, just as importantly, connect with my students. Not only do the checklists give me a prompt for the individual conversations, but they are a lifeline of communication between me and my students that's there 24/7. They can use it to tell me things that I'm sure I wouldn't otherwise ever find out about. Sometimes it's a difficult situation they're going through, sometimes it's a suggestion they have for our class, and sometimes it's valuable feedback, good or bad, for what I'm doing. There are even times that a student checks "need help" on something, but by the time it's their turn for help, they've forgotten all about it. Good thing they wrote it down somewhere!

VoiceThread comments:
Students are required to leave a comment somewhere in the VoiceThread. If their comment is a question, I either answer right away in the VoiceThread so everyone can see, or I might do so during individual help time.

Class blog and student blogs:
These are for communication of a different nature than students generally provide via the VoiceThread or the checklist. Blogs are a good tool to use for deeper levels of learning, such as reflection, or posting a finished project.

The Class blog: At the beginning of the year, I create the class blog, the students create their own blogs, and then I link the class blog to all of their blogs. I use the class blog to post information that I want all my students to see, such as instructions, or exemplars of good work, or a collection of their own words, taken from the current week's checklist. On one checklist, they submitted their tips for remembering the important angles on the unit circle, which I then collected and posted on the class blog:

Amanda, on how she remembers the radian angles by their denominators:

"Basically, I separate the circle into sections; the "over" 1s, 2s, 3s, 4s and 6s. Then, in my mind I visualize the lines that would be there and place my values."

Jessica, using a visual relationship to remember the radian angles (and not the one we talked about in class, either):

"I have worked on the Ferris wheel with Javiera and we have both realized that there is a mirror image (for the denominators) from left to right. Also, we have realized that the fractions that are the same color all around the circle, have the same denominator."

Cassandra, another memory aid for radians:

"My tip is that the first is a red cross which represents the quadrantal angles. Then we separate this cross into 4 pieces with yellow lines. Then we split the 180 degrees into 3 with pink lines. And finally we separate the 6 angles into halves with green lines."

I did this because I was having a hard time getting them to read each other's blogs and to comment on them. I wanted it to happen organically, rather than for marks. I wanted to show them that other peoples' ideas were worthwhile reading, as it gives them the opportunity to compare with and assess their own ideas. I had some success, but there is still room for improvement. An unexpected advantage was that this turned into a good opportunity to talk about how to comment.

Flipping 2.0

The class blog also serves as a subtle hook for web tool use. I often embed a video, a VoiceThread, or a Geogebra applet, in the hopes that someone will find it very cool-looking, and ask me how to do that. It has worked a few times!

Student blogs:
I encourage my students to blog whenever they feel like it, but only a handful blog on their own initiative. Usually I had to assign blog posts in order for them to use their blogs. Those assignments ranged from homework problems to in-depth chapter summaries, and even long-term projects. I also encourage them to use web tools, such as codecogs for math and science notation, so that their posts have a more finished, professional look, as you can see in this student's post about identities:

$$tanx(sinx + cotxcosx) = secx$$

$$(\frac{sinx}{cosx})((\frac{sinx}{1}) + (\frac{cosx}{sinx})(\frac{cosx}{1})) \qquad\qquad = \frac{1}{cosx} \checkmark$$

$$\frac{sinx}{cosx}((\frac{sinx}{1}) + \frac{cos^2x}{sinx})$$

$$\frac{sinx}{cosx}((\frac{sin^2x}{sinx}) + \frac{cos^2x}{sinx})$$

$$(\frac{sinx}{cosx})(\frac{sin^2x + cos^2x}{sinx})$$

$$\frac{sin^2x + cos^2x}{cosx}$$

$$\frac{1}{cosx} \qquad \checkmark \qquad\qquad QED!!$$

In case any of my students ever wonders why I'm so keen on them blogging, they have only to look at my own professional blog, which is also linked to the class blog. I can't think of a better or more authentic way to model for them the benefits of reflecting on one's own learning than practicing what I preach.

On Pacing

I would suggest that during any given week you:

- leave at least two days where most of class is given over to students doing their own thing, and you're having those individual conversations with them
- have at least two days of planned class activities
- assign no more than three lessons
- have at least one conversation with each and every student. It may not be as good as having one every single day, but it's way better than I was ever able to do pre-flip.

FLIP AGE 3: THE BIG BEAUTIFUL BLUR

I call this stage the blur because it's getting difficult for me to tell where the lesson ends and the help or activities start. I try to design the activity so that the learning takes place there and then, with me and the rest of the class together. I am trying to cook my lessons down, as much as possible, to the bare bones. If it's possible for my students to learn it in class, by doing something, then that's where I'll put it, rather than in the recorded lesson. If it's better to reinforce via group collaboration, I'll move that into class time. The best evidence I have that this merging of learning-and-doing is happening is that I now have a new folder name in the file structure on my computer: "activities". I have been teaching for over 25 years, and until last year I never had a folder with that name.

This is one area in which I don't honestly have a lot of concrete suggestions, because I feel I have only just begun this phase myself.

All I know is:

- I'm chopping up my lessons by moving parts of them into the class, or replacing lessons with class activities.
- I'm taking long lessons and splitting them into two or three shorter ones. I do not wish to reveal how long they were to start with, but okay, there was one with 104 slides in it. Sorry, students of my past.
- How to decide what to move into the class: anything that involves the higher-order thinking, the things that are more likely to require support, should happen when that support is more available, and that's when you're all together at the same time.

A lesson through the (Flip) ages

In <u>flip-age 1</u>, my unit on trig functions looked something like this:

1. Unit circle angles
2. Exact values of coordinates
3. Here's what the graph looks like when you plot angle vs. x-coordinate
4. By the way the "cos" is x and "sin" is y...
   [*Several weeks later....*]

10. Applications like the height of a car on a Ferris wheel.

As you can see, it's so flip-age 1 because:

- All of the info was delivered via the VoiceThreads, so all the emphasis was on the delivery of content.
- Students' work was largely practicing, memorizing exact values
- There was no opportunity for students to explore, let alone wonder about circular motion, or how different it is from linear motion.
- They never had to wonder what the trig function graphs were going to look like, because I showed them in the VoiceThread.
- The values that were used to make that graph were the exact ones, like $\sqrt{3}/2$, which were quite abstract to them.
- The sequence was from abstract to concrete.
- They had no concrete situation to which to compare it until the very end.

In <u>flip-age 2</u>...Same sequence, but I moved step 3, the graphing, into the class. The change was not so much about what I did, but who did it and when. One class was spent plotting points and joining them, without any prior knowledge of what the resulting graph would look like. The only problem was that they were still graphing the exact values, which were difficult to wrap their heads around, let alone locate them on a graph. It was still way too abstract.

In <u>flip-age 3</u>, about which I blogged a lot this year, the sequence, the approach, the central characters, the tools, everything was totally different. I used Geogebra to create a virtual Ferris wheel activity.

Here's a Ferris wheel where you can make the car go around by dragging it:

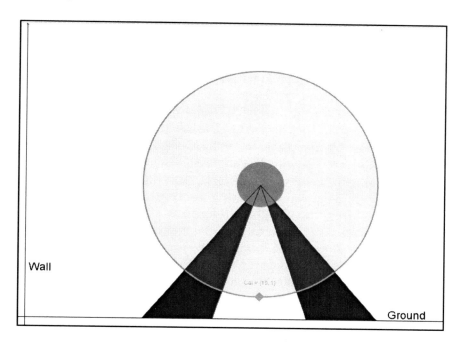

And as you do that, you can always see how far it is from the wall, and how high above the ground it is:

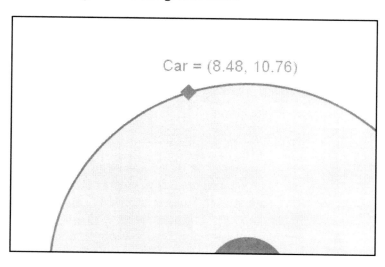

Flipping 2.0

The Tasks
In your group,
1. Plot the height of the car against time.
2. Compare your graph with other groups.
3. Upload to Google Docs so we can all see them.
4. Which one do you think is right?
5. Figure out how to get a function that makes a graph like this.

I completely reversed the sequence in flip-age 1:
- We moved from the concrete to the abstract.
- In making up the table of values, they stumbled upon the convenience of knowing the angle at which the car was
- They got to discover the wave form from their very own data
- They then discover that using *sohcahtoa*, we can define a function that graphs height as a function of angle.
- Later, as we progressed to the very abstract, they had this very concrete framework to hang ideas onto, for example, when we got around to the exact values, which I moved much later, they could see them as merely coordinates on the Ferris wheel.

There were other key differences, but as mentioned, I wrote a lot about this unit on my blog:
- "New intro to trig functions" (bit.ly/flipping41)
- "Follow up on new trig activity" (bit.ly/flipping42)
- "A week without homework. Sort of". (bit.ly/flipping43)
- "It almost looks like I know what I'm doing" (bit.ly/flipping44)

I'm sure next year, if I get to teach this again, I'll tinker some more, but even if I don't, at least, I hope, someone somewhere will use it and improve it for me, and for all of us!

Audrey McLaren *has been teaching high school math for over 25 years. Since 2008, she has been teaching in a live, virtual classroom for an organization called LearnQuebec, which supports the English educational community in Quebec, Canada. Find her on Twitter @a_mcsquared, or on her blog at audrey-mcsquared.blogspot.ca. or at about.me/audrey_mcsquared.*

Math
John Stevens

Math is hard, but there's no mystery in that. As students, we were drilled and killed, and we repeated that cycle for twelve years (or more). As students, we didn't understand why we had to learn so much in so little time. As students, we deserved better. Couldn't they just slow down and make sure we got it? Wasn't there a way for the classroom to be adapted to make sure that we had enough time to ask questions and dive deeper into the content?

Near the end of my 6th year of teaching, things had to change. Algebra wasn't going to change. We still needed to cover 21 standards of complex material that students had never been exposed to prior to that school year. We still had 51 minute class periods that nobody was about to extend to allow for the depth of conversation that is necessary to truly master a standard or concept. Being a teacher can be difficult due to the constraints that we are under and the variables that we are not allowed to vary. The traditional school system is what it is: stable. Therefore, something else needed to change: me.

After attending the CUE conference in March of 2012 and listening to Ramsey Musallam talk about the flipped classroom and its benefits, my mind was made up. If the system wasn't going to change, I was going to do my best to adapt. From there, the flipped classroom for my students was developed. In this chapter, I will walk through the steps that were taken to establish a flipped classroom and some of the advantages of moving to the flipped model. To be warned, it isn't easy. There are times where, especially in year one of a flipped classroom, the work gets overwhelming. Just like anything, start in moderation and learn from others as you go.

THE VIDEOS

Let me start by saying this: the flipped classroom model is not about the videos. It is not about technology. Taking the same boring lesson, recording it, then sending it to YouTube so the kids can watch it at home; this is not the goal of the flip. For me, taking the chunk of the content that students really need to understand, teaching it to them at home, then having them come back with questions, is what I love about having a flipped class. Video allows me to do that, but it isn't the focal point.

In the short amount of time that I have been doing the flipped classroom, there have been a number of experiments. As teachers, we have a unique chore of finding programs, apps, and platforms that allow for the best possible outcome. To me, this seems even more difficult for math teachers because of the formulas, exponents, and graphs. This challenge is something that we get the pleasure of sifting through for best practices.

In the beginning of the flipping revolution, I was using an iPad with the app called Educreations. It was an ingenious plan because Educreations came with a coordinate grid background. I could easily screencast all of my lessons, especially the graphing problems, upload them to the Educreations server, share or embed the videos, and have students rejoice. The problem? Students were having trouble watching the videos on any sort of iOS device.

One student in particular, Janet, would get onto Edmodo on a regular basis and let me know that my attempt to flip my classroom was being blocked by a glitch with her device not being able to view the videos. She was a motivated student, wanted to do well in the class, and had bought into the concept of the flipped classroom. By now, this issue has been resolved, but I've since moved on to different apps and ways to record.

For quick tutorials or on-the-go flip lessons, I love to use the ShowMe app. It's free, of course, and it is very easy to use. There is an eraser in the mighty rare, yet seemingly often, case of an error. There is no graph paper background (as of this printing), but I can pause the recording while I meticulously sketch out the graph that I'm hoping for. When finished with the video explanation, the files automatically get stored to the ShowMe server and I can upload them into Edmodo or embed them into my website for students to view. It is truly a perfect solution for those times when students need help with a few problems and typing/writing it out just doesn't do the concept the justice it deserves.

This was all good in theory, but there was some resistance from my classes. The quiet kids did what they were told, but the ones who took ownership of (and pride in) their learning started to speak up. Anthony, a strong math student, pushed back against this idea of the flipped classroom. *"Stevens, why can't you just teach us in person?"*, he asked. After talking to him about how the flipped model allowed for more time, I started to realize what he was really saying. See, all through school, Anthony was used to a teacher standing in front of him and delivering instruction. All of a sudden, the teacher was gone. Without compromising the advantages of this new style for my classroom, I made a deal with him. "What if I record myself going through the instructions at the whiteboard instead?" Bingo.

I'm all for optimizing the voice of my students, so I listened to Anthony and the others who felt the same way. Armed with a Flip Camera (purely coincidental in the name...or is it?) and a crate to make sure that it was at eye level, I began recording single-take lessons at the whiteboard after school. Since then, I have moved into recording with my iPad using the following setup: a Makayama movie mount adapter, basic tripod, Samson USB microphone, and my whiteboard. Once I'd get my setup in order, I would spend 15-20 minutes planning out what was to be taught, working the problems out ahead of time to ensure that the solutions are what I was looking for and there weren't any hiccups in my instruction of the material. As instructors, we do this anyways in traditional instruction, so nothing really changed here.

After the planning came the camera time. Starting out, it was embarrassing. I've never been afraid of the camera, but the thought of making something that needed to be perfect made for a difficult taping process. Once the first couple flipped videos were out of the way, I stopped worrying and started teaching like there was a room full of students listening to my every word. The videos ranged (and still do) from 6-12 minutes, doing everything I can to stay under the 12 minute mark. My goal is to be as concise as possible without plowing through the content. 12 minutes should be sufficient for one lesson, while many of them will be under.

Helpful Hint: If you are a little bit camera shy, ask a couple students to come in and be a sample class for your first few recordings. Two students who would typically have nothing to do after school got roped into my room, sat down, and pretended to be my students while I got comfortable teaching to an empty room. It was perfect timing!

In the videos, I introduce vocabulary, discuss real world applications of the standards, teach the formulas and how they are derived, and work through practice problems. Once the video is done, it's off to watch the video to make sure that it's what I was looking for all along before it gets uploaded. I've tried a number of ways to upload videos for student viewing and each has its advantages. Vimeo, YouTube, Weebly's video uploader, and TeacherTube are all good options, depending on your site's network firewall and students' access.

As a firm believer in Weebly (education.weebly.com), a free website creator, I now have an option to record my lessons and upload them directly to the Weebly server. It does require the upgrade of $29 per year, but the cost is well worth the lack of headaches of students not accessing the videos because YouTube and Vimeo are blocked (which they were). The downside to this is that they files have to be under 100 MB and most flipped videos exceed that limit.

Helpful Hint: To shrink the size of your videos, open them in iMovie (or a similar PC video program), and export as a QuickTime movie to reduce the size of the file. It doesn't deplete the quality of the video to where students couldn't watch and ensures an easy upload.

BENEFITS OF THE FLIPPED CLASSROOM IN MATH

Time

In 180 days of school, we may only get 120 days of high quality instruction before the state tests come across our students' desks. Between early release days, assemblies, review and assessment days, state testing, end of the year, beginning of the year procedures, and other unforeseen days where we don't get that A+ lesson delivered, the true 180 is unrealistic. Understanding this is paramount to buying in to the flipped class concept.

The bottom line is this: we simply don't have enough time to interact with our students. In a 51 minute class, I typically give a warm-up exercise (Estimation180.com, 101qs.com, etc.) that runs close to 10 minutes when all is said and done. I use the last four minutes (give or take) for closure and Ticket Out The Door. Removing the beginning and end (and assuming that there are no interruptions during class), I have my students for a total of 37 minutes.

In traditional mathematics classrooms, including mine prior to the flipped model, a typical day may look like this *if* all goes well:

- **12 minutes** of the introduction of the concept, including formulas and definitions
- **5 minutes** of questions and clarification of what was just taught
- **10 minutes** for the first example problem done by me intertwined with questions and clarification
- **10 minutes** for the second example problem done with the class with randomized questioning

Just like that, the class period...IS...OVER. I would catch myself thinking, *"What just happened?! How did I run out of time so quickly?"* As a way to combat this, my first response was to send students home with questions that they could practice and we could discuss them during class the next day. *"Yeah"*, I thought, *"they'll get those two examples and we can have a high quality discussion tomorrow"*.

Interaction

If you've been in the classroom for any amount of time, the above philosophy holds true in about 1% of classrooms and mine is part of the 99% of that unofficial statistic. The reality of the scenario described above plays out much like an educational train wreck that was destined for failure from the onset. However, I never knew how to avoid it. I had 21 standards to cover and I wanted my students to be exposed to as much of the content as possible without losing those who were struggling to keep up. All in all, I was the engineer of the train wreck, so it was time to switch tracks.

If you look at the breakdown of time, I would typically have 20 minutes to review two example problems with the class. Considering that this is Algebra 1 and such a new concept for all of the students in the room, a single day on Mixtures, Inequalities, Quadratics, and so many other powerhouse standards wasn't going to be enough. Truth be told, a *week* wasn't going to be enough. I needed to find a way to interact with my students more about the content that was being delivered. Their brains were only turned on during the 10 minutes that they had a chance to work through the problem.

With the flipped model, the time allotted looks much different. We still have the warm-up and closing, but the guts of the lesson are far from teacher-centric. Once again, *if* all goes well, here is the breakdown of time:

- **3 minutes** of peer sharing about their notes of what was discussed in the assigned flip
- **2 minutes** of sharing out to the class with their best answers in the group or pair
- **7 minutes** of showing students how to do a problem similar to the flip content
- **25 minutes** of students working through problems related to the flip content (quantity of problems will vary based on the standard and pace of each student)

"Wait, did I just read that right?" you might be thinking. *"You're meaning to tell me that a flipped classroom has you 'teaching' for a total of seven minutes?"*

Yes. I've already delivered my first instruction with content vocabulary, real-life applications, formulas, examples, and/or practice problems during the flipped content that students were required to complete prior to class starting. In total, I am able to review one problem with the class, which doubles as a way to ensure that all students see the instruction at least once before trying it on their own. I'm not naive to the concept that I won't get 100% turn-in rates, so this is my way to deal with it. More importantly, look deeper into the breakdown of time.

Out of the 37 minutes that are dedicated to student learning, 30 of them are the students interacting with each other and the content directly. I'm not delivering a "one size fits all" model where advanced students are bored out of their mind and struggling learners are counting dots in the ceiling panels. We have a great conversation for three minutes that ensures all students have an opportunity to interpret the day's content and another two minutes to refresh the memory of the entire class.

> *"Class, turn to your partner and discuss the flip, then share the big idea and any questions you still have with your team."*

It isn't often when we can give students a voice like that. Andrew, a student who struggled all year with completing the flipped portion of the class, was still able to be surrounded by, and embed himself into, the conversation within his group. He still did the work that was required, but the conversations were the most beneficial part of his learning.

During the 25 minutes of student work time, this is my opportunity to have the interactions with the students that I have never been able to get to this often before. Gone are the days where I feel bad about not getting to a student's question or feeling like I missed a group. With that 25 minutes, it is much easier to progress monitor all groups and individuals in the class and motivate them throughout the period. For example, Amber, a notoriously high-volume questioner, took advantage of this extra time to pique her curiosity. Where would she have been able to ask those questions if the time wasn't available?

What else this model eliminates is the need for as many multiple day lessons. When planning lessons, many math teachers (including myself) will plan two or three days for a section, knowing that there will be a lot of questions at the onset. With a seven-minute flipped lesson, I've found that this eliminates almost a half-day of paced instruction needed for that section. The reason for this is simple. As we introduce a concept, there is confusion and the necessity to go back to the previous step or example for clarification. We fumble over the correct way of explaining it, losing peripheral students who either don't understand the question or "get it" and have checked out. All a student needs to do now is rewind, re-watch, review, and write it down. It may not be that simple for every student in every lesson, but small victories are worth celebrating when they appear!

Archiving of Information

When we teach a typical math lesson, the content is taught and leaves as soon as the students pack their bags. Every now and then, there is a certain lesson that really sticks with the majority of the class. The reality is that these lessons are so few and far between that the traditional style of teaching is extremely ineffective. What if students could easily access all of their previous lessons with simple clicks of a mouse or taps on a tablet?

Using Weebly, my students now have constant around-the-clock access to all of the flipped lessons that have been created from the beginning of the year. Before we study for tests or benchmark exams, students go back through the videos that have already been created as a reference of what has been done thus far. It isn't a perfect system, and I'll be the first person to admit it. There is always something more effective, something more dynamic, and something that will allow students to retain more information. What I have to look at is the time invested with the flipped classroom compared to the traditional model of instruction.

Ramona, a great student who fell on some tough luck, had to be out for a long stretch in the middle of the school year. Usually, we send students a few worksheets that may or may not get completed during Short-Term Independent Study. Using the flipped classroom, all she (and others who missed days of school) needed to do in order to stay caught up was check the site, stay in touch with me about questions she had, and complete the work like the rest of the class. She missed out on some of the face time with her peers, but she was still able to work through the material in a similar manner as the rest of the class.

With the archives of information, I'm spending about the same amount of time in planning and prepping for the next day's lesson. What I get out of it is an archive of videos and flips that ensure all students have a level playing field of access to the instruction of standards throughout the school year.

In review for a big test (or "the state bubble race"), struggling students or students eager to review content can now access an entire database of lessons that they have already been taught, going back through the most challenging and getting what they need at a pace that works for them. When we archive our flipped lessons, we put the control for the learning of content back into the hands of the people doing the learning- the students.

Alex, a struggling student all year, wanted to do well on the state test, but hadn't really given his full effort throughout the year. He approached me about three weeks before we started taking the tests and asked if there was anything he could do to study what he had missed. I'm all for 2nd, 3rd, and 15th chances, as long as the student shows that he/she cares. In this case, it was a pure longshot that he would score proficient. My recommendation was to go online, get caught up on the flipped content, and come back to me with 1-2 questions from each unit. The thought was that he'd watch a few videos, get bored and overwhelmed, then quit. You know, like "the usual". The next Monday, Alex showed up with questions from four different units about lessons that he needed help with. There is no possible way I could've seen this turn-around had it not been for the flipped classroom.

Redefinition of Homework

I get defensive when it comes to the homework conversation and the other teachers look at the math department with a scowl. Even worse is when every teacher is giving their students "only" 30 minutes of homework per night. For one, this is ridiculous. Giving a time-based homework assignment simply because this is the way it has always been done could not be further from real learning. Second, it's an invalid barometer. My advanced students are going to fly through the homework in 10 minutes. Some will show work, while others will do it in their head. My middle-level students will struggle with the work, spending anywhere from the estimated 30 minutes up to an hour (or more) trying to finish the work before the due date. Worse than that, my struggling learners or homework tyrannists won't even bother trying the work.

If you analyze what just happened there, it is very interesting to address the issue of why we give homework. The advanced students flew through the homework because they already knew it, proving that the assignment was unnecessary for them. The middle-level students struggled with it, some spending more than an hour on an assignment that was meant to reinforce the learning. These are the students that we typically try to reach with the homework assignments. Then, for our worst offenders of the missing assignments, the students who never turn in the work simply don't get a chance to practice.

Being math teachers, we can all agree that practice is completely necessary to master almost any standard that is in our grade level or subject area. Some standards take more time than others, but each one comes with its own hurdles. Instead of giving traditional homework from a worksheet, textbook, or even self-created content, the flipped classroom model has students watch a video that provides foundational knowledge and ancillary support, creating experts before class even begins.

Once you have flipped your classroom, everyone who has completed the assignment has been provided with the same foundation in which we can differentiate to the needs of each student. They have all copied down the definitions, examples, or had a chance to think about the essential question that was posed during the flip. What happens from this point forward is when students begin to differentiate for you.

Your struggling learners will be a focus group during the class period and the majority of attention will be spent ensuring that they understand the core of the lesson being taught for the day. In a traditional setting, we lose our struggling learners because there just isn't enough time in the day to nurture them into what we know they can become. In my class of 39 students, there is no mathematical way I can address the needs of each learner with any sort of authenticity. However, if I'm given those 25 minutes during the day to work with students who really need the personalized instruction, it is well worth the work.

Your small group of students who refuse to do the "homework" are given the time during class to watch the flip and get caught up. While this is best suited for classrooms with access to computers or devices with internet, teachers can anticipate this (hopefully) small group of students and send them to the library to access the content that the rest of the class has already been able to access. This also clears up the issue of not having access to the internet outside of school.

Your advanced learners are internally jumping for joy that they can finally challenge themselves and not be held back by their classmates who don't get it, ask too many questions, and keep the class from getting to the practice that they're already chomping at the bit for. These are the students that I feel the worst for in a traditional math class because they aren't being challenged at the level in which they need to be. It isn't the fault of the teacher, even the best teacher. It is the system that we have in place where students sit in a room with four walls and listen to a cookie-cut lesson because this is what we're supposed to do. In a flipped classroom, those advanced learners become the experts, get their practice done right away, and begin assisting others or picking up challenge activities that stretch their brains and force them to *think*.

Students Who Refuse (Or Are Unable) To Do Homework

In a flipped classroom model, how are you supposed to deal with the students who simply don't complete the assigned content before the lesson begins? If a student didn't complete the homework assignment in the traditional setting, this only meant that there was a void of practice that needed to get filled. We supplemented that by letting students turn the assignment in a day late or punishing them by assigning a detention to complete the assignment in class.

With a flipped classroom, the "homework" is actually the instruction for the lesson. If a student misses this, how can the lesson go on? In my math classes, students don't have the opportunity to complete an assignment in class until the flip is turned in. This may not work for every teacher or every student, but it is my way of keeping some control of the situation. Instead of spending the 25 minutes practicing the content, students who haven't completed their assignment will get a device and watch the video, answer the questions, and/or complete the notes for the day. Since my lessons are less than 12 minutes, there is still ample time to practice what the rest of the class is practicing without losing an entire day of instruction.

Prior to flipping my class, I had never had a 100% completion rate for homework assignments. Even if it was a simple worksheet, there would be one hungry dog, one water bottle that would ruin a paper, or one backpack responsible for losing the work. Now, 100% of my students will complete the assigned work before practicing. No excuses.

Elvia, an English Language Learner who is timid and low-key, had some trouble getting the flipped videos completed on time. She wasn't the strongest student in the class, but she really cared about her education. She was the one who, no matter how hard she tried, just seemed to have "average" pre-printed on her papers. When I asked her about her failure to turn in the video forms, I felt terrible when she explained that she had no Internet at home, had to take care of her brother and sister until her mom came home at night, and rode the bus to school in the morning. Unfortunately, some kids just get dealt a botched hand. To help her out, I set time aside during lunch and before school where Elvia could come in, get the content, and also have some one-on-one Q&A time with me to help her out. It may or may not show up on a standardized test, but that girl gained some serious confidence and true understanding of the content.

DIFFICULTIES OF PREPARING FOR A FLIP

Anticipating the Rich Questions

Flipping a math class can be more challenging than traditional instruction, where the teacher can plan a great lesson and feed off great questions that students pose during the lesson. Even more effective is adjusting the lesson to meet the needs of the students as the lesson develops. If you are in the middle of graphing inequalities and it is clear that the class as a whole struggles with finding the slope, it doesn't take long to audible and change the plan into a brief lesson about slope before carrying on with graphing inequalities.

To assist with the anticipation of the rich questions, it is imperative that the teacher understands the students who will be watching the videos and truly understands the content that is being delivered. While it may not be necessary to script out the entire flip video, a successful flip will anticipate and address some of those questions.

If the video or method of flipping cannot address those questions, this is what the additional class time is for! Instead of asking the favorite student of yours to stay back after class to continue the tangent you were about to be directed in, go for it. I have always been the teacher who will take the bait of a good tangent because I was that kind of student. Alysa was that student this year. *"Hey Stevens, what happens if there's... (insert your crazy question here)?"*, she would ask. While the rest of the class is practicing, I can address her (and anyone else's) curiosity with that question without losing valuable instruction time.

If there is a question about *"when am I ever going to use this?"* in the middle of a Systems of Equations lesson, it ruins the entire original lesson plan to review cell phone carriers and options. You have to explain the concept of cell phone plans, research the numbers for each, come up with a solid example, and present it. The translation of this process: one more day gone from my pacing guide.

With the flipped model, ride that tangent as far as you can! While students are working through their examples, huddle around the group asking the question and get into the details of how financial firms or businesses will generate graphs of systems to compare and contrast price points and profit margins. You will either knock your students into a corner of amazement or pacify the students who have historically challenged the need to know such arbitrary procedures.

Unfortunately, math is almost always the subject that student feel the least connected with and it's understandable as to why. As Dan Meyer puts it, "I teach high school math. I sell a product to a market that doesn't want it but is forced by law to buy it."[4] Quite frankly, there's no mystery as to why students feel this way—there is rarely any meaning placed with examples of mathematics. As math teachers, we have to try hard in order to come up with projects that include the math necessary for each grade level.

Say you were doing a lesson about fractions and you wanted your students to understand the order of fractions dependent on their denominator. This is a 6th and 7th grade standard in California, but we never really have time to get deep into the "why a student would ever need to know this" of the standard. Instead of spending an entire lesson with a number line from 0 to 1 and having students

---

[4] "Dan Meyer: Math class needs a makeover | Video on TED.com." 2010. 31 Mar. 2013
<http://www.ted.com/talks/dan_meyer_math_curriculum_makeover.html>

place marks for each fraction's location, do that during the flip. When students come in to class, there are wrenches (or measuring cups). Have them experiment with the different sizes and understand why each is ordered a certain way. It's all but guaranteed that even the snarkiest student will walk out of class without asking that question about fractions and their applications in a real-life setting.

WHAT A MATH FLIPPED LESSON ISN'T

A lot of folks on Twitter have initiated chats, blog posts, debates, and research studies about the flipped classroom and its effect on education. The cliché of "It's not the tool, but how you use it" may be played out but it is incredibly true. Just like anything else out there in any industry, the best of tools can be misused and misinterpreted. Even with the best of intentions, the flipped classroom leaves itself vulnerable for criticism, especially in the drill-and-kill department that is mathematics.

"How cool would it be to have a model of teaching where students could get a chance to do 20 more problems?"

Yes, technically, the flipped classroom would open up the possibility of students completing more problems. But, for the teachers who already give unruly amounts of busy work, what is another worksheet of 20 going to do that the first 20 didn't? The flipped class model is not a free ticket to stand in front of the copy machine. It is a chance to cultivate rich discussions during class about the steps and processes of the standards that students are struggling with.

"Thank goodness I'm flipping my classroom. Now I just teach through video and have them work out of the book during class"

Someone had said that doing something different isn't a good thing unless you make it something different. Whoever said it, this is where it takes shape. Flipping your math classroom is not the inversion of what you're currently doing. Recording your lessons so that you don't have to answer questions during Direct Instruction isn't the faithful implementation of the flipped model. This was designed to create discussion and get to the heart of where students need the most help. Likewise, students will pick up pretty quickly that the flipped model for them is the exact same thing as what they've been taught their entire life and check out.

The goal is to do something different as a way to make change. Flipping your math classroom can be a rewarding experience for all stakeholders if you make it meaningful for everyone. After two weeks of flipped instruction, my students were coming up to me and requesting that I showed their other teachers how to do this. It isn't crazy to think that our students are smarter than we give them credit for. They want to learn. They are begging for someone to set the hook.

WRAPPING THE FLIP IN A BOW

To continue the discussion about the flipped classroom, do yourself a favor and join Twitter. Once you have done that, follow every author of this book, as well as @ramusallam. I have learned an incredible amount from their tweets, blog posts, and ideas posted on Twitter. If that isn't enough for you, search for the hashtags #flipclass, #flipmath, or #flipchat and read up on what people are saying about their flipped classroom experiences. As I was in the middle of flipping my classroom, this was a comforting and educational opportunity to learn what others were doing to successfully flip their classrooms.

If you are taking the first leap to a flipped classroom, go in with the expectation that there will be styles that work and others that don't. Failing is the best part about life because it's where we learn, so don't be afraid to fail at a flipped lesson. A little secret? If the flip fails, you still have all of your class period to make up for it by using traditional instruction!

Another tip is to not attempt a 100% flipped model the first year of making the transition. I found myself getting burnt out with video production and the quality of flips decreased tremendously. Stick to no more than one or two flips per week as you and your students ease into this new style of learning that benefits everyone. As you get more comfortable with it, so will your students. As your students get more comfortable with it, they'll start asking you to ask their other teachers to flip their lessons!

Finally, have fun and be yourself. When I first started making videos, I transformed into this narrator that my students didn't even recognize. When they came in questioning whether or not it was my voice in the videos, I knew that something had to change. I relaxed more, spoke from the heart like I do during the face time my students receive, and the learning became more authentic for everyone, including myself.

John Stevens *has taught secondary mathematics since 2006, ranging from 8th grade basic math, algebra, and currently high school geometry. He has a passion for trying new ideas that will engage and provoke meaningful conversation among his students. Find him on Twitter @jstevens009, or email him at stevens009@gmail.com. Also find him on his content website mrstevens.weebly.com or his professional blog www.fishing4tech.com.*

Science

Marc Seigel

A Flipped Classroom, by my not-so-technical definition, is 'A blended learning model in which typical instruction occurs outside of class while review, homework, critical thinking, inquiry, and one-on-one teacher time happens during class.' Those who attempt to report on it, but have never actually done it themselves usually say that teacher lectures are recorded on podcasts, which the students watch at home. Then, upon returning to class, students complete problem sets and other classroom activities to reinforce what was seen in the video.

The key aspects of a true Flipped Classroom are two things: 1) instruction that involves low-level cognitive function (low on Bloom's Taxonomy) like lectures or rote note taking is moved outside the classroom, and 2) class time is spent on higher-order thinking activities that are completed in a collaborative environment.

FLIPPING THE MINDSET

When I first began flipping my classroom in 2010, I did what the media has come to define the Flipped Classroom and what Bergmann and Sams call "Flip 101." Students watched my podcasted lectures which were placed on my YouTube channel and completed labs, homework, quizzes, etc., usually during class. I changed nothing about my class except where the lecture and the homework took place. Assignments were identical to the year before, labs were to be performed in the same amount of time, and the unit was to be completed in the same amount of time. It started out fine. My first podcasts were long (to be honest, one of them was an hour!) which the students immediately made me shorten for future units (never make them more than 15 minutes for high school students. Less than ten minutes is the preferred). Students were completing assignments, I was giving immediate feedback, and we were moving through the curriculum.

Things went like this for about a marking period (nine weeks); students come in, mostly having watched the videos, they complete a quiz, lab or review sheet problems, then they leave. Next day, lather, rinse, and repeat. It was toward the end of the term that I noticed I was beginning to lose track of the days; every day looked exactly like the one before. The only difference was occasionally we had a double lab period in which there was a sudden flurry of labs being completed. My class runs asynchronously so students could be at a variety of different points in the unit as I only dictated due dates, not daily work. The class began falling into a regimented routine, and it was *BORING*. The students were so focused on just getting the work done, that the goal of learning the material was lost. Unfortunately, I was running out of time in the year to make significant changes, but I knew a major shift had to occur in the fall.

The problem that I kept encountering was that my students had a clear expectation of what was *supposed* to happen in a science classroom. They knew there would be lectures, homework to practice what was taught during the lecture, labs to demonstrate how the material could be applied, and chapter tests to measure understanding. Every unit, same structure. This could not be their mindset in my chemistry classroom if the flipped classroom was going to succeed.

As strange as it may sound, the first thing I changed was the sign on my door. Instead of it saying "Welcome to Mr. Seigel's Chemistry Class!!" it now just reads "Welcome to Chemistry!!!" (The extra exclamation mark makes all the difference.) On the first day of school, I show them the sign and tell them that this isn't *my* class, it's *our* class. While I have some guidelines for them to follow, everyone is expected to learn from each other and be an active participant on a daily basis. Chemistry is a contact sport; they are expected, actually *required*, to get their hands dirty.

The room is arranged in learning pods of 4-5 desks all facing each other, not facing necessarily facing me. The idea is for them to work collaboratively on everything they do for class. The students also understand that the desks are not the only place that work gets done. I had students who like to lie on the floor, some who like to make the area under the lab benches their personal "learning cubbies," others who sit in bungee chairs that I purchased at Target. When desks are in nice, neat rows, it sends the message that the teacher is the most important person in the room, and I want them to know it is the learning that takes priority.

FLIPPING THE RULES

Classroom Rules are a thing of the past (except for lab safety; never ignore lab safety). Rules have punishments that must be handed out when they are not followed, almost all of which result in a loss of learning time. Late to class: Go to the office and get a pass (loss of learning time). Raise your hand to ask for permission to use the restroom: interrupts the lesson and distracts everyone in the room. Forget your pencil in your locker: can't take notes or complete classwork (loss of learning time). Now I have four Classroom *Guidelines*; a small but important difference. Guidelines are a way to live your life better, to be a better person in the classroom.

1. **Be Respectful**
   No matter what is happening, everyone is to treat each other with respect. My number one goal every year is to build a strong rapport with my students so that the classroom is a comfortable learning environment. This cannot happen if we are insulting each other, placing blame, and are generally disrespectful of each other's opinions and ideas.
2. **Take Initiative**
   There is no question that chemistry is hard (and science in general). Students need to take the initiative to speak up when they are confused, when they do not like an assignment, and when the class is not meeting their needs. Too many students have become good at the game of school and that is detrimental to their learning. My students are encouraged to speak their mind and know that I will listen to their ideas no matter how much I disagree. Then we will work toward a compromise.
3. **Be a Critical Thinker**
   Science, by its very nature, is a curiosity driven subject. You cannot sit passively in my class and just expect to get it. You need to analyze problems and develop creative solutions. As I will discuss later, my students perform guided-inquiry labs throughout the year that have them extending their learning to novel situations or just creating them 100% from their own

interests. The students who learn the most in my class are the ones who spend the majority of their time outside the box.

4. **Dare to Fail**

   Robert Kennedy said, "Only those who dare to fail greatly can ever achieve greatly." Failure happens and it's how we react to it that makes us who we are. I want my students to fail because we learn more through failure than success. Also, in today's grade-driven world of high stakes testing, many students simply won't even try if they feel they might get a low grade. However, if you set audacious goals for yourself and are not afraid of what happens if you don't reach them, then you have a better chance of reaching your full potential.

Now, what happens if you don't follow the guidelines? Nothing, except that you won't be able to reach your full potential as a learner in the chemistry room. Simple. My students are told this on the first day of school and reminded whenever they make poor choices.

FLIPPING THE RESPONSIBILITY

On the first day of school, our students have certain expectations when they walk in the room. They have heard the good, the bad, and the ugly from their peers, and they have mentally prepared themselves for what they think class is going to be like. They are ready for the teacher to tell them what to do and what to think for the next 180 days. So, on the first day of school, change all of that; let them have a say in how the class is run.

We have a Personal Electronic Device (PED) Policy in our classroom that governs all electronics used in the class from cell phones to iPods to laptops. I got the idea from Carolyn Durley's blog (bit.ly/flipping72). In every pod, is a large (16"x24") whiteboard that I cut from a larger piece of Melamine board purchased at Lowes home improvement stores (another idea that I stole, but from Twitter). On the boards are written either 'OK', 'Inappropriate' or 'Trust.' I explain to the students that the computers that they carry in their pocket are an extremely powerful learning device and that 'with great power comes great responsibility.' Within their pods, they develop a list of ways that their PEDs are acceptable in the classroom (OK board) and ways that are inappropriate (Inappropriate board). Also, I don't define Trust, but let them come up with the definition. When discussing this later, many decided that

TRUST meant that I trust them to act responsibly and as adults, so they came up with ideas related to that. I give the class about ten minutes to brainstorm ideas and then we compile everything into one class list. All of the ideas of my six classes are put onto one poster that is hung on the wall.

When they return on the second day, I project onto the front screen what the poster looks like and give them a chance to read through everything developed from the other classes. I then ask them three questions:

1. Are you ok with me, the teacher, holding you accountable for this? (*lots of nodding heads*)
2. Are you ok with holding each other accountable for this? (*a brief pause then the heads start to nod*)
3. Are you ok with holding me, your teacher, accountable for this? (*you could hear a pin drop*)

This is where the mindset begins to shift and they look at me differently. Students are not used to being the ones to holding their teachers responsible for classroom rules. When given that responsibility, they really don't know what to do. After a discussion, the class agrees to call me out whenever *I* am not using *my* device appropriately.

About a month into school, I knew the students had truly taken on this shared expectation when the principal came to observe me for my first of three formal observations. The lesson included a lab activity and in the middle of the activity, the principal's phone rang and he answered it. I have been doing this long enough not to let this kind of thing phase me, but I realized that all of the students had stopped working and were looking at me. One of the students pointed at the PED Policy on the wall and it clearly indicates no phone calls except for emergencies, and the principal was clearly not handling an emergency. So, I reminded them that on the second day of school they agreed to hold everyone who enters this classroom accountable for following the classroom guidelines. When the principal hung up the phone, one of the students politely told him that 'in this classroom, we are not allowed to make phone calls except for emergencies.' The principal stared at me for a second, smiled and apologized to the class, then turned off his phone. The students then turned back to their lab, picked up their phones and finished documenting the results of the experiment.

All of this happened well before I moved to a fully-flipped classroom. The key is to get them seeing your classroom as a completely different learning environment before you really change instruction. Once that has occurred, everything else is a lot easier.

FLIPPING LABS AND ASSESSMENTS

Hopefully, the primary component of your class time is spent in lab. But, if you are in a district where there are district-wide exams that cannot be changed by the teachers, you spend more of your time covering content than practicing skills. Regardless, laboratory investigations usually serve two purposes: to apply the content the students have been learning to a lab setting, and to teach them laboratory skills that they wouldn't learn in other classes. In the traditional classroom, labs come in the middle or the end of a particular section of a unit because they reinforce the 'real-world' application to everything the teacher has been teaching. Labs are usually done in groups of two or three, completed on a lab sheet, and each student submits his/her own copy.

When you start moving your instruction to outside the classroom, there will be more opportunities during class for meaningful learning. Traditional labs help reinforce the content through hands-on experiences, but rarely provide for novel learning experiences. Use the class time for extension activities that occur at the end of an activity and that bring the real-world into your classroom. For example, learning to make a solution is a very important skill, in my opinion. When we discuss solutions, I have my students create Sucrose solutions (sugar water) in different concentrations, taking pictures of their work when they are complete. They compare the different solutions based on Molarity and Molality to demonstrate not only their ability to follow directions, but also that these are different concepts despite having similar procedures.

At the end of the activity, they are given a container of Kool-Aid and using the procedure on the back of the package, they are to calculate the Molarity and Molality of the final solution. For those unfamiliar with powdered drinks, the directions on the back have you measuring a certain number of scoops, pouring them into a pitcher, and filling with enough water to make a certain volume (usually in quarts or gallons). So the questions that immediately come up with are 'how much is in a scoop?' and 'where's the pitcher?' In order to calculate Molarity and Molality, you need to know grams of the sugar and the amount of water (or total volume in liters). This requires the students to weigh a scoop of Kool-Aid and convert quarts to Liters. Then they want a pitcher, but I only provide them with beakers and none of them are big enough to hold a quart (approximately 946mL). Plus, that would be a tremendous waste of Kool-Aid if every group made a quart. So now the students must find the right ratio of Kool-Aid to fit in the beaker size they have chosen. That covers everything they need to find Molarity. Molality, on the other hand, requires you to know the exact amount of water used where Molarity is only concerned with the total volume. That Kool-Aid they added takes up space in the total volume so they need to find a way to make their solution, but identify how much water they actually used.

This activity is in no way difficult, but it does require the students to think creatively about their methods before proceeding. I use Kool-Aid and sugar because there is a lot of experimentation that takes place and using expensive chemicals that may require disposal is a waste of school funds. You can also see that these guided-inquiry labs take up a lot more time than traditional activities. The students need to come to class prepared with a method of attacking the problem because if they don't, an activity that should take one block suddenly turns into two or even three.

In today's world, teachers need to make a connection to the students' lives. Sometimes this is difficult or even impossible. Food, however, is the great equalizer. Many teachers or schools outlaw food in the classroom, but nothing connects better with students than food (teenagers especially). The way to a kid's brain is through their stomach. A traditional method for teaching isotopes in chemistry is using different types of beans. Well, why not use M&Ms instead? Teaching thermochemistry? Find the calories in food by burning Doritos (also a great way to get the kids to stop eating junk food once they see what their bodies can't digest) or determine the specific heat of cheese by making grilled cheese sandwiches in class. And, who could pass up liquid nitrogen ice-cream when connecting freezing point changes and thermochemistry. Biology teachers usually have students create scale models of the cell. Why not tell the students to make it out of food? What better way to celebrate their hard work than by eating the project? Physics teachers can talk about force by smashing watermelons with mallets (and don't forget to show a clip of Gallagher first!); the cleanup will be the best part.

Inquiry drives science. That natural curiosity to dissect and understand the world around us is the primary reason most of us studied science in the first place. But now textbooks, standardized tests, and note-taking have taken over. I want to tell you a story about curiosity:

Ryan and AJ don't need teachers to learn. These two honors students could get an A in a class if a monkey was in the front of the room. Not only are they naturally-gifted, they truly like school and want to learn more. In fact, the only teachers that they ever complain about are the ones who aren't teaching them *enough*. I decided to experiment with guided inquiry labs with their class. The assignment was to measure the volume of CO_2 gas produced from the reaction of vinegar and baking soda and compare it to the predicted volume found using Gas Laws. They could use any equipment and materials they wanted as long as I had it in the classroom. Now, there is an easy way to solve this problem: conduct the reaction in a flask with a balloon on the top, measure circumference of the balloon, and use the circumference to solve for the volume. But, I didn't tell the class this; I wanted them to create the procedure on their own.

Not known for every taking the easiest route to a solution, AJ decides that they should use the water displacement method for determining the gas created. Gases float so that meant that the reaction would have to take place under water. But, water would ruin the reaction so it would have to take place in a flask with a balloon on the top, under water. I really wish I had a picture to insert here because my description will not suffice. They assembled the entire thing in a 4L container filled with water, and using several classmates, managed to invert it in a water bath (to keep the water inside). The reaction immediately starts and the balloon inflates, pushing the water out. The boys were so excited. I had been watching this with fascination the entire time so now it was my turn to point out a major flaw in their setup. The elastic on balloons puts a force on the gas, compressing it so the volume they were looking at was not the actual volume. They needed to pop the balloon.

Well, to make a long story slightly shorter, after a quick scavenger search around the school, they found a wire coat hanger, sharpened it with my triangle file, and managed to pop the balloon. This whole endeavor took the better part of three 45-minute periods. Could I have given them a step-by-step procedure that made them do what everyone else did? Absolutely. But they were far more engaged by being allowed to use their ingenuity to solve the problem.

Inquiry activities and student-driven assignments are not unique and may be the type of activities that you already use in your classroom. However, what the Flipped Classroom allows for is the time; the time to experiment on new techniques, the time to improve upon what you already do well, and the time you so desperately need to get your students to that deeper level of understanding.

FLIPPING ASSESSMENTS

As an AP teacher, I prided myself on being able to write test questions that integrated as many topics together as possible. The problem with this method is if the student is weak in one topic, he/she may not be able to complete the rest of the question. Even if he/she understood all of the other parts and how to do them, he/she would lose most of the points because of one area of weakness. So I started wondering: what are my tests really measuring? I thought a good grade on the test meant my students were mastering the unit objectives. But there were always those students who did well on the homework, but performed poorly on tests. I chalked it up to test anxiety until I started thinking differently about assessments. Now, all of the questions on my test are directly linked to both the objectives and instructional videos. If a student doesn't answer a question correctly, he/she can go to a specific video lesson and fill the knowledge gaps.

Something else you will want to consider is moving away from written tests and quizzes. Chemistry classes are known for their demonstrations, so why not turn the demo into an assessment? Instead of explaining the science behind the demo, have the students do that for you. This is also a great way to transition students into watching instructional podcasts for homework. Assign the videos over a couple of days, then do the demo and ask the students to write down their scientific explanation. The first time you do this, have someone record the demo so you have them for later years to use as examples in your videos or to have the students watch online and answer their questions digitally.

No matter what you decide to do, the key to success is to abandon much of what is traditionally used in science class and embrace the new. Can you use what you made previously? Absolutely! Start small; add one non-traditional assignment in each unit, then a 2nd, then a 3rd. Or, pick a unit that you are really comfortable teaching and change assessment there. Whatever you do, just do it great.

OTHER FLIPPING CONSIDERATIONS

Flipping Instruction

While many of us (myself included) continue to use videos for basic instruction, there are other methods to choose from. Incorporating inquiry-based assignments, Problem-based learning, Process Oriented Guided Inquiry Learning (POGIL) or any other student-driven activities is definitely the preferred method for not only reinforcing material, but also teaching the material from the start of a unit. Videos should be reserved for the low-level information, the stuff that is procedural-based, as much as possible. Leave higher-order thinking for class time.

While on the subject of instructional videos, if you are going to make them yourself (the preferred method), make sure you keep them short (absolutely no more than 15 minutes, but under ten is the ideal). A general rule of thumb is 10-15 minutes for high school students, 7-10 for middle school students, and five minutes for elementary. If you are not tech-savvy enough to pull this off, bring in a video camera and simply record class. Or, search through YouTube for someone who has already done it.

Before you use someone else's work, however, make sure that it aligns completely with your curriculum by watching the video completely first. Too many teachers make the mistake of not watching the videos and it causes problems in the classroom. There are also a number of video editing options out there that allow you to take a piece of another video to use in class (search for tubechop.com). And, I cannot fail to mention TED-Ed videos (ed.ted.com). These short (less than five minute) videos are a great way to spark discussion for your DO NOW (or starter activity) and transition students to watching videos for instructional purposes.

Mastery Learning

How do you know if a student has learned the material? We all say that if a student passes a class, he/she has mastered the content. But is this really true? The central idea behind Mastery Learning is the students must complete all work to a certain standard before moving on or receiving credit. If you have a very flexible curriculum or teach a class that doesn't have an advanced level, this may work well. My program has an extremely tight curriculum and district exams, so I had to modify this philosophy. Students in my course have the option of resubmitting work that falls below my benchmark (65%). When failing work is returned to them, they fix their mistakes, study the material more, and complete an alternate version of the assignment. Sometimes it is the exact same question with different numbers/chemicals; sometimes it is an entirely new assignment. No matter what, they are forced to gain a better understanding of the material before the grade is entered into the grade book. This forces the students to go back, examine their mistakes, and fix misconceptions before moving on to more difficult work.

Pacing

Who drives the pace at which the students master the material? In my class, every student is given an assignment chart which details all work that needs to be completed before the end of the unit with the expected due dates. My class runs asynchronously, meaning everyone finishes the material at his/her own pace. There are no late assignments as everyone may complete them at different times depending on how comfortable they are with the material. Other teachers like to keep the entire class as close together as possible, having them finish specific goals every week. You also need to take into consideration your lab schedule. If your school uses a double lab period every week or some form of block scheduling, you will need to help your students plan their schedules so they can be at the right point in the unit to perform labs on the double lab days.

Student Driven Assessment

Do you stick with traditional assignments or move to standards-based grading? Discuss with your colleagues and supervisor on this one as shifting to SBG will require major buy-in from all invested parties. While much of the work in my class is the traditional homework, lab, quiz, test, I give the students a list of "alternative assignments" in case they want to try something completely different. For example, they might create a bulletin board that teaches unit objectives and count that for a homework grade. Or after watching a YouTube video that they found, they repeat the experiment as a demo for the class to replace a lab assignment. The key is to open the students' mind to different ways of demonstrating understanding. Also, give the students a choice for how they want it to be in corporate into their grade. Is it an extra grade in the quarter (not extra credit, though) or can it replace something that you assigned?

This past year, I had a student, Rachel, who was not into Chemistry the entire year. She did her assignments well, but she never connected with any of the material nor made any attempt to. She was a B+ student and was perfectly fine with that, never making any effort to strive for the A which she definitely had the ability to achieve. At the end of the Solutions unit (the last day to take the Quest), Rachel came flying into class, nearly at a run. She was already two minutes late, but that didn't bother me as my attention was focused on the very large colorful poster that was trailing behind her. With a smile on her face, she handed me the poster. She said that she couldn't stop thinking about the Kool-Aid activity when she went home so she decided to use the extra time she had to make poster describing the entire solution making process. The poster was gorgeous, with panels that you had to flip up to get more information. But the best part was that it contained more information than what was in the unit. Rachel had gone on the Internet and did extra research to learn more about how different substances dissolve and how you can maximize the dissolution process, complete with molecular illustrations. You must provide opportunities for students to demonstrate understanding in whatever ways work best for them. This goes beyond simply assigning a variety of assessments. You must give them choice so they can become invested in the material.

Paperless

Money is in extremely short supply, so paper is typically one of the first things to run out in schools. And nothing is worse than taking home those monstrous piles of labs and tests to grade. Add to this the fact that many states are moving their standardized tests online. The need to transition your students to completing and submitting their work online is an absolute necessity. Instead of just having a website, consider moving to a Learning Management System (Edmodo, Moodle, MyBigCampus, etc.) where your students can access class files, complete assignments, and engage in online discussions. An LMS will also allow students to post questions to a forum for anyone in the class to answer which frees you up from being the person all students turn to for help.

Google Apps for Education are another great alternative for going paperless. All of the labs in my class are completed on Google Drive. The student can access the files from home or school, complete the questions on their schedule, and submit them to folders you share with them. You can also use the forms feature to create quizzes that can be accessed from any Internet-ready device. One of my students said that he preferred this method over traditional paper quizzes because he could complete them on the bus ride back and forth from baseball games. Using Google, time that was normally wasted could now be spent demonstrating learning.

While this chapter may have moved away from a traditional how-to manual, I hope to have expressed the true beauty of the Flipped Classroom: you can make it whatever you want it to. Be creative, be innovative, be bold (Dare to Fail). I want to end this chapter with a story about what true learning looks like.

The lab I use for stoichiometry has the students reacting vinegar and varying amounts of baking soda in six test tubes. The students measure the balloons attached to the top of the test tubes, perform mole conversions, and explain the effect of varying mass to the amount of product of a reaction. I came over to check the progress of a group of three boys who finished performing the lab and seemed to be up to mischief. They were measuring a large amount of baking soda into a balloon which was clearly not what the lab told them to do. When I interrupted them, they said they wanted to know what the largest amount of gas that could be produced from a balloon completely filled with baking soda. They thought I was going to get upset, but instead I told them that if they performed the stoichiometry calculations to prove how much vinegar was necessary to react with what they already measured, they could perform the experiment. Immediately they jumped into the calculations. I happened to have an extremely large test tube to perform the reaction. Words cannot express what happened next so I will let the following picture do it for me.

Now that's the face of an engaged learner.

Marc Seigel started teaching chemistry in 2000 at a Magnet School in New Jersey. A few role changes later, he is in his third year using the Flipped Classroom model in the Chemistry classroom. Marc has spoken at several conferences including EdcampPhilly, Edcamp Leadership, the NJSTA conference and the 2012 Flipped Classroom Conference. Marc writes about his experiences on his blog aflippedapproach.blogspot.com and can be found on Twitter @DaretoChem.

Science
David Prindle

When I was first asked to write this chapter on using the flip class method in the science classroom I had some trepidation. I say trepidation since many of the students I teach are At-Risk, special education or low motivation students. Much of the time these students don't do tasks outside of class like homework. So to convince them to watch videos might be an uphill struggle. This doesn't mean that all my students are like this and in the end this was not an issue.

In the State of Michigan in order to for students to receive a state endorsed diploma they need to take and pass a chemistry or physics class. For this group of students we created a class called General Chemistry. This class focuses mainly on the state standards that will be tested on the Michigan Merit Exam given each March. Most of the students in this class will not be attending college. Pure lecture doesn't work well with most of these students so I decided to flip my class during the 2012-2013 school year.

Before I go any further let me delineate details about this class. We started out with 34 students. I say we because a few days before the school started another teacher and I were told we were going to co-teach the class. At first we tried to teach them as one large group but that did not work out well. After that we split the class in two and I would be responsible for the content and she would be responsible for the labs. I had 16 students in my section. Three were seniors and one exchange student that transferred in from college chemistry due to language issues. Of the remaining twelve juniors four were special education students with IEP's (including one with Autism) one of which dropped out at the semester. Two others left at semester to attend the local intermediate school districts online school. Two transferred to our Alternative school, however, one did stay in the class. Of the remaining four students two had motivational issues, one is "low achieving low" (low achieving low means that a student is working at the level that fits their abilities) which denies them special education services, and one did everything requested of her at a high level. Due to the diverse educational needs I have decided to flip my class. During the flip our classes remained split for a majority of the time. I was responsible for the "content" of the class and my co-teacher was responsible for the laboratory part of the class. This coming year I will be responsible for the entire class due to budget constraints I will not have a content area co-teacher but a special education teacher as a co-teacher. This year the class won't be split either so rather than each of us have 15-17 students in class we will have a class of 27-30+. Although not ideal using the flip will aid in letting those that can move forward and those that need remediation get the help they need.

MY FLIP

Early on I determined that flipping this class would take a change in the vocabulary I used and the length of the videos I made. The rule of thumb for the length of the videos is no more than one minute per grade level. Thus for my juniors and seniors this would mean videos of 11-12 minutes long. However, I found out early on that five minutes was even too long for these students. This comes back to the type of students I have not really wanting or doing work outside of class. Also chemistry is a totally different science than the students are used to and trying to put too many concepts into one video was too much for my At-Risk and Special Education students. However this did not slow down the students that could handle more they just advanced through the lessons faster.

I broke each unit or concept into short three minute videos. Each video was accompanied by a WSQ form. WSQ stands for Watch, Summarize and Question. I got this idea from Crystal Kirch (flippingwithkirch.blogspot.com), a Math teacher in California. (You can find her form by following this link: bit.ly/flipping45) During the Watch—the W in WSQ—phase of the form the students are instructed to watch the video and use pause and rewind as needed. I do ask if the students watched the video or not and students will actually answer no to that question. This is valuable data from the standpoint of the teacher. I now know who is prepared for class and who isn't. I also ask if they did use the pause and rewind buttons. If they said they used the pause and rewind button that lets me know that they actually took more time on the material and they concentrating on the material presented. I modified the WSQ form from the way Kirch does her and students take their notes in the Summary section. This was done so students have one set of notes that get sent to their email when they submit the form. However, this year I will be modifying the form even more. As in Kirch's form I will either leave the Summary (the S in WSQ) open-ended and let the students enter their own notes, or I will ask direct questions to help guide them. In the Question (the Q in WSQ) section I have students enter questions that they did not get answered or were raised by the video. The next time we have class these questions are the basis for our class discussion or I will present them to the class so others can answer or discuss them for the entire class. An example of the type of question would be: "Why use molarity for concentration? If there are no questions then we use class time to apply the concept in class or practice problems.

I don't use terms like tests, quizzes or assignments. Thanks to Brian Bennett I use the terms Entrance Survey (Formative Assessments), Checks for Understanding (quizzes), Exit Surveys (Summative Assessments), and tasks (assignments). Using this terminology I have found that my students don't stress as much over these common classroom activities. I believe this is because the entrance surveys don't count on their grades and tasks are only 5% of their total grades. Forty-five percent of their grades are on Exit Surveys and Checks for Understandings. Checks for understandings are very low point and let me and the student know where their weaknesses are before they take the Exit Survey. Students are given three times to pass these exit surveys with an 80% or higher and it seems to take the pressure off of them. Before they take a retake (when needed) they have to review their material first. What I saw as the semester progressed is there were less and less retakes mainly because they didn't want to take the time to do the retake but they still had the security blanket of a retake if needed. In the end the change in terminology, point values and retakes lessened the stress of passing the class. The rest is split between lab and writing grades. All of the surveys and checks for understanding are done through Google Forms. Using Google Forms lets me give the students immediate feedback by using Flubaroo to grade them and then email them their grades.

As you know, Chemistry is a paper-and-pencil problem based class. However, I have converted my class to a paperless and student turn in their work either through Google Docs or forms. Some students objected to the paperless classroom but for tasks or surveys that involved calculations students still can use paper. However, their answers are still submitted via a form for quick grading and immediate feedback for both the student and me. This aids in immediate feedback; however, students still turn their work in just as a check for me to make sure they understand the problem solving process and are not depending on the "kindness" of others for their answers. In the end a majority of the students liked the paperless classroom. Students that didn't still took notes on paper but most switched to Google Docs. My autistic student took a mix of notes with his paraprofessional or they printed responses to the forms. I would say that he was the exception rather than the rule since he had different needs that most of the other students.

As soon as I started flipping in my General Chemistry class a majority of the class took off with it. Due to the diverse learning abilities in my General Chemistry class many of the higher level students took and ran with the flip to the point I barely could keep ahead of them. However, for a few (about 10%) in the class the flip was not a good fit but because we were flipping my co-teacher and I were able to help them individually. Flipping the class also had an unintended positive consequence in that many students started working together collaboratively. They were not copying each other's work but truly helping each other learn and problem solve. This collaboration left time for us to help others but eventually other students started helping those that were either behind or needed extra time. Students in a flip especially in an At-Risk class need to have their progress closely monitored. If not some of them will hide and not complete the work. They are not completing the work is either due to they get too far behind and feel that they can't catch up. Some of those that fall behind are those that have spent their life hiding from school. However, the beauty of the flip now we as teachers can find these issues and correct and catch them up. This worked out well because of the 30 students we finished with 28 passed the class. The two that didn't pass the class pretty much chose not pass the class on their own.

MY TOOLS

I use many different tools and platforms for my flipclass (*Figure 1*). The main reason for this is I don't want to give a student any reason for not getting the material ("the site was down"). The first one stop shop for my students is my self-hosted Wordpress website davidprindle.com. When students access this site, they have access to my other sites, the class LiveBinder or Edmodo page, or Facebook page. At the end of this year and starting next year each unit of each of my classes will be on learn.davidprindle.com first. They are duplicated on the class LiveBinder by date. This works out well for students miss class for one reason or another. Students no longer ask what they missed they can then go to the LiveBinder to see the daily agenda and associated materials. Everything is then duplicated on the class Edmodo and Facebook pages. I will talk more about why I use Facebook in the next section of this chapter. I also use sophia.org and TED-Ed (ed.ted.com) to make tutorials or flip lessons that embedded directly into all four of my student platforms. I use four platforms to prevent "the site was down last night". The students also can use the platform they are most comfortable with whether it be LiveBinders, Edmodo, Facebook or my site. Sophia allows me to create a space that includes my videos, WSQ form and any other media or material I need in one continuous tutorial. It also allows me to add a quiz if I wish. TED-Ed works slightly differently in that I can flip any TED or YouTube video by letting me include a quiz (multiple choice or short answer), a Dig Deeper section, and add a Discussion thread or threads. (Here is a link to one of my TED-Ed flips: bit.ly/flipping46) Finally this is all tied together with Google Apps for Education (GAFE). We are lucky to be a GAFE school in a one-to-one environment. Each student has a Gmail account that is connected to a Google Drive, Blogger and YouTube account. Students turn in all work via a shared Google Drive folder with me or via a Google Form. At times they will upload a video lab report to their YouTube channel and using a Google Form report the URL to me.

Finally, I have started having students create video lab reports. In creating a video lab report makes students take their time during the lab because each step of the lab is video recorded and they have to make sure they take time following all of the procedures. In the past students could brush off poor lab process to "human error". Student also have to think about putting the lab report together and take their time of any and all calculations since these will also be available to the world online.

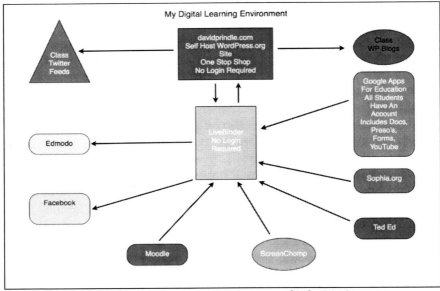

Figure 1: My Digital Learning Environment as of July 2013

THE FLIP CLASSROOM AND AUTISM

This last school year I had a student on the Autism spectrum (he also had a one-on-one paraprofessional that was a relative tech newbie). This changed how I thought about how my class and web resources worked. He kept me honest and thinking about accessibility for students with special needs. By keeping me honest he would let me know when access to class materials and resources it either took too many clicks to get to them or they were not written very clearly or the directions were complicated. He is fairly high functioning but had issues with too many places to access class resources. He was able to access his Google apps account but his life was on Facebook. This means that he was not comfortable using the Google app account supplied by the school. He preferred to use Facebook for everything. This was more of a comfort level thing for him rather than rebelling against what the school supplied. However over the course of the school year he with the aid of this paraprofessional was able to get more comfortable with his Google account. This made me think about the rest of my students. Some had said, "Why can't our assignments be on Facebook?" So I created pages for each of my classes and duplicated everything I did on my site or LiveBinders to Facebook and Edmodo. I chose to also use Edmodo because this is the LMS of choice of other teachers in our school and some students prefer it to Facebook, LiveBinders or my site.

Back to my autistic student and class resources and assignments. Each assignment I created I had to think how he would react. I say "react" because he had this ability to look at an assignment and say it was too complicated. In some cases he was right especially if it contained math. I will be changing the way I present material this year and make sure it is accessible to all students regardless of academic level.

When we had to use other sites (TED-Ed, for example) he and his paraprofessional would use his same username and password that he used for school. This helped his stress of having to go to another site. After a year he and I worked things out really well. Any time a new site was needed to be accessed links with instructions were put on all of the different platforms.

STUDENT ACCEPTANCE, RESPONSE, AND ONE NEW IDEA

For the most part my students accepted and embraced the flipping of my classes. The students that wanted to work ahead really loved it and it put less pressure on the students that needed to move slower. Students who could work faster were getting bored in the traditional classroom as we had to move at the pace of the slowest student. However, some of the slower students could move faster if they had more one-on-one help but this was at a premium in the traditional classroom. But by flipping my class the all students could move at their own pace and one-on-one time was no longer at a premium but became common place. As with anything some students were resistance but that was mainly because they have been well trained in playing the school game and wanted to be lectured to and worksheets. However, over the course of the year nearly 100% of my students adapted and did well in the flip environment. Many of my high academic students really loved the flip. They were able move faster and keep their interest in the class high since they didn't have to sit and wait for the others to understand the material and complete the assignments. The mid-range students could also work at their own pace but had time to ask questions when they got stuck but then move on quickly when they got them answered.

Because of the flip I had an idea gleaned from Twitter: Video Lab Reports (VLR's). I instituted them toward the end of the year and they were a hit for the students. Creating these lab reports made the students to think more about the process of the lab and their results. This was because the reports were uploaded to YouTube and they knew others could be watching. In the VLR students have to video and edit the procedure/process and then put it together with their results and conclusions using iMovie. The VLR's added one more layer of student collaboration to my flip.

CONCLUSION

Finally, I will continue to flip my classes. I thought that flipping an At-Risk class would pose some interesting challenges. It did in some ways but for the most part it was a very positive experience for my students and the teachers. I would recommend flipping At-Risk classes but with careful progress monitoring. It is very easy for students to hide during the flip if they are not monitored for progress. I will continue to change what I do each year. I have a great PLN that is willing to share their ideas and resources. I love many of the things that Crystal Kirch does in her math classes but I will be modifying those resources to fit my classes and my students. To follow my classes and what I do please go to learn.davidprindle.com. If you are planning on flipping your classes just know it will be more work the first couple of years. As in teaching in a traditional learning environment some things may not work the way you thought it might. If you choose to flip you will be tweaking and changing things on the fly and each summer.

David Prindle *teaches Forensic Science, General Chemistry and Credit Recovery at Byron Center High School in Byron Center Michigan. He uses the flip method of teaching in a 1:1 MacBook Air environment. He writes for the edreach.us Disruptors blog, the Sophia.org's School of Thought blog and co-hosts the #21stedchat Twitter chat on Sunday nights with Jill Thompson. You can find out more about him at davidprindle.com and on Twitter @dprindle.*

Technology for Students

Thomas Driscoll III and Brian Germain

Scenario #1

Mr. Educator is ready to deliver a technology-rich presentation that he perceived to be a highly-engaging, knockout lesson. He has transitioned the traditional PowerPoint to the flashier Prezi, and he thinks this will really up the engagement. The Prezi has images, audio files, and YouTube videos embedded throughout. He also uses his interactive whiteboard to toggle through several tabs on his browser to illustrate his supposedly salient point. Despite his best efforts, the class displays lackluster effort. Some students who quickly understand the content are bored. Others who think it moves too fast become frustrated and tune out. Then, for whatever reason, there are the select few who decide that disrupting the presentation is a wonderful idea. Mr. Educator's technology-infused lesson failed to hit the mark.

Scenario #2

Mrs. Educator has adopted principles of the flipped classroom into her instruction. She feels that transitioning her lectures to online video is a great idea and dives into the concept. She will use quality screencasting software along with a reputable learning management platform to deliver content in a high-tech way that will surely engage students like never before. She quickly realizes how doing so frees up much needed class time and reduces classroom management issues. It also enables students to progress through the lectures at their own pace. Although students are comprehending and retaining more of the course content, engagement remains lackluster and Mrs. Educator feels that there is still something missing.

While educators across the nation have most likely experienced the first scenario in their careers, those who have begun implementing flipped learning have probably experienced some of the version of scenario number two as well. The initial stages of the flipped classroom, which for most educators means shifting direct instruction online through screencast videos, may prove more effective. Many of us however, have been left yearning for more. What is missing? Unfortunately, and despite our best intentions, the allure of modern educational technologies often blinds educators from an important aspect of these digital tools; they are of best use when utilized effectively by the students themselves.

Over the past few years, we have had the fortunate opportunity to learn with teachers experimenting with the flipped class concept through a continuously reflective process to improve our instructional practices. The two of us teach social studies at Putnam High School in Putnam, CT, a small town of modest means in Northeastern Connecticut. Although the state classifies the district as high-poverty, we have witnessed the strong sense of pride in this historical community in Connecticut's "Quiet Corner." We believe that the economic struggles faced by many of the students in town should in no way deter them from experiencing a rich, technology-infused 21st century education.

When reflecting upon our practice, we have realized that instructional technologies have never played a more substantial role in learning than they do right now. The question is therefore not whether we *should* utilize these instructional technologies, but rather *how* we should use them. Teachers can now leverage digital technologies to enhance everything from traditional content delivery, to skill modeling, to formative assessment and feedback. Educators also recognize the need for students to leverage these technologies as they engage in complex tasks that encourage higher-order thinking. We make the case that flipped learning helps create an environment conducive to such student-centered technology integration.

FLIPPED LEARNING AND TECHNOLOGY INTEGRATION

Before venturing into effective student use of technology, let us first discuss the ways in which we as educators have used instructional technologies in our flipped classrooms. When it comes to technology integration, most educators first think of ways that digital tools can make direct instruction more effective and engaging. For example, consider what many, including flipped learning pioneers Jon

Bergmann and Aaron Sams, consider the "traditional" conception of a flipped class. Their description starts with the teacher identifying which direct instruction could be shifted out of the classroom's group setting. The method for accomplishing such a task is creating instructional videos, typically with screencasting software, that are then archived online. Some teachers have gone a step further with this approach by incorporating online assessment tools and data analysis software to accompany their videos.

We have gone through this process of archiving direct instruction online and still employ these methods in our classes. First, we began recording lectures, tutorials, assignment instructions, reviews, and other forms of direct instruction using screencasting software. After much research, as well as trial and error, we have concluded that Camtasia Studio, a screencasting program by TechSmith, is the best software out there. Camtasia Studio does an excellent job not only with the screen capturing, but also regarding the video editing capabilities built into the program. There are also options to incorporate embedded quizzes and interactive hotspots, features that will be further explored later in the chapter. For those teachers who are not very tech savvy or those who are just venturing into screencast technology, the program can seem a bit overwhelming at first. TechSmith, however, has developed a great series of video tutorials to help both beginners as well as those with more experience who want to make their videos even better (bit.ly/flipping47). For teachers and districts that lack the funding to purchase Camtasia Studio, Screencast-O-Matic is a free and relatively simple web-based screencasting software. Although the editing capabilities are limited, this is often a good place to start out before investing in full-featured software such as Camtasia.

Although this chapter is focused primarily upon student-use of technology, we have a few tips for those venturing into developing screencast videos. First, invest in quality audio. For our first videos, we used a cheap, $7 analog mic. Little did we realize that the audio came out terrible, because most analog mics actually pick of the internal sounds from the computer. Although we tried to improve the audio in the Camtasia editor, we still sounded terrible. Students could make out what we were saying, but they also commented how distracting it was. Therefore, before investing in a high quality HD webcam, which is increasingly unnecessary due to the improved quality of built-in webcams, make sure to invest in a USB mic. One can typically be found for under $30. If you want to step it up a bit, there are podcasting kits that can be purchased for around $100. Brian and I use a podcasting package by Samson and have had great results.

Another option that we often overlook is bypassing screencasting and creating videos with an HD or basic standard-definition camera. For example, if you are demonstrating an experiment, touring a historical site, or creating a video introducing a big idea or addressing a class misconception, creating a traditional video may be a better approach. Any video editing software has the ability to insert text and basic graphics, and you could always incorporate images or clips from web video as well. I prefer to use Adobe Premiere Elements for my editing. It is certainly a step-up from Windows Movie Maker and is reasonably priced.

One nice feature of this software is that it is easy to create multiple audio and video tracks, along with the ability to create "green screen" scenes (*Figure 1*). If interested in utilizing a green screen for your or your students' videos, consider having your district purchase a basic lighting kit as well. A cheap option is to find a wall that is one solid color and that is free of any shadows. Good video editing software gives you the ability to remove the background regardless of color, so you therefore do not technically need a "green screen" at all.

Once you have recorded and produced your video, you have to decide how students will view or interactively engage with your videos. Although Tom has created a YouTube channel called FlippedHistoryVideos (bit.ly/flipping48) to host and share videos, YouTube is blocked for students in our school district. We have spent countless hours trying to find ways around this, but in the end we just began uploading copies of each video to Vimeo, a website that is not blocked in our school. Our advice would be to find out what students have access to beforehand, a simple preliminary step we wish we took ourselves. If you choose Screencast-O-Matic.com to create your videos, there is actually a very simple way to share. After producing the video, the website provides you with a link to your videos that you can then share with students. There is also an embed

Figure 1: Using green screen techniques, a PHS student "attends" the press coverage during the fall of the Berlin Wall.

option if you would like it to appear directly in your blog, website, wiki, or LMS. As part of a flipped learning training session, I created the following video quickly demonstrating how to do this with Screencast-O-Matic (bit.ly/flipping49).

> *"I use these video lectures as a resource to help learn many of the unit objectives. I like how I can go back to use these videos and review them until I really understand them. For instance, in class lectures can go too fast so I can't take all the notes in time. But in our flipped class, when I am about to work on an objective or take a test, I can go back and listen to them over again if I need to."*
>
> *Steven B.*
> *Putnam High School Student*

Of course, there must be some online space for students to view and engage with your instructional videos. The typical options include blogs, wikis, basic websites, or learning management systems. Although we encourage students to create blogs and wikis for different assignments, we have ourselves chosen learning management systems for our courses. Brian uses Edmodo mainly for its user friendly interface. The setup is very similar to Facebook in both appearance and function which has made it very easy for students to use effectively. Adding to its convenience, many other teachers in our school use Edmodo as well. The major drawback is in

Edmodo's assessment feature, a component of the LMS which definitely needs some re-tooling to be more teacher-friendly.

Tom uses the Flipped Social Studies LMS (flippedsocialstudies.com) which is built on the EDUonGO platform. (eduongo.com/v2/). He chose this newly developed LMS due to its collaborative nature. For example, its video notation feature, built-in e-reader with interactive note taking, and streaming module creates a very active and participatory blended learning experience. Another advantage is that it is simple for users to develop their own "online school." For instance, Tom will soon be adding Brian and fellow department member Garrison Rose's courses to the Flipped Social Studies LMS. This is a great feature for departments, schools, or entire districts seeking to gravitate towards a common LMS for all educators and students.

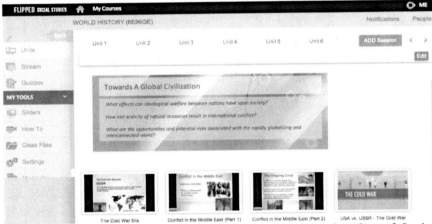

Figure 2: Screenshot of the World History Course on the Flipped Social Studies LMS (EDUonGO Platform).

Brian's assessments are developed and delivered through Edmodo's built in quiz feature and occasionally through the brilliantly simple website testmoz.com. Testmoz leaves the frills out of backend quiz building, but still offers excellent data analysis with results. The teacher can view a chart that has all the questions lined up with notation indicating a correct or incorrect answer. If a column is filled with red X's, it might be a signal that this concept needs reteaching.

Question #1 (1 point)

The influenza outbreak of 1918 was considered an epidemic because the disease

○ affected an extremely large number of people at the same time.

○ spread through the air, quickly and unknowingly.

○ stumped medical experts, who found no vaccine and no cure.

○ doubled the death rate in large urban centers.

Question #2 (1 point)

Why did Great Britain and France finally declare war on Germany in September 1939?

○ They had formed an international army to fight Hitler, whose forces trapped thousands of soldiers in Czechoslovakia.

○ Hitler signed a non aggression pact with Stalin, threatening the Allies.

○ Hitler signed an alliance with Mussolini, forming the Axis Powers.

○ They had pledged to defend Poland against Hitler, who attacked it from the West.

Figure 3: The simple outlay of an assessment on testmoz.com

Jacob F	✗	✓	✓	✓	✗	✓	✗
Jennifer B	✓	✓	✓	✓	✓	✓	✓
Jeremy M	✓	✓	✓	✓	✓	✗	✗

Figure 4: One of the data reporting features on testmoz.com that allows teachers to search for testing patterns.

Tom's assessments are created with Google Forms and the Flubaroo grading script. First, since Tom utilizes Google Drive for all of his documents and presentation, the forms and graded spreadsheets help keep everything in one organized location. To make these quizzes easily accessible for students, they are then embedded directly into the Flipped Social Studies LMS. The Flubaroo script provides item analysis for the video quizzes, a useful tool for gauging the performance not only of individual students, but for entire classes. Creating a Google Form is a relatively straightforward task, but using the Flubaroo script can be a bit tricky, particularly for those new to scripts. Tom has created a video tutorial that explains each step of the process (bit.ly/flipping50). In Figure 5, you can see the quiz embedded in the course LMS, while in Figure 6, you can see how the Flubaroo script graded and provided item analysis for the quiz entries.

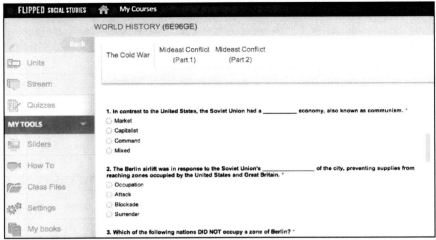

Figure 5: Screenshot of an embedded Google Form Quiz in the Flipped Social Studies LMS.

Figure 6`: Screenshot of the grading analytics provided by the Flubaroo script.

The common theme here is that flipped learning, at least the initial conception of it, is primarily focused upon teacher use of technology. Although this approach is preferable to more traditional "chalk and talk" varieties, students largely remain the consumers of direct instruction, albeit through a modern digital medium. Flipped learning, however, does enable educators to move beyond this teacher-centric technology use. We strive to make the point that the flipped model of education enables technology to be student-centered, which should not simply be appealing to teachers, but a concrete pillar that their curriculum is formed around.

STUDENT-CENTERED TECHNOLOGY INTEGRATION

Why The Shift?

You may be wondering why we place such an emphasis upon student use of technology vis-a-vis teacher use. First, we believe that modern digital technologies are pervasive in today's society and offer incredible opportunities regarding communication, productivity, and innovation. With an unprecedented number of students with internet access enabling them to create and post original content for the world to see, it is important for students to develop the knowledge and skills necessary to make use of these technologies in effective and responsible ways. If most of the technology use is implemented and controlled by the educator, students will lack the experience needed to develop such skills.

Another reason is that many of today's curricular standards, both at the local and national level, place a heavy emphasis upon effective student-use of technology and development of the many skills involved. A brief examination of excerpts from the Common Core State Standards, The Partnership for 21st Century Skills' P21 Skills Framework, and ISTE's NETS-S Curriculum Planning Tool clearly illustrate this fact. A common theme that emerges is that the focus is not on the teacher, but on the learner. In particular, these standards concentrate on students' ability to utilize digital technologies for a wide variety of essential uses. If there is such a growing emphasis upon such student use of technology, it is therefore increasingly vital for educators to develop the expertise needed to effectively incorporate these skills into their curriculum and daily instructional practice.

Student use of technology will also lead to higher-order thinking and increased curiosity both inside and outside the confines of a school's walls. In 1956, educational psychologist Dr. Benjamin Bloom organized a team of fellow psychologists to establish a classification of higher-order thinking that could be employed in school to extend learning beyond a simple consumption and regurgitation of facts. Bloom's group set their progression of principles into a pyramidal hierarchy where the levels at the top reign supreme. The lower levels form an important base, but without the ability to extend learning to points of analysis and evaluation, what good is all the information in the world? This taxonomy has evolved into a full-blown educational paradigm that puts pressure on teachers to make sure they can design lessons to focus on skills of an upper echelon. Many will say that rote memorization has its place in tasks like learning the anatomical bone structure of homo-sapiens. Assuming that to be the truth, the ever important extension question becomes: What do we do with this information now that we know it? It is clear that simply remembering falls at the bottom of Bloom's Taxonomy and in the 21st Century and the world of Google, students can no longer get by with simply knowing. Realizing the shifting nature and demands of an ever evolving world, Lorin Anderson, a Bloom's disciple worked through the 1990's with a team to ensure the taxonomy was reflective of modern times. So, as is seen in *Figure 7*, the change made was to transform "synthesize" into "create" and place it at the top of the pyramid. Emphasis has been given to write, design, construct, and to mix knowledge with dreams to make something tangible.

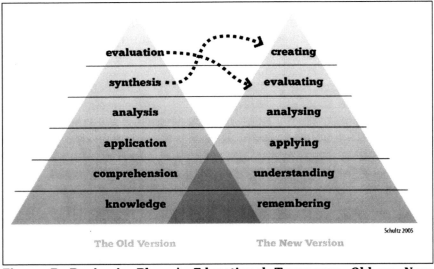

Figure 7: Benjamin Bloom's Educational Taxonomy: Old vs. New. (From: Petram, Kim)

With the face-to-face time and individualization that a flipped class offers, students will have more time to create. They can make their own blogs, videos, websites, and so much more. The options are virtually unlimited, but when students are in control of technology, they are much more invested in the content that goes with it. Brian's favorite example is his project about U.S. westward expansion in the mid-late 1800's. Students wrote their own songs about moving to the west, applying the content they had learned from flipped lectures and structured research in class to create an original piece of work. They then proceeded to set up a recording studio in class, lay down a track, and edit some excellent effects into it. Students did not stop here because they had become totally invested into the overall awesomeness of the assignment. Music videos were made that blew Brian's mind away. Some filmed at locations around town, and one student even made a puppet to be the star in their video. This was a five week unit with this capstone project taking no more than a week. Not only do students pick up the requisite information listed in sometimes antiquated curricular documents, but they learn valuable tech skills such as recording, editing, and creating a real production that they are fully invested in.

History class has been paired for years with the negative stigma of reading textbooks and answering questions. While this pedagogy certainly may have its applicable uses at times, nothing can measure up to the empowering experience of letting a student take hold of their education by creating their own content. This streams into project-based learning and when executed properly, learning happens through creation that is driven by personal inquiry. In a unit on WWII, for example, a student will find the internal motivation to answer a question that they themselves pose. Maybe they are curious about the man who designed the landing crafts at Normandy. Instead of telling them about Andrew Jackson Higgins and the LCVPs that were first tested in Anzio, let them *find* an answer they will remember. After all, students are curious beings; why should teachers be the ones who ask all the questions in class? Welcome to the new Bloom's.

EFFECTIVE TECHNOLOGY INTEGRATION
Technology Integration Matrix

Although there is no step-by-step procedure that would work for every learner in every situation, there are several guiding principles to effective integration of student-centered technology use. One of the best resources out there is the Florida Center for Technology Integration's "Technology Integration Matrix (2013)." They have developed a continuum that is both grounded in theory and offering practical classroom applications for educators. Their "entry" level is described as a situation in which "the teacher begins to use technology tools to deliver curriculum content to students." This describes the teacher-centered technology use that even the most tech savvy teacher may be described as employing. It also describes that category that many people new to the flipped learning approach would fall into. Although you are integrating modern technology into your curriculum, it still serves as a relatively basic content delivery system.

Transformation, the highest level of technology integration according to this matrix, involves "the teacher encourage[ing] innovative use of technology tools" and "technology tools are used to facilitate higher-order learning activities that may not have been possible without the use of technology." This transformative environment, which is increasingly possible when implementing flipped learning principles, is what all educators should aspire to. This goes beyond delivering content with modern technology. It also pushes educators beyond simply teaching students how digital tools work. In sum, transformation leads to a degree of relevant, engaging, and rigorous learning that would simply not be possible without the existence and effective use of modern digital technologies.

EXAMPLES FROM THE CLASSROOM
Utilize Learning Management Systems

When educators hear of learning management systems, or even simple class websites, they think of a place that students can access course documents, view calendars, or in a flipped classroom, receive direct instruction via video. Learning managements systems, however, offer much more than this, including many tools that are more student-centered than one may think. Although there are several ways to do this, Tom has focused upon the use of interactive video features and discussion forums. One critique of flipped classrooms is that it is propagating bad pedagogy, the passive act of students receiving information via lecture. One way to avoid this trap would be to create interactivity with your videos.

Tom has used Camtasia Studio to add interactive "hot spots" to some of his videos. When students click on the "hotspot," it opens up a browser tab with a relevant online resource. Also, quiz questions are embedded into the video at particular points. Therefore, students cannot simply just skim through the video without really understanding the content. If their answer is wrong, it will direct them back to the point in the video where the answer was located (bit.ly/flipping51).

Another way to increase interactivity is to utilize video notations. In the EDUonGO LMS, which Tom has adopted this past year, students have the option of asking questions during the video in a discussion area. When other viewers, including the teacher, watch the video, this discussion stream will appear at that particular point. Teachers can also pose open-ended questions at certain points of the video that you expect each student to respond to in the video notation area. This will help students engage in the group dialogue that is typically a missing component of instructional videos.

Discussion forums are another way that students can use technology to converse and collaborate in ways that may not be possible in a traditional classroom setting. An important element of digital citizenship is the ability to engage in dialogue in online settings, and this is a way to help teach students how to use this medium in appropriate and effective ways. Beyond this, students will most likely encounter discussion forums in college. There are few higher education institutions that do not require students to post questions and responses to discussion forums.

A Babson College study entitled *Going the Distance: Online Education in the United States* documents the number of college students taking an online course experiencing double digit percentage growth each year. More than 30% of undergraduates with an enrollment in Fall 2010 will take an online course. To extrapolate growth at a conservative rate, that percentage could easily double to 60% by 2015. With such a large population of students moving on to college and destined to encounter at least one online course in their career it only makes sense that they learn the basics of internet learning along with digital literacy, safety, and etiquette. With many class levels around the country titled "college prep," we as educators should certainly be prepared to adapt to continuously make that not only a title, but a mantra.

Student Screencasting

Many educators around the country are unleashing the power of screencasting technologies by putting it into students' hands. This tends to be a simpler approach than one might think. First of all, since flipped classrooms often have students view or engage with videos created with screencasting software, students are already relatively familiar with this technology. You have been inadvertently modeling this skill all along which is a wonderful part of the hidden curriculum in flipped classrooms. Some teachers have been known to facilitate student creation of videos to teach other students. Beyond the empowerment factor, when a student provides instruction, he or she is forced to really know the information they are trying to convey in order to do it effectively. Frank Oppenheimer, world renowned particle physicist and brother to J. Robert Oppenheimer of the Manhattan Project once said, "The best way to learn is to teach." Anyone who has ever tried to teach a concept, skill, or entire class knows just how true this can be. As educators, let us help our students put this mantra into action.

For example, Tom has students create screencasts as a way to teach concepts to others in the class. Additionally, some students who were uncomfortable presenting in front of large groups had the option of creating a screencast presentation instead. The remarkable thing was that some of these students who were apprehensive about speaking in front of the class later asked if they could publish their screencast videos on YouTube! This also serves as a viable form of differentiation, one that Special Education departments embrace as well.

"From the perspective of a special education teacher, I see the flipped classroom as differentiated instruction at its finest. This model also exposes students to different technologies, which for special education students especially, gives them more tools to put into their arsenal in which to apply to other classes and projects. I've seen improvement in my students' understanding of technology, writing and analysis skills this year. But the most important improvement that I've observed in the flipped classroom has been their confidence."

Sarah Pellegrino
Special Education Teacher
Putnam High School

What are the logistics of student screencasting? First, the tech equipment we referred to earlier in the chapter when discussing flipped video creation applies. There are, however, a few things to consider. First, what are your available resources? For districts that cannot afford to purchase Camtasia Studio, I would highly recommend having students record with Screencast-O-Matic. As previously mentioned, it is free and relatively easy for students to use. Tom has actually created a "Five Minute Guide to Screencasting" (bit.ly/flipping52) video tutorial for students that walks them through the steps necessary to create and share videos with Screencast-O-Matic. Regarding student submissions, they can either download and share the actual video file, or simply copy the link and send it to the teacher. For students who have more technical skill or those who are more heavily invested in a particular project, Tom has them use the more advanced Camtasia Studio. This full-featured screencasting software typically produced the highest quality videos, something that most students truly pride themselves in. If interested, here is a playlist of student screencasts on our Flipped History Videos YouTube channel: bit.ly/flipping53.

"The presentation on the historical inventions let us choose how to present our knowledge with technologies. We chose to make a screencast so we could show images and explain the old and new inventions. We also were able to show everyone what we did by posting it online."

Travis S.
Putnam High School Student

"With the screencast you can really be yourself. You can express yourself more by making a video than just writing it down. There is more personality and viewers can see things differently."

Brendan H.
Putnam High School Student

Figure 8. Putnam High School student creating a screencast.

"I started by creating a PowerPoint and used Screencast-O-Matic.com to record the presentation. I liked how I could do this instead of speaking in front of the class since sometimes I have stuttering issues in front a group. The screencasting has actually helped me with the public speaking though because I could practice and hear what my voice sounded like when presenting. I also like how the video can be easily shared with people that I would like to see it."

Kayla K.
Putnam High School Student

Collaborate With Google Apps

Once students in your flipped class begin spending considerably more time engaging in collaborative problem solving and other higher-order cognitive tasks, online tools such as Google Apps will prove invaluable. Students can collaboratively develop documents and presentations in real-time, which is a benefit both during class time and outside of it. For example, all of the students in Tom's AP European History course recently developed a single document simultaneously. In the end, a 70-slide review presentation was collaboratively developed in less than two class periods (bit.ly/flipping54)! In another example, students typically share their Google documents with Tom early on in their research projects so that he can offer commentary and guidance at several points in the writing process. Many students also liked the research feature that is built into the Google Drive app. This reduces the number of tabs and windows open, allowing students to maintain focus on the research and writing. Students in the class have created a brief video explaining how they collaborate with Google Docs during research (bit.ly/flipping55).

> *"Google drive has simplified the hassle of having group members get together to do a group project. In the past, when my teacher gave the option to work in groups, I would always pick solo because I knew that with my busy schedule it would be difficult to get together with the other members to do true "group work". Now, however, I will always pick working in a group because I know that it will be as simple as going online to do the project and the other members can change/add/suggest ideas to put on the project as I am working. Google Drive also eliminates the hassle of having to save...upload...and email friends just to show them the rough draft."*
>
> *Mikayla V.*
> *Putnam High School Student*

> *"Connections are key. Being able to use technology to establish connections with other students is very useful and improves the chances of succeeding at what you attempt to achieve."*
>
> *Angelo D.*
> *Putnam High School Student*

Leveraging Social Media

Brian had a professor in college for a class called, *The History of Religion in Early American Society.* The very structure of every single one of the professor's assignments got under Brian's skin. The syllabus had a list of ten books each student was supposed to read and then summarize in an essay; only the essay wasn't an actual essay at all. The first "essay" started off as a 400 word limit, and each subsequent "essay" had a lower limit than the one before it. As a history major, common belief was that this was an extremely unjust way of judging anyone's understanding of the content. All of us history majors had excelled in a world of written text where the more words typed positively correlated to the level of comprehension. This professor taught everyone a valuable lesson. Memories of lamenting over a laptop one night after reading the 240 pages in *The Times and Trials of Anne Hutchinson* and having to write a 300 word summary still haunt Brian. He had to choose each word carefully; not only did content have to be mastered, but cultivation of the skill to present a succinct and logical flow of text was forced.

Not every assignment in socials studies needs to be a huge essay. In many assignments, the ideology of this formerly infuriating professor that sometimes less is more needs to be embraced. Concise summaries have less fluff and really force a student to know what they are talking about so they can appropriately represent that knowledge with words. For this reason, Brian has been a big proponent of Twitter in the classroom. Not only is it used as a forum for collegial dialogue, extra credit options and so much more; it's a piece of educational technology that students can utilize to make learning more relevant to them. The best part is that Twitter has a 140 character limit to the messages (tweets) that are posted. If a student can't make a clear message in 140 characters, an essay of 14000 words will be no less jumbled or confused.

In the early Civil Rights movement in American History, students are exposed to two prominent African American leaders with conflicting ideologies. While most are familiar with the names Martin Luther King, Jr. and Malcolm X, few know anything about Booker T. Washington and W.E.B. DuBois who paved the way for the Civil Rights movement in the 1960's. Throughout the course of a comprehensive unit, one of the assessments students must pass is to have Booker T. Washington tweet at W.E.B. DuBois and vice versa. Drawing from our studies and primary sources like *Up From Slavery* by Booker T. and *The Souls of Black Folk* by W.E.B. DuBois, students must make a statement in the first person point of view to accurately characterize the position each took on the types of rights African

Figure 9: A student created Twitter conversation between early Civil Rights leaders.

Americans should strive for and how these rights could be realized. Furthermore, each student has to think of a creative Twitter name (handle) for both Civil Rights leaders. Working with a socio-economically diverse rural demographic, where many kids don't have home access to technology, an immediate roadblock is that not everyone is familiar with the inner-workings of the Twitterverse. Embodying further 21st Century skills of collaboration, those who have mastered the communicative skill of tweeting, take the new learners under their wings. The final tweets are a great product of knowledge and skill intricately woven together using a base of peer guidance. Hashtags to indicate subjects like #TalentedTenth #Tuskegee appeared regularly, while the showing of Twitter handles added a twist of historical creativity to the assignment. Final results were a complete understanding of concepts with brains fully at work and a range of cleverness of which there was no precedent.

The first time through an exercise like this requires close instruction to make sure the process is carried out properly. However, it opens the door for quick and meaningful assessments down the line and can be used simply as an exit-tweet, similar to an exit slip. Teachers can easily track these by having student enter a unique hashtag indicated by the traditional pound sign # and accompanying text. Questions can be posed by the teacher to assess the day's learning, such as "What would John Adams have said about the WWI Sedition Act?" or questions posed by students such as a great one I got recently: "Who needs the other more- USA or China?" Students took the viewpoints of Barack Obama, Wal-Mart, Mao Zedong, and a whole slew of other characters. When students are allowed to embrace technology in the classroom, there is a real sense of empowerment in the air, and everybody wins.

Fostering Inquiry, Autonomy, and Empowerment

Brian definitely experiences a level of frustration when not meeting students' desires for instant gratification by answering their questions on the spot. The best he does is guide them to a particular resource (which may be another student) to help them find the answer. In flipping the classroom, this is something that teachers should be prepared for; the fact that you will not immediately live up to your students' expectations of what a teacher is and does. It's important to keep in mind that as educators we must give students what they need, and often times that is the opportunity to develop autonomy. Teaching in the age of technology and instant access to answers should no longer be about the recitation and regurgitation of facts; it's about the skill to research, assess a source's validity, discern fact from fiction, and most importantly answer the question, "Why does this matter?" Brian trains his students to always be able to answer the question "SO WHAT?!" as that is always the question posed to them when they make an assertion with textual support in writing. If a student cannot go a step further and explain why their statements are relevant and important, the whole idea of 21st Century learning begins to crumble.

When Brian started student teaching in New Haven, CT, the district gave all new teachers a book called *Motivating Students Who Don't Care* by Allen M. Mendler. With references to educational demagogues, Robert Marzano, Howard Gardner, and Carol Tomlinson, it was pitched as a cure-all reference guide to engaging all learners and eliminating behavioral problems. What this book fails to mention in its nine chapters is the concept of empowerment. Much like the doctrine of traditional education, all the focus is on what a teacher can do in given situations to ensure proper classroom management. Educational prophet and professor at Sacred Heart University, Dudley Orr always used to say, "The best discipline plan is a good lesson plan." What the flipped classroom offers in terms of cutting down on distractions, interruptions, and misbehavior is amazing in its own right. However, students are also empowered to harness the power of modern technologies to have an active role in the construction of their learning. Here's the key to motivating students who don't care: help them find a way to motivate themselves. Provide the scaffolding that will make them successful for life after high school when they will need to follow the compass of their inner drive because very few people on the outside will be offering directions.

One particular project in Brian's immigration unit jumps out as having a high level of student empowerment and autonomy. In a jigsaw like design, the class is divided up into groups of four and handed a large envelope containing information on a different topic related to immigration: Countries immigrants came from and reasons for leaving, the trans-Atlantic passage to get to the US, the journey through Ellis Island, etc. There are checkpoints or formative assessments embedded in the process so progress can be closely monitored. To play to multiple intelligences, there are several suggestions of how students can show mastery of their given topic, and the group must decide what fits their needs and learning styles best. Furthermore, included in the envelope are roles that individuals must choose such as group leader, secretary, public speaker, and artist. Groups decide amongst themselves who has what role and then with a little time and the urging from the teacher that they should use whatever resources available, they start doing miraculous things.

Students use the SMART Board to pull up a website that compares the height of the Statue of Liberty with other monuments and lists a ton of facts about Lady Liberty. The group then goes through, highlights, copies and pastes the facts that they think are the most interesting, take notes with the SMART Board pen in a document that then converts it to typed text. They then print copies to distribute to each group member and the group leader divides up new research tasks based on these newly found facts.

Another group has a member that makes a connection to steerage (the low class passenger quarters the poorest travelers were relegated to) and pulls up a clip of the movie *Titanic* on their smartphone to show the others. They say to the others that steerage was just like the area that Leonardo DiCaprio traveled in. Another group member counters by pulling up pictures on their phone to say, "Yea, except steerage wasn't nearly as nice because the Titanic was a luxury ship, but steerage was way below deck." They proceed to show the others pictures of what actual steerage conditions were like. They get the general size and capacity of these travel quarters and are asked them to map out an area on the floor to simulate how close people would be. What really hits home is when they start to describe how scarce light, fresh water, and bathrooms were...and how frequent illness was. They all start to cringe when they think about someone vomiting in the tiny little space they were in with no option of escape.

Students start to understand the enthusiasm with which immigrants regarded the Statue of Liberty and Ellis Island simply by understanding how awful the travel to get to the US was. Other groups find this important realization by reading about the potato famine in Ireland in 1847 and using laptops to research what strain of bacteria destroyed the potato crop, postulating whether or not this could happen again, and diving into the importance of diversifying a country's agricultural growth. The constant "ah-ha's!" and beautiful moments of discovery that take place for the duration of this project would be constricted by a normal curriculum. One of the best parts about this three day research period is that students have to discover information about their topic that interests them. They must meet a quota each day of a certain number of questions they have about their topic. These questions then become the basis of their project as they are fully invested in finding answers to the questions they asked. Say hello to inquiry-based learning. Flipping a class, even just partially, and embracing the student use of technology has freed up time to make this all possible.

OTHER STRATEGIES AND TOOLS

There are, of course, many other ways to leverage student use of technology that are beyond the scope of this chapter. We will therefore provide a brief overview of some others out there for your consideration.

Content Curation

Since searching for information on the internet often seems the equivalent of drinking water from a fire hose, curating relevant and reliable content is a vital 21st Century skill. Student creation of websites and wikis are two of the myriad approaches to content curation. Here is an example of a wiki created by AP European History students at Putnam High School as part of their exam review:

apeuro-review.wikispaces.com. There are also emerging social media tools that can be leveraged for this task. For example, Pinterest and Tumblr can be used for students to quickly and easily organize and publish their findings.

Content Creation

Beyond curating content, we want students to create content as well. They can do so with presentation software such as PowerPoint, Prezi, or Google Presentations. Another approach is to have them create their own websites, wikis, or blogs with original content. Depending upon you and your district's privacy preferences, you will want to research which platforms are open to the public and those that have strict limitations on the audience. Here is an example of a student-created wiki developed by an entire class at Tourtellotte Memorial High School as part of their Climate Change Project (climatechangedebate.wikispaces.com).

Programming and App Development

Many of our students continue to amaze us with their knowledge of programming. Although this may be advanced for most students and teachers alike, providing students with the skills and drive to develop these tools will certainly enhance engagement and perceived relevance. There are also new websites out there that provide free app development services without any prerequisite programming knowledge. One example of this is the new website AppMakr.com.

Gamification

One movement that has caught fire is educational circles is gamification. Although we can only graze the surface here, we see three basic ways to leverage gaming. First, you can use an existing game to help teach a particular concept or skill. An example would be using MineCraft to teach problem-solving and collaboration skills. A second approach is to use games specifically designed for educational purposes. An example of this is iCivics (icivics.org), a great website with citizenship-based games and simulations.

Lastly, you can incorporate gaming principles into your instructional design. For instance, you can implement a mastery-style "leveling" in your units while offering multiple pathways towards achieving a particular learning goal.

CONCLUSION

At the onset of the TED Talks 2013 Season in February, a $1 Million award was given to Sugata Mitra for his educational research he refers to as *The Hole in the Wall Gang* (bit.ly/flipping56). In multiple poor, rural areas of India, Mitra set up computer in a wall and tracked what happened as uneducated and poverty stricken youth began to access a machine they had never even knew existed. Amazing things started to happen as children learned and taught each other how to surf the web, discovering that their computer was slow and leading them to request new specific parts. By the end, the Hole in the Wall Gang had explored advanced topics like DNA replication learning terms like protein synthesis at the ripe old age of eight and posing insightful questions. Oh, and one more detail: these children only surfed the web in English, a language they were unfamiliar with in the beginning. Let's piece all of this together and try to wrap our heads around it for a moment. Not only did a group of children learn to use a computer at a young age, but once they understood the mechanical operations of the machine, they had to learn English so they could use its processes to complete something worthwhile. Only after these two steps were complete could they consume a seemingly limitless amount of information leading to advanced topics most can agree is well beyond their years. The initial experiments were so successful and intriguing that funding was secured to replicate them in several different countries across the world, all of which validated the insanely captivating story of this self-organized learning.

So what? Why does this matter? Allow us to answer the very questions we demand of our students in making points of relevance. This story originally came to our attention because CNN ran sensationalist headlines insinuating that teachers inhibit learning. As an educational researcher, Mitra himself understands the value of a teacher, but firmly believes that as technology shifts, so too must the teacher's role. In his studies, he hired many adults (usually retired teachers) to provide virtual encouragement to these groups of kids via Skype. They lauded the accomplishments of these young learners and motivated them the way an effective office manager would his workers.

Mitra stresses how vital autonomy and curiosity are and that top-down instruction by itself does not get the results in education that we so desperately seek. The adage that we must transform our instructional practices from "sage on the stage" to "guide on the side" shows its face here. There is no authority that has a more diverse or quicker line of information and answers than the web. Not even Ken Jennings could beat super computer Watson on Jeopardy. Google has become the answer to all of our information woes, which is both scary and exhilarating. Mitra argues that the computer has become the center of the education domain. How can anyone who has been exposed to modern technology really argue with him? The world has drastically changed, but for the most part we continue to employ an industrial-age, transmission model of education. Teachers need not provide answers for every question, but we better ask some good ones ourselves. We must minimize the emphasis on basic content acquisition and instead focus on fostering student-driven inquiry, collaboration, creativity and innovation. To truly embrace the rapidly changing world and apply these changes to education, we must also empower learners through effective student uses of technology. Changes in the world of education sometimes move as slow as molasses in a New England winter, but as educators we must keep pace with these changes and embrace them, the stakes are too high not to.

Thomas F. Driscoll III is a Social Studies Teacher and Technology Coach at Putnam High School in Putnam, CT. He has implemented flipped learning in his courses since 2011 and regularly presents and conducts professional development workshops regarding instructional technology. Find him on Twitter @Mr_Driscoll, email him at thdriscoll@gmail.com, or check out his blog www.flipped-history.com.

Brian Germain now teaches at Putnam High School in the Quiet Corner of Connecticut where he serves as Social Studies Department Chair and was recognized as the 2012 Teacher of the Year. He has been experimenting with varying levels of technology integration and flipped learning after stumbling upon a TED talk by Salman Khan in March 2011 and finding the principles of more intense technology integration both intriguing and inspiring. Follow him on Twitter @Mister_Germain, or email him at brianfgermain@gmail.com.

PART TWO:

Can Anyone Flip?

Collaboration: Co-flipping

Andrew Thomasson and Cheryl Morris

CoLab Partners from Across the Country

Collaboration always seemed like an amazing idea...in theory. Over the years, both of us had been on grade-level or subject teams that shared curriculum, assessments, or even a strict pacing guide. We have been in Small Learning Communities (SLCs) and Professional Learning Communities (PLCs), and worked cross-departmentally, and sometimes even with teachers from other schools in our district.

And most of those experiences were a chore. They were what you did because you were told to collaborate. So someone wrote an agenda, full of tasks that administrators or district staff felt were important for us to "collaborate" on, and people reluctantly showed up, where they graded papers covertly, or checked their email, or played Sudoku. Very few meetings ended with anyone having been inspired or motivated to make their practice more collaborative. And over time, even the sound of the word collaboration began to make many teachers cringe or sigh in frustration.

At some point in the last year, we coined the term "CoLab Partner" to talk about our cross-country collaborative partnership. We felt like collaboration had such a bad reputation that we needed a whole new name to describe the EduAwesomeness of the work we did together. By removing an "L" from "collab" we got something that sounded more like a team doing experiments where they got to blow things up and talk about it. It describes two people who enjoy each other's company, and who inspire each other to learn and grow.

That's why we are CoLab Partners: our partnership has been fun, we have become close friends, and we have inspired so much growth professionally and personally that the teachers we are today bear little resemblance to the ones we used to be. Cheryl had a teacher-centred classroom where there were strict rules, but also a love for language and its intricacies. Andrew ran a chaotic classroom that was designed more like a college seminar, featuring discussion and high-level analysis of texts. We both were successful, to a degree.

Now, the classrooms we run together are very different. It's not like we took the two styles and mashed them together, with many of the original features intact. No. We created something new, together; there are no seams where you can see evidence of the distinct classrooms we used to run. Now, despite the fact that the physical buildings in which we teach are 2,700 miles apart, we have classrooms that beautifully reflect both of us, equally.

To us, collaboration does that—it takes two disparate elements and teaches them how to become something brand new, together. The result of the last year is that we have become better people, better teachers, and better friends. And while our students certainly benefitted from that growth, we benefited from it far more. The best part is that our journey together has just begun.

THE BEFORE TIME; THE LONG, LONG AGO

The story of how we met is actually pretty simple: on Twitter. Through a series of inconsequential tweets, Andrew found Cheryl's new blog and read some of the entries. After a direct message exchanging basic information, we decided to talk as face-to-face as we could get: FaceTime. That conversation turned into a video series. That video series became a life-changing relationship. Everything we have done over the past year is a reflection of that relationship, but none of it would have happened without the risk of contacting an Internet Stranger and asking questions.

I'm sure neither of us expected that a year later, we would be best friends and team-teachers. In fact, neither of us really wanted a collaborative partner. We *did* want someone to help us make videos, though. As early-adopters of flipped learning in English, neither of us found many videos online that we could use in our context. Each of us had made a few videos on our own—Cheryl used ShowMe, an iPad app that is an interactive white board, and Andrew made screencasts of a PowerPoint lectures for his AP class. However, the thought of filling an entire year worth of videos for multiple preps was intimidating to say the least. Flipping a class is really hard work, and though there is no how-to binder, subjects with sequential content, like history and algebra, or subjects with tons of content that is typically delivered through lecture, like science and foreign language, at least have models to work from. There are hundreds of teachers flipping Algebra, but very few flipping English, and even fewer who post and share their content for the general public.

TMI: THE EARLY DAYS

There was a lot of talk about collaborative videos during FlipCon12 (which we both attended virtually, and was responsible for the tweet that launched our partnership), so we figured that if we found someone who would work with us, we could cut our individual work in half. One of the main reasons Andrew contacted Cheryl was that she had the necessary technology to record more elaborate video, and he didn't. Cheryl had little experience with 11th-12th grade English, so needed someone to help her talk through what was different at that level...and it just so happened that Andrew had primarily taught those levels. So while we both needed the other, we soon came to realize that there was no way we could just divide up the work equally and end up with a product we liked.

The main problem was in the video production process. The original arrangement we made included Andrew doing the planning and scripting, then both of us recording the video, with Andrew as the "teacher" and Cheryl as the "student," and finally, Cheryl doing the editing and finally uploading it to YouTube. The problem quickly became apparent that it didn't work for Andrew to plan alone, as both of us needed to know what the video would be about. And editing without Andrew's input made no sense, so we exchanged hundreds of direct messages about each draft of the early videos. Cheryl would do the first round of editing, then would upload it to YouTube as a private video, and Andrew would send comments. Draft after draft would be posted, repeating until both of us were happy. Neither of us was all that happy with the byzantine process though.

Working that way felt like the way our students usually approach a group task. They will divide up the work, and then each do only their own part. When the time comes to assemble, they realize that without having worked together for the whole task, they now had to revise extensively to match their part into the whole project. They end up either turning in an incoherent project of individual pieces, or they spend twice as much time in revising and making it all into a unified product. Neither model produces work that is efficient AND high-quality enough to satisfy two OCD perfectionists. So we had to find a better way.

THE RULES OF INTERDEPENDENT-NESS

The better way turned out to be tweaking the process to be more collaborative at each step. After the first few videos, we started to plan together before starting the video recording. Then we would talk at the end about the editing—which parts should be included, which parts should be cut, what title screens we would need, etc. Cheryl would still do the editing, but it was generally planned and outlined, and Cheryl's skill with editing increased, so the task went quickly. After a few videos of incoherent pieces, we found a way to make truly collaborative videos that reflected a completely joint effort.

It did, however, create a problem that could have easily destroyed our partnership before it really started. Since we were now planning together, Andrew was doing "less work" in terms of time commitment. Editing took time, especially because Cheryl was learning Camtasia on the fly, and working on a computer that just couldn't handle that kind of task; that meant that Andrew started to track the deficit of his own effort, and inflate the metric of Cheryl's effort.

In reality, there would have been no work without the partnership, and it took many, many conversations to reach the point where we no longer viewed the work as a transaction. In a transactional relationship, each person is trying to give the least in order to get the most. Most collaborations operate transactionally, probably because most human relationships are transactional, too. We don't want to love someone who won't love us back. We don't want to spend time with someone who will later ditch us. We don't want to help a friend move because they failed to help us move the previous month.

So much of life is transactional that it is hard to break out of the transaction. To be true CoLab Partners though, we had to find a way. We began to address this with the creation of rules for our work together. While we never sat down and wrote out a list of rules and norms, we did use arguments as opportunities to discuss the problems we faced, and as a consequence, we developed rules that would protect the partnership from conflict and dissolution.

The first of those rules was that anything we created or worked on together was not Cheryl's or Andrew's. It belonged to both of us, and because of that, we couldn't break it down into individual pieces to assess who had done more. Outside of our collaboration, none of the work would have existed anyway, so by trying to claim the larger portion of credit for a project, we were actually destroying the entire thing. It took both of us several months to fully accept this and act out of that belief. Occasionally, the idea that one of us does more work is brought up, but we are skilled at defeating that thought with the truth: neither of us could do this alone, and none of it would exist if we were on our own. Believing this is a form of self-preservation, actually. You cannot have a partnership of this kind where one person secretly believes that they are carrying the other person; those thoughts will lead to the death of the relationship.

Other rules we made became equally as important. The second rule we have is that there is neither an insignificant contribution nor an insignificant person. To that end, we don't allow self-denigration, even in a joking way. As teachers, we are constantly being assessed and criticized, and that has a tremendous impact on our confidence in the classroom. Neither of us has had all positive experiences in our career, and the balance is far greater on the negative side than the positive. It is not difficult to make either of us feel like we aren't doing enough, or that we are failing to measure up to the impossible standards we set for ourselves.

We hold the "insignificant contribution" rule to be so important because if the work is a product of the collaboration between two people, then allowing one person to negate their contributions negates the entire sum of the collaboration. There is no way to make ourselves smaller and less important without making the project and relationship small and less important. The idea of ubuntu, which comes from South Africa, fits here perfectly: we are all people through other people. An injury to one is an injury to all. That is never clearer than when one of us has a bad day or a lesson fails, or we are muddling through a life that is hard and full of disappointment. By supporting each other, we are supporting ourselves and the community around us.

That kind of support translates into the exciting feeling that we're getting the better end of the deal in this relationship. It's a pretty amazing blessing to get to work with someone who respects you so much that they believe they are lucky to get to work with you. That's not to say we don't see each other's faults. It's impossible to work this closely and not run into conflict. But when you would rather have them win—because if they lose, it feels like you lose even more—it helps stop conflict before it escalates.

That feels a little granola to a lot of people, but one of the major benefits of having a collaborative partner is that they are there when everything falls apart, and they will help you put it all back together again. We are each other's lightning rod—when storms roll in, we are the person at the front lines, seeing the anger, the turmoil, and the intensity. We absorb some of that so the storm can quiet down and eventually pass. Being a lightning rod for each other is one of the most meaningful roles we have, and it's the reason we are now just as close as friends as we are as team-teachers.

FRIENDS FIRST

We also have a rule that governs the amount of work we do. We believe that balance is important in life, and that we need to be careful to not let school take over our entire priority list. Having time for eating, sleeping, and exercise is just as important as having time for friends and family. Now, we're lucky enough to be friends, rather than just teaching partners. But when those two roles come into conflict, there is no question which one will triumph. We are ALWAYS Friends First.

That means that sometimes, the work is unfinished. We show a movie instead of the intricate lesson we wanted to do, but didn't have time to plan. We reuse a lesson we wanted to revise more extensively. Class is more chaotic because we got less sleep as we worked through an issue in our lives together.

Friends First is a commitment we make to each other that if one person says, "Hey, I can't do this right now. Can we just hang out for a little while and be friends instead of teachers?" the other person is happy to comply, even if it means personally sacrificing time spend on their lesson planning. When one partner is not fully present because of the drama and trauma of life, it impacts the other partner and the work at a fundamental level. Being friends first is often inconvenient, and rarely comes at a low-stress time where we have nothing to do except hang out. But the payoff of sacrificing time spent on work is that our friendship is mature, healthy, and robust. The closer we get as friends, the better the work; it's not why we became friends—that was because we genuinely enjoy hanging out together—but it's a by-product we happily accept.

CONFLICT RESOLUTION

Those rules, along with lots of others like them, have kept our friendship vibrant and our work exciting for the past year. Those rules have also prevented plenty of fights, but there are times where conflict within the partnership is unavoidable. As teachers, we work with students whose emotions are far more raw and immediate than ours. Every year, we get more distant from what it feels like to be young, and the assumption society makes is that there is some point where we magically grow up and know how to be a Full-Fledged Adult With Responsibilities And Emotionally-Mature, Healthy Relationships.

The reality is that we have had to learn how to work closely and be vulnerable with each other, but also deal with arguments, disagreements, and hurt feelings. Fighting is not something most people would include in a chapter on collaboration, but it's perhaps the most important result of our CoLab Partnership. This is probably made far more intense by the fact that we usually can only see each other's faces, and that means we have learned how to read each other pretty accurately. If one of us is angry about something, the other tends to notice within five seconds of starting the Google+ Hangout. Neither of us can count the number of times this has happened:

> *Google Hangout initiated, calling other person*
> Partner 1: *Hi. What's wrong?*
> Partner 2: *Yeah. I'm having a rough day.*
> Partner 1: *What do you need?*
> Partner 2: *I don't know...trying to figure that out. Help?*

Most people get used to hiding their emotions so that conflict is minimized. And it's certainly true in our relationship that knowing how to read each other's mood accurately leads to having to face conflict more regularly.

So over the course of the last year, and lots and lots of fights, we have learned some important things in relation to managing and resolving conflict. The first consideration is security. If the relationship is secure, then each person is committing to not pulling the eject button on the partnership, regardless of the argument and how angry we are. There is no back door, and both of us are convinced that the other is committed to working it out, no matter what. Secondly, we trust each other and assume positive intent, even when we hear malice and intent to cause pain. It is difficult to always assign a positive motive to the other person when they hurt us, but doing that stops resentment from taking over and rotting the partnership from the inside out. Finally, we commit to saying what we actually think. If we're not fine, then we don't say "I'm fine." If we're angry about something, we tell them specifically, without waiting for the other person to convince us that they care enough for us to grace them with the truth. We say what we mean. And often, that's enough to stop the argument entirely.

Those practices protect this priceless relationship, and even though it's difficult to follow them all the time, doing so demonstrates that this isn't a transaction, and that we are grown-up enough to fight in a mature way. These rules also make it safe for us to take risks with each other, and be vulnerable. If you trust that nothing you say will cause them to walk out the virtual door (or slam the laptop cover shut and turn off their phone), then you are more likely to be honest. Slowly over time, these positive patterns replace the negative ones, and it starts to impact our other friendships and our classrooms as well. In a relationship where one person could turn off their technology and disappear forever, it's even more important to be good at resolving conflict without bitterness or resentment developing.

Here is the bottom line about the friendship: it is hard work, but it is incredibly worth it. We are clearly better together than we are alone. We have someone to support us when we struggle, to challenge us when we get complacent, and motivate us when we get weary. And that changes everything.

WHAT DO YOU NEED?

In the imagined dialogue above, there is a phrase that we use a lot: "What do you need?" What we have learned through working together is that the other person will not always take care of their needs, or recognize our needs when they arise. It sounds like a simple question, but it is as profound as it is simple. When is the last time someone asked you what you needed to make your classroom better? If you're like us, there are very few people who ever venture into our classrooms, let alone ask us what they can do to help. We are regularly pushed through training that is neither what we need nor what we want to spend time on. We spend hours grading essays alone, for students who only care about the number on the top of the page. We are taught to be as self-sufficient as possible, both as teachers and as human beings, because counting on someone else is dangerous and even scary.

It is that isolated, self-sufficient tendency that drives out half the teachers who enter the profession within five years. In fact, before we met, we wondered how long we could keep going on our own. Cheryl was even at a collaborative school with a strong department of well-meaning and intelligent colleagues for her first year flipping, but most of the teachers in her department were new mothers, or involved in so many leadership roles that they didn't have time or energy to experiment in their classrooms. Andrew was at a school that actively tried to divide-and-conquer so that their teachers were easier to control when they didn't like something. So neither of us knew what we were getting into when we decided to team-teach.

We also didn't know that the relationship, not the work, was what we really needed. Had you asked either of us a year ago what we needed, it wouldn't have been "a new best friend who is also helping you collaboratively plan, teach class, and assess students." But sometimes, not knowing what you need is okay. Some needs are so glaringly obvious in hindsight, but impossible to see in the present. Now, the answer to the question of "What do you need?" in the big picture sense at least, is "Each other." We are both decent writers, but the writing we do together is always better. We are both decent teachers, but together, we are better at every aspect of the teaching profession. There are so many things we've done that would have seemed impossible before we met. Currently, there is very little we can't accomplish together.

IMAGINING OURSELVES AND EACH OTHER COMPLEXLY

The actual decision to team-teach came after Cheryl met Jon Bergmann at a one-day CUE event in California. He had seen our videos, and had asked us to make a video about our process so that other flipped teachers could try the same sort of thing. In the advanced session that afternoon (for anyone who had already flipped, of which there were three of us), Andrew joined Cheryl on a note-taking Google doc. We use this structure a lot—because we attend professional development and conferences separately, we will either bring the other person in on a hangout, or through a collaborative note-taking document. Jon was talking about data, and asked us to survey our students at the end of the year to see what they thought of the other person, the teacher not physically in the room. He wondered if they would see us both as their teachers.

That got us thinking: What if we both WERE their teachers? Rather than just making videos together, what if we actually planned our classes collaboratively, and observed each other as often as possible through Google Hangout? As far as we knew, no one had ever tried something like that. We knew of a few collaborative partnerships, like Katie Regan and Shari Sloane, or Zach Cresswell and Steve Kelly. But both of those partnerships were created off the basis of meeting in person and living within driving distance. They also didn't plan every aspect of their instruction together; the focus was more on the flipped videos that they created and shared with one another.

What we wanted was a person to help us design the course, plan daily, assess frequently, reflect thoughtfully, and create content for every class we taught. There were three obvious complications:

1. Time
2. Amount of work required to sustain it
3. No one had ever done this before.

First of all: collaboration of this magnitude takes a lot of time. We will talk about the logistics later in this chapter, but the ballpark figure for how much time we spend on school is about 15-20 hours a week, divided into "lunch" and "evening" hangouts, spread over six days. We won't lie. This takes a lot of time. Honestly, if we weren't friends, we would never put this much time into team-teaching. The friendship makes the work fun, and the work keeps the friendship fresh. But there have been lots of times when we just ran out of hours in the day, and we had to do some planning or preparing on our own.

Near the beginning of the year, both of us were worried about the amount of time we were spending on work. We were teaching for 6-7 hours actively, working together for another 2-3 hours a day, spending an hour (Andrew) to three hours (Cheryl, for the first few months of school) commuting, and we both have "real lives", too. We are also legendary project-starters, but not so much project-finishers, and we were worried about getting bored with the work if it wasn't sufficiently novel to hold our interest. Once we got through the most intense and difficult period of August to October, the work started to feel more manageable again, and the fear we had of getting bored or burning out slowly faded.

The strange thing we've found is that, while neither of us is naturally gifted at seeing a project through to completion, together we could make it happen. Somehow, our similar personalities—if you're an MBTI fan, Andrew is an INFP and Cheryl is an INFJ—took our individual lack of motivation to finish what we start and transformed it into a shared work ethic that has seen us finish nearly every major project we've started. Perhaps we don't want to be responsible for letting the other person down. But I think the truth, as with all aspects of life, is far more complex than that.

Before we met, we would each have these Big Ideas that we'd get halfway into before realizing it was doomed to failure because we hadn't foreseen that problem, or that objection, or we just didn't have the time, energy, or motivation to follow it to completion. So one benefit of our collaborative partnership is that we always talk through ideas completely before committing to them. That naturally limits what we are able to do because we don't have infinite time to talk through every idea, but it also gives a second perspective on the idea and its benefits and costs. There have been dozens of ideas that we've thought through and rejected because the deeper we get into it, the more clear it is that it will never work. We are also very aware of our time being limited, both with each other and with our students, so we have to be really discerning when choosing projects.

Neither of us can think of a project we started (let alone finished) before starting our collaboration that was as large-scale as the Blank White Page Project, the Flipped Learning Journal, or the CoflipReads Book Club (all of which we will discuss later in this chapter). It's equally likely that we would have burnt out on flipped learning without one another. Any flipped teacher can tell you that the hours spent making and editing videos is exhausting, and changing nearly everything in your practice takes a lot of time and energy. There are very few teachers who can sustain a flipped classroom without some help from other people; some are lucky enough to have another flipped teacher at their site or in their district, but at the very least, most flipped teachers engage on social media or in communities like the Ning or on Edmodo.

The problem with the way many PLNs function is that the focus is on sharing, and most people would rather talk about their successes than their failures. It is easy to share a blog post about how amazing it was to have every student pass an assessment, or sharing the results of a big project. It is easy to give pithy advice, especially on Twitter, where the 140 character limit doesn't lend itself to complex conversation. And frankly, we all want to seem successful. We believe that if someone knew what it was REALLY like in our classrooms every day, they would expose us as being the fraud we really are. So we edit out the struggle, the failures, the mess, and "sharing" with our PLN just makes us feel more alone.

Something we learned pretty quickly is that teaching, as in most aspects of life, resists simplicity. The simple story of our #CoLab Partnership is that we met, we got along great, had an amazing year where we were innovative and dynamic team-teachers and all of our lessons and ideas ended up being 100% successful. That is why this chapter, along with all the other attempts we've made at sharing openly about our work together, has been so difficult to write. Our natural tendency is to make the story about us, and about how special we are, and how many successes we've had, and how amazing it is to have such a perfect partner and a perfect year of teaching. The truth is far more complex.

This relationship is special, but it's also a hell of a lot of work. There have been plenty of times that we wondered if we were strong enough to overcome the challenges we faced. Both of us have had moments where we want to have a surface-level friendship where we ignore the simmering resentment and paper over it with platitudes. It's true that we've been successful on many fronts, but we also have failed. A lot. The first six weeks of school was a gigantic train-wreck of failure. Some ideas only showed a glimmer of their full potential because we lacked the time or resources to make them as good as we wanted them to be. We both struggled with colleagues or administrators to get them to understand the work we were doing, with limited success and even more limited appreciation or recognition.

When we reflect on the past year, it's easy to gloss over the things that didn't work and focus on the huge amount of success. Choosing to share only our successes creates a situation in which we are actually alienating people who we want to help. We've had teachers tell us that they could never do what we do; in that statement is the implicit comparison between their own flawed and messy practice to their belief that our practice is Made Entirely of EduAwesome. So we fight against that constantly. Failure is not only an inevitable part of life, but it's also how we learn and grow and mature. If we had given up every time something failed, we'd have quit teaching years ago...or would have never started in the first place.

Teaching isn't something we're born knowing how to do. While some people have natural gifts and tendencies that make them skilled at various aspects of the profession, every teacher has to learn how to deliver instruction, create lessons and assessments, build students' skills by working with them where they are at, motivate reluctant learners, manage a classroom, organize the lesson and the physical space, and hundreds of other things we do every day. Flipping the learning in the classroom adds an entirely different set of skills to master, and it takes time and a lot of failure to figure out how to do it well.

That's why we share the mess in our classrooms and our relationship. We fight. We have lessons that fail. We lack follow-through or even start-up motivation. We wish we were more like x person or less like y person, or just less like us. But the only way to collaborate effectively is to let someone else into the mess and ask them to help you clean it up. And they might fail you, or hurt you, or abandon you. Real relationships have real risks. But the risk is worth it, especially when you end up with something as life-changing as the CoLab Partnership we've built.

How Do I Get What You Guys Have?

We're pretty confident that it's not possible to completely replicate the relationship we have, but we do think that every teacher should have room for a collaborative partnership in their practice. Teaching alone is difficult, but manageable. However, teaching a flipped class alone is nearly impossible. There are just too many possibilities and too much work for one person to do it entirely on their own. We know that most flipped teachers currently work alone, in large part because of few willing colleagues, but we don't know of many flipped teachers who don't engage with the PLN for new ideas, support, and reflection. We also don't know many flipped teachers who can sustain a flipped class indefinitely. Teaching the traditional way, with the teacher at the front of the room, and students furiously copying down lecture notes so they can later study for an exam on the material, is much easier than creating an extensive video library and redesigning class time to be learner-centric.

So we need each other. Where we started was Twitter and the Monday night #flipclass chat (at 8pm EST). Both of us had participated in the chat prior to meeting, and we also were following the #flipcon12 hashtag while watching the conference live. By engaging with other educators on Twitter, we had access to hundreds of teachers who were as passionate about these ideas as we were, and didn't need to be converted to the benefits of a flipped classroom. There is also the Flipped Learning Network Ning, where there is a large community of teachers looking to interact with other flipped teachers. Any of these places work for building your PLN.

However, more care is needed before anyone begins a collaborative partnership. Collaboration can happen in a large group of people with vaguely similar goals; collaborative *partnerships* happen when a pair or small group of teachers intentionally choose to work together closely because there are so many things made possible when they work together that would never be possible alone. It is of vital importance that we choose our collaborative partners carefully. You have to respect the work they do. You have to trust that they will be honest, even when the honest answer is the more difficult answer. You have to trust that they will support you and work well with you.

None of those are easy things to find, and we encourage teachers to be selective before agreeing to collaborate. There are also curricular considerations, such as the level or grade, the specific subject, and the type of school environment in which both partners teach. Finding a partner whose teaching context is a perfect match to yours is probably not possible. In some courses, you might not find someone at all. For Cheryl's San Francisco Stories class, there were literally zero other teachers in the world who taught that exact course, or even one of the novels. There are really two options here:

1. Find a collaborative partner who will plan with you regardless of how different your classes are, or
2. Choose the subjects or units for which you want a collaborative partner.

Either option is better than flipping alone, but as we've taken the first option, we're clearly biased. For English teachers, it is sometimes easier to find teachers who want to collaborate on a single novel or text. We know a group of teachers who planned their *Of Mice and Men* unit collaboratively, and taught it simultaneously. After the unit ended (and was incredibly successful!), each teacher resumed planning on his or her own, but made plans to collaborate again in a future unit. There really is no wrong way to collaborate, and if you don't see a way to fit a CoLab Partnership into your practice, then finding collaborators for books, subjects, units or even lessons is a good way to start.

If you are aiming for a CoLab Partnership, then there are several important considerations. The first is the interpersonal dynamic. The time commitment is so intense that, on top of respecting and communicating well with them, you have to really, *really* like the other person. You also have to have a schedule that is compatible so that conversations aren't always rushed through between events. Ideally, you also need someone who is good at what you're not, and vice versa. If you both aspire to making engaging videos, but neither has video editing skills or motivation to learn, then the partnership isn't ideal. If both of you are incredibly Type-A personalities and get so focused on the details that the big picture is completely ignored, then the partnership won't be productive.

Finally, test it out before committing to an intense close relationship. Jumping into a collaborative partnership without adequate time to get to know one another, not just as work associates but as friends, is like moving in with someone after the first date. It took us about five weeks to decide that we wanted to team-teach, and in that time, we had progressed from making a few instructional videos together to writing course maps and planning units. It took that much time for us to test out the dynamic and be sure that it worked. There are so many factors that go into human relationships, and this kind of relationship is no different.

Here are some questions to ask yourself before deciding whether or not to commit:

- When I have a problem, do I feel comfortable raising it with them? When I do, are they likely to react in a positive, constructive way?
- Is the work we do together better than what I can do on my own? Is it better than what they could do on their own?
- Do they add value to my life and my practice? Do I add value to theirs?
- Is this someone I can trust and with whom I can take risks? Can they trust me and take risks with me?
- Do they make me more excited to do my job? Does our partnership translate to success in the classroom with students?

If you can't answer all or most of those with a positive, unequivocal YES, then you should give it more time. If you have serious reservations about the relationship after answering those questions, you should consider moving on. The point of a close collaborative relationship is to make both of you better at your job and at being human. That's important enough to get it right.

LOGISTICAL AND PRACTICAL CONSIDERATIONS

Once you've found the right person, you have a lot of considerations for how the collaboration is going to operate. We can't tell you the "right way" to collaborate, but we can tell you how ours progressed and what was helpful at each point along the way.

We started with a single project—a series covering the research process—and worked on it pretty solidly for about a month. We posted our first video on June 30th, and the final video, which was the 20th in the series, went live on July 28th. The videos alone total about 170 minutes of instruction, which is probably about half of what we recorded. Once we started doing all the planning together and making editing notes at the end of the recording session, it probably took about 2 hours to complete a 12 minute video. Those two hours were broken down roughly like this:

- Start hangout, review from the last video, open the document with all our notes, and do a rough outline of what we would cover (15-25 minutes)
- Begin recording and talk through the process, sometimes once and sometimes twice depending on how the first time went (35-45 minutes)
- Stop recording, make notes on the document about what the next video would include, then talk about the video we just recorded and how it should be edited (15-30 minutes)
- End hangout and begin video editing. Post final video to YouTube (1-3 hours, depending on how much the technology cooperated and how intensive the editing)

We filmed the first ten videos in the series in four sessions; in fact, videos five through ten were all filmed together and edited in one very intense day (the times of upload to YouTube are, in order: 1:31 AM, 2:58 AM, 2:55 PM, 5:57 PM, 9:21 PM). Our goal was to finish as many videos during the summer as possible, and both of us had a lot of time in July, so marathon video-making and editing sessions were a regular occurrence, and were actually quite a lot of fun...even if sleep played a supporting role in our lives during those times.

The summer provided the ideal time for us to begin our partnership. After FlipCon12, we had the motivation to tackle this kind of enormous undertaking, and the schedule to facilitate that. Had we met during the school year, it would have taken months to do a project of that scale. That is why we advocate finding a collaborative partner during the summer if at all possible. Most teachers work ridiculous hours during the school year, and the stress of building a relationship with a collaborative partner on top of the pressures of teaching and trying to have a "real life" outside of school, would be overwhelming, at least for us. Meeting at the beginning of summer also meant that we had not done our planning for the upcoming year either, and that gave us the chance to work on it together, rather than trying to shoehorn something into an already existing plan.

As we completed the research paper series, we turned our attention to long-term planning. We had a total of nine courses to plan, although only six of them began in fall. When we committed to team-teaching, we didn't know if it would really work. As far as we knew, no one had ever attempted anything like it, and we certainly had no idea what we were getting into. The logical place to start was by writing course maps of the skills, standards, texts, and themes for each class. We hadn't started out with the intention to teach exactly the same material at the same time, but as we wrote the course map for Andrew's class, we began to see how it was possible. While we knew there would be different novels for each class, the progression of skills we wanted to teach seemed to match perfectly. In a discipline like English, where curriculum varies wildly from school to school, we were surprised by how much we could have in common instructionally.

One thing that distinguishes English from other subjects is the amount of creative freedom often afforded to English teachers. Other than novels required at each grade level, many schools have few mandates about what must be taught in what course. However, it makes English teachers far less likely to collaborate outside of their department or school. While many English teachers teach classics like *Of Mice and Men*, *To Kill a Mockingbird*, and *1984,* every district places them at slightly different levels or courses. We were amazed that within our discipline, we could find so much crossover in what we taught and when.

The first step was to create a course map of the skills and standards in each unit. *Figure 1* shows the first unit from the Skills Map we wrote in the summer of 2012 for Andrew's 10th grade English class.

Using that course map, we started planning out a semester where we would be teaching the same skills simultaneously. We outlined the entire year—seven units—in which we would share assessments and assignments, with just the names associated with the reading changed. With both of us using the Common Core State Standards, and with few district or site mandates on curriculum, it was fairly simple to coordinate objectives and standards. (*Figure 2*)

First Unit:

Snapshot of a Modern Learner/Introduction to Procedures

In this unit, students will be introduced to the concept of a flipped classroom: how it functions, how their role will change to accept responsibility for their own learning, how they will be assessed, and how they will access the content for the course. Students will also be introduced to the various technological tools which we will make use this term. The skills focus of the unit will be in developing the ability to conduct research on a variety of topics and in a variety of ways. They will learn how to summarize information accurately, synthesize content effectively, and use evidence to draw inferences from the material. They will read several texts around the theme of identity, specifically their identity as a learner. Students will complete several writing assignments on that theme, and will work on their use of language, both implicitly in multi-draft essays, and explicitly in Daily Oral Language assignments and skill-building in areas students show need.

Direct Instruction (via video)
- How to set up accounts/services for technology used
- How to use the reading strategy of Patterning
  - Available here:
    http://www.youtube.com/playlist?list=PL35BDA021465E7A57
- How to write a research paper (series)
  - Available here:
    http://www.youtube.com/playlist?list=PL1AD0016A263E3C9A
- Basic Concepts in Grammar

Challenge Activity (for students who complete the unit early):
- Work on next BWP (Blank White Page project. Defined shortly.)
- Find an article about learning and critique it based on personal experience. Write an article that describes the way in which technology shapes culture (or youth culture)

Figure 1

When the school year started, we didn't realize just how difficult our task was going to be. After all, we had spent almost a month planning, and two months making video content for our classes. We had prepared everything we could. Our impression of how the first few weeks would go was that while our students were working through all the content we'd prepared in a self-paced mastery model, we would use our planning time to get ahead and prepare unit two. We really believed that we could launch into a fully flipped, fully mastery classroom at brand new schools. We were excited and passionate about it, and we showed our enthusiasm to our students from the beginning. But no amount of passion was going to move them from their desire for a traditional education, where they could fairly accurately assess their ability to get the grade they wanted with limited critical thinking required, to embracing the very different education we were offering.

Standards to be assessed for mastery:
- apply basic patterning strategy to a text (RL 4)
- provide objective summary of text (RL 2)
- make inferences drawn from text (RL 1)
- conduct short research projects to answer a question or solve a problem (W 7)
- demonstrate understanding of the subject under investigation (W 7)

Standards assessed, but not mastered yet:
- assess strength/limitations of each source (W 8)
- synthesize multiple sources on a subject (W 7)

Other standards addressed in unit, but not assessed yet:
- gather relevant information from multiple sources (W 8)
- use advanced searches effectively (W 8)
- cite strong textual evidence (RL 1)
- use info clearly and accurately through effective selection/organization/analysis of content (W 2)
- analyze impact of specific word choices on meaning/tone (RL 4)
- choose relevant/sufficient evidence (W 1)
- use technology to produce, publish, and update individual/shared writing (W 6)
- write routinely over various time frames, tasks, purposes and audiences (W 10)
- demonstrate command of standard conventions when writing (L 2)

End of Unit Assessment:
1. Use the text "How to Become a Writer" by Lorrie Moore and have students apply patterning to a section of it, write a summary, and choose one piece of evidence. They will make inferences about the evidence and how it relates to the overall message.
2. Students will complete two small-scale research projects that show mastery of research skills - one will be Artistic, and one will be Analytical. The projects will also function as a formative assessment for the rest of the term, where students will be required to complete one more of each type of project.

Skills to be Demonstrated (from GCS Pacing Guide):
- I can use textual evidence to make an inference.
- I can choose several sources and synthesize information to answer my research inquiry.
- I can demonstrate understanding of the subject under investigation.
- I can integrate appropriate digital media in a strategic manner to improve my presentation.
- I can present my information in a sequence that allows the listener to follow my line of reasoning.
- I can demonstrate correct use of standard grammar and conventions.

Figure 2

As our students grew more frustrated with our desire to change ALL of the things at one time, we faltered. That wasn't how we thought the first unit would go. While there were solid activities and the overall design was clear and compelling, it didn't fit the needs of our students. We introduced too much too fast, using technology with which we were barely comfortable, and they were wholly unfamiliar. We had to change what we were doing. A lot. We limped through the first unit, but started looking forward to the relative fresh start of the start of the new unit.

In Real Life, You Can Sometimes Get a Do-Over

Once we regained our footing from the first unit, we fell into a fairly consistent pattern that held for the majority of the school year. Andrew would be preparing (he had first period off) while Cheryl got ready for school. He was teaching by the time she left home, and we would check in about any last minute planning decisions during the window between Cheryl waking up and leaving the house. Cheryl taught from 8:00-12:00 most days, and by that point, Andrew was done for the day. The first hangout of the day would happen then—after school for Andrew and during lunch for Cheryl.

This hangout largely was to debrief what happened in each class. Cheryl had one class afterwards, but for both of us, the day was mostly over so we could look through the formative assessment we had gathered during class and help each other make meaning of it and decide what came next, instructionally. However, these conversations were often more about troubleshooting than instruction. Andrew's classes were at a much lower level and behaviorally far more challenging than Cheryl's. Cheryl's classes tended to move much faster, but students were content with surface-level understanding and had to be challenged to move deeper with the material.

Therein lies the reason we were so successful together: each of us had something the other didn't. Cheryl spent most of her career teaching lower-level 9th and 10th graders in urban, under-served environments, and had only taught two upper level courses in nine years. Andrew had taught 11th-12th grade primarily, but also a large number of AP courses, and had worked in environments with students passionate for knowledge and a propensity towards "point prostitution" (the tendency for students to debate the finer points of every grade given, regardless of the skill or understanding they demonstrated). Our roles were so completely reversed, it was almost comical. There were plenty of times we wished we could trade assignments; there's no doubt each of us would have found the other's classes easier to teach. However, that turned out to be more of a gift than it seemed at first. Without being pushed so far out of our comfort level and instructional practice, we would not have needed each other.

There is no doubt that we would have benefitted from the relationship and collaboration without both of us feeling so overwhelmed with our teaching assignments. Neither of us felt qualified to teach the classes we were given, and knew enough to know how much we didn't know. And while we both knew we could do it alone, we were relieved to not have to. Collaboration, for us, became not just a survival strategy, but part of our professional DNA. Once we saw the benefit we gained from working together so closely, it became much harder to do without it.

Around the sixth week of school, we realized that it wouldn't work to continue trying to teach the same skills at the same time. The needs of our classes were so different that we needed to adjust. We made the choice to continue planning together, despite the fact that all six classes needed individual lesson plans. By that point, we had departed from the pacing set out in the course map, but that didn't seem to matter. We were no longer tied to doing the same thing, which freed us up to be far more creative in our planning. The classes we taught slowly shifted from flipped mastery to predominantly student-centred and project-based.

We started to realize that our classes had to reflect the skills, themes, and topics most interesting to each individual group of students, rather than some master plan we developed before meeting any of them. Even though writing the course maps was a lot of work and represented some great ideas, we eventually abandoned them in favor of a class planned day-by-day, directed by the students and our assessment of their educational needs. This kind of planning was often difficult; it means that if you have other things to work on or talk about, sometimes classes didn't get planned as well as they should, or sometimes even at all. That doesn't mean we showed up to school without a lesson plan—it just meant that we would do our lesson plans individually (Cheryl had time to work in the evening, after Andrew went to bed, and Andrew had time to work during his first period prep). That happened occasionally, but we made an attempt to plan every class together every day because it became clear early in the year that the classes planned collaboratively were almost always more successful than ones planned alone.

So we would spend two or three hours most weeknights on Google Hangout, talking through the next day's lessons and discussing the unit goals and objectives. These hangouts rarely had a clear agenda and were not the same night to night. Some nights, we would talk generally through our classes and make an outline in a document we shared. Other nights, we would write tests or essay topics. Other nights, we would spend hours planning one class, and a few minutes on others. The point is this: we prioritized our work, and worked through the list in that order. And the list changed day to day.

When we add up the total time we spent together this last year, it's a little staggering. However, our workload was equally staggering, and our friendship was in its infancy and needed a lot of maintenance. We're pretty sure that we could have operated with less time together, but are equally sure that we don't regret any of it. Most teachers don't have the experience of finding someone with whom they work so well that often, words are unnecessary. Someone who is a witness to your life, who helps shape your institutional memory of what happened in your classroom. We both remember our year fairly clearly because of the time that went into planning, teaching, and reflecting on every lesson. Unlike in previous years, where we could likely give you a rough outline of the major topics we covered, we both remember our curriculum in great detail because it was purposeful, intentional, and communal.

The logistics of our planning seems overwhelming, even to us. We know that very few educators would knowingly sign up for a scenario where they gave up so much time, energy, and control in order to collaborate with someone else. We also know that most educators haven't experienced the joy, the freedom, and the amazing results of this kind of collaboration...which is the only thing that makes the investment of time, energy and resources worthwhile.

Now What?

In this chapter, we wanted to convince you first of the why before we discussed the how. Collaboration isn't something most of us do naturally if the school environment doesn't mandate or encourage it, and especially for new teachers, it can be intimidating to work with people entrenched in the institution and instructional pedagogy. We also know that we tolerate change and chaos in our classroom better than 95% of teachers. Some of that is personality, and some of that is pedagogy. Our students are constantly changing, and to be the best possible teacher, we have to be flexible with our methods, and open to changing our minds when we are persuaded of the merit in the opposite point of view. By collaborating so closely with each other, we've learned to be more flexible in many ways, but also we've had to articulate the merits of all of our instructional practices. That has led to some intense reflection and self-examination, and often has resulted in a change in what we believe about education. In a world as constantly shifting as the one our students occupy, it is our job to learn to take the shifting movements in stride, and to stand firm on only the positions and practices that are most educationally sound.

For us, that means that we won't do long-range planning again. While we will have an outline of what the course should look like and include, we will not make all the decisions before meeting the students. In fact, the most important assessment comes in the first few weeks, where we get to know our students, their skills, their needs, and their educational history. Alone, neither of us would be able to make sense of so much data, so our collaboration is necessary for a day-to-day planning structure to work.

Additionally, a lot of long-range planning actually creates an absence of this kind of formative assessment. If you have the exam written before the students start the unit, how do you know what you've taught or how well they've learned it? You can certainly assess how much they know. But without the formative assessment gained throughout a unit, you have no idea how effective your teaching has been for each student. We do believe in having a roadmap, but it has to be more like Google Maps than the paper variety: adaptable, often changing, and far more accurate.

WHAT'S POSSIBLE?

The kinds of projects you can create through collaboration are endless. There are a few that have been incredibly successful and instrumental in shaping our collaborative partnership and helped us redefine what we thought was possible.

The first project was the Blank White Page project. There is a lot of press and excitement around the idea of a 20% project, and so last summer, we built one that would fit our class particularly. Students choose a topic or question, then find answers and build a project of their choosing with the results. What makes this project most remarkable is that we had four teachers from across the country participating, and students from 9th grade to 12th grade, from AP to low-level, and with vastly different interests. This would have been a fun project had it been limited to our own classrooms, but the idea that students would share their work with students from around the country raised the stakes and produced some incredible projects and a lot of incredible thinking.

It also was a low-risk project with which to start a collaboration. The project required little administration, and was almost entirely in the students' hands to make successful. It brought other teachers into our classrooms and into our practice. It also demonstrated to our students that we were part of a network of teachers that went far beyond the school walls. Seeing the collaborative relationships we had with other teachers started a lot of conversations and helped students understand why we focus so strongly on collaboration and use so much technology to facilitate it.

Another project we collaborated on this year was the Flipped Learning Journal. With a small group of flipped learning teachers on Twitter (using the hashtag we created, #coflip), we built a website that could collect meaningful and practical advice on what to use the newly-freed-up face-to-face-time with students. There was plenty of information on the internet about how to start making flipped videos, but we wanted a resource that would help teachers reimagine what is possible in a flipped class. This project is ongoing, and the relationships we developed with other teachers through creating the FLJ is another great model for our students of what collaboration and friendship can create. In a way, it was OUR first major Blank White Page project, and we shared it with students to show them that our learning didn't stop once we graduated from college.

Through the FLJ, we started another BWP project: CoFlipBooks Reads *The Fault In Our Stars*, by John Green. It started with seven teachers who committed to making collaborative videos about each chapter. We divided up the chapters and partners, and started reading and recording our thoughts. Some of our students got involved as well, and even made two of the chapter videos for the group.

None of these projects is that extraordinary outside of the context in which they were created. All were produced because of the collaborative partnership we have forged; while we aren't the only teachers responsible for these projects, our collaborative partnership has been a driving force in making all of them happen. These projects, just like our relationship, are much bigger than just two teachers making instructional videos together. They also remind us that so much more is possible, and that all the struggle and the difficulty are definitely worth it.

WHAT'S NEXT?

As we move into our second year as collaborative partners, we don't know what the future will hold for us. There is very little overlap in the courses we taught this past school year and the courses we will teach in the upcoming school year. What that means is that we will be back to daily planning, and will use some pieces of courses we've taught previously, though much of what we use will be brand-new. We also want to build on our strengths:

- Making video: collaborative video is where we started, and we both believe that there is much we can still do in that format
- Helping facilitate collaboration and professional development: we will continue to moderate the Twitter #flipclass chat, but we also want to share our story as widely as possible to help inspire teachers to try it for themselves
- Relationships with our students and each other: relationship is the heart of what we do collaboratively and professionally. That is one place where our energy is never wasted.

We believe strongly that collaboration is the best way forward for us. We know that some teachers will disagree, and many have over the last year when we've presented our work together. But we also know that what is more important than the work we do together is modeling for our students what collaboration and friendship looks like. For many of our students, they have not seen adults work together in any capacity, and so they regard us as an aberration. By opening up our lives and work and inviting students into the mess, we show them that we—like them—are human and flawed. We make mistakes. We fight with each other, and annoy each other, and take care of each other. That kind of relationship is difficult, but is always worth it. We want them to see both sides—the difficulty, and the degree to which we believe it's worth it.

Our hope is that one thing they will take away from our class is that we are ALL Better Together. Maybe you don't have room in your practice for a team-teacher, but you do have a project that you've always wanted to have help executing. Maybe you are at a school where you are the only one interested in flipped learning and by finding colleagues on Twitter to interact with occasionally, you can feel more supported without needing a collaborative partnership. Having a CoLab Partner won't solve all your problems. But a real CoLab Partner will make those problems seem less intimidating, and help you manage them better. We know that we could not have continued teaching forever without this partnership, and that is exactly why we keep telling our story.

We hope that by sharing our story, we can make it possible for other teachers to recognize the places in their lives and practices that could benefit from collaboration, and then find someone who is willing to help.

What happens from there, we hope, is personal and professional alchemy.

We know alchemy is possible, and that when it happens, it's worth fighting for.

Part-time Flipping
Kenny Bosch

When I began teaching in 1999, the technology available to me as an instructor had little improved since I was a student in the classroom—chalk, sometimes a whiteboard, an overhead projector and a teacher's computer. My collegiate training to prepare me for my profession did not include a single aspect of technology.

The fastest area of change in our profession, much like the rest of the world, has been in the area of technology integration. In the first few years of my career, the resources available to me were filmstrips, VHS tapes, and the occasional opening in the computer lab. If I wanted our learning community to explore outside of the textbook, any internet lesson almost always had to take place at school, as most students did not own a computer.

One of the first computer-based projects I had my students attempt was a PowerPoint project where they worked in small groups and had to combine their work into one final presentation. The technological hurdles we had to overcome were many: it took four floppy disks to save the work, loading was painfully slow in class, and students had varying versions of the software, making editing a nightmare. I knew that the project idea itself was good; the technology needed time to catch up, however.

To me, flipping is a way to create an idea, project or lesson, to alter an existing idea, project or lesson, and to find new ways to give students the freedom to learn and present what they have learned in a form that fits their needs and styles. As technology continues to change, I change with it by finding more opportunities for my students to learn and present what they have learned.

HOW MUCH DO I HAVE TO FLIP?

In my conversations with educators, many of us feel pressure to go "Texas Hold'em" and be all-in! I do not think that we have to. The beauty of flipping is it allows *you* more options, not just your students. If your preferred instructional practice is to have discussion, maybe you flip how you do the background work, or as I call it, front-loading. You assign the reading material at home and then use Edmodo, Todaysmeet or Poll Everywhere and give the students some questions to look at, answer and prime their thoughts for the discussion the next day. You are still able to keep intact the part of the lesson that you enjoy and the students are more prepared for the discussion as well. If you feel overwhelmed trying to flip ALL of your lessons, then don't. Flip one lesson per chapter or unit and eventually you will have them all done. If you don't want to flip everything, don't!

WHAT IS FLIPPING AND PART-TIME FLIPPING?

Flipping can be explained in two ways. First, you can flip when you take information that you would present in class and present it as a video, podcast or other version that the students view or experience prior to coming to class, thereby allowing more class time to handle the more difficult course material. Second, you allow multiple options for the students to be able to prepare and the present their work for an assignment. With more options for the students, class time can be utilized to handle questions they have with research, guide them to new learning, and allow the group time to meet and exchange ideas.

Part-time flipping is another option for teachers to consider and is my preferred method for flipping. Part-time flipping is flipping only portions of your classroom, but not all of it. As a professional, each of us knows what is best for our class and students. Technology might not always be the answer or the best way to instruct or share ideas. As I said earlier, it may be a scary and daunting task to flip your class 100% due to a lack of technology, a lack of technological skill, time to practice your skills before instruction, time to create flipped lessons, students' lack of technological skill and access to technology, and so on. Part-time flipping allows you to flip at your own pace, finding ways to incorporate new technology as you see fit.

Teachers often describe their skill sets using a tool box as a metaphor. When we first start out as teachers our tool box has fewer tools than we possess after a few years. Part-time flipping may make some of us feel as if we are starting out again as professionals and this may be an unnerving feeling. Instead, look at part-time flipping as an exciting way to reinvent your classes and content using your full tool box of skills and utilizing those skills in new ways, at the pace you decide. Just as a new teacher is starting to amass new tools for their tool box, a teacher new to flipping may be part-time flipping until they feel they have all the resources necessary to completely flip their class.

To better understand the concept of part-time flipping, I would like to go back to the example from earlier regarding a PowerPoint project. I flipped the assignment by presenting the rubric to students through Educreations and posting it to my Edmodo page. Prior to class time, the students were directed to view the video on the overview of the project and the rubric specifically. I included exemplars to help them visualize the process including some "not there yet" examples as well. When the students came to class the next day they were able to immediately work while I was able to walk around the room and field questions. This process allowed for more work time and individual attention while allowing all learning community members the chance to work and do so at their own pace.

Technology allowed us more flexibility to flip when our school added a Student Drive (S: drive) where they could save and share their work with other students. I created a "Teacher Folder" in the S: drive, divided by hour and group. Each group could then save their work to the folder and combining work was able to take place whenever a group member had a chance. Again, the work was no longer controlled or dictated by our class period being in the library at the same time or availability of the library. Due to this flexibility in student choice, some students needed a computer, others used books, some were putting data into their presentations, and some were exploring new presentation formats like Prezi, Google Presentation, or Symbaloo. (If your school does not have an "S" drive or is transitioning to Google Apps for Education, as is my situation, you can use your Google Drive and sharing capabilities in the same fashion.)

In our classroom I wanted my students to feel safe in experimenting with new ideas and technology. I began to take time, one day a week, to model ways I have tried new technology and how I used it. I began by having the students explore new technology options, presenting chapter content utilizing the new technology and grading them on attempting to use the technology. I did not grade them on how precise and deeply they use the technology. In subsequent technology projects, I encouraged students to again try new technology ideas to present their learning or to use the same technology, but in new ways.

The classroom environment was one of exploration and collaboration. We became a learning community where the students began to take the lead and teach me and their classmates new technology ideas. In creating an environment where creativity is fostered and students feel safe to experiment with new ideas, the students feel empowered to learn about topics they enjoy. They feel more comfortable presenting knowledge they have gained by taking ownership of their education.

HOW CAN I USE FLIPPING TO MY ADVANTAGE?

You can use flipping to your advantage if you continue to think of creative ways to incorporate new options. In my AP course, I continued to plead with my students to read the "Chapter Highlights" sections of our books. After I assigned the reading, the next day in class I would lead a discussion asking questions regarding the material only to discover, to my frustration, that they did not read the material. I would tell them, "The pages are yellow, similar to a traffic light, so that you slow down, not run through them." Despite my pleas, students did not read the sections, and I became more frustrated in class when trying to discuss material they did not read.

I used flipping to my advantage by taking the material, creating a lesson and making it available to them online to view when they were ready. I felt empowered because I still covered the material, but now it was truly up to my students to view the lesson. I felt that flipping worked to my advantage because we did not cover the material in class, which freed up more time for more important information. The students had the responsibility to learn the material and freedom to learn it on their timetable.

After flipping the content of these sections, more students viewed the lesson than read the actual section of chapter. Students sent me emails the very first night telling me they really enjoyed learning the material being presented in the flipped format. The next day, I had greater student participation in class discussion than in any previous lesson and flipping the content was the catalyst for this change. While these online lessons are important to our class content, they are not as important as other material. Flipping these lessons enabled me to remove them from the main focus of classroom discussion, devoting more time to more difficult material that needed our attention. As my class sizes continued to increase over the years I needed to find new, creative ways to free up more class time for the most pertinent information. Flipping portions of my lessons was the way to accomplish this goal.

Another example of how I used flipped teaching was through PowerPoint lessons. I have taken some of my traditional PowerPoint lessons and uploaded them as a Google Presentation, and then linked them to my Edmodo account. Now my students can preview the lesson at home, they can view it anywhere if they were absent and, on occasion, I have had the students work in small groups in class and go over the lesson at their own pace. Flipping the lesson and making it accessible from anywhere has made my students feel more connected to the class, and each other, and made me more accessible as well.

The goal behind previewing a lesson is the same concept as a pre-test. Students are able to preview or look over the upcoming lesson and PowerPoint online to prime their knowledge and upcoming in-class discussion. When my students preview the lesson at home they have already looked over the topics, pictures and higher-level questions and come to class more prepared to participate in class discussions with confidence. Another example of a benefit of flipping my PowerPoint lessons is evident when students are absent from class. They often feel anxious about being behind and missing information that we covered as we move on to the next section. By having the lesson flipped, the student can access the information from home and keep up with the class. If they have questions, they can post them to Edmodo or send me an email and still feel a part of the class while away. Often times in our flipped classroom, when a student poses a question to Edmodo, other students answer the question posed by their classmate before I can get to it, thus furthering the feeling of a learning community and staying connected.

One example of our flipped classroom community helping each other was when a student was absent from school for three days. From home, this student was able to watch the same PowerPoint lessons online via Edmodo that we were discussing in class. Then, the student at home posted a question regarding the date of the upcoming test asking if it was still taking place on the scheduled date. Other students in the class posted a response noting that the test was moved back a day. The student sick at home was able to be a part of the classroom lessons and stay alerted to classroom events without being in class. The students in our learning community answered the question before I had time to see the question and answer.

Another way flipping my lessons has been beneficial to students is when we have small group discussions about the flipped lessons posted on Edmodo. The students enjoy working with classmates of their choosing and moving at their own pace. Some groups will need more time on topic A, while another group can quickly move through A, B, C and focus on the area where they struggle.

In my A.P. class, my students formed groups of their own choosing and began to discuss the PowerPoint. One small group had two advanced learners, and they concluded after a few minutes that they understood topics one and two well enough to move on to topic three. After their ten-minute discussion on the National Bank stalled, they asked me for some guidance on the topic. Our flipped classroom allowed them to focus on the areas they needed the most work instead of the entire class being at the same point at the same time. In the previous example, while my advanced group quickly moved through topics A and B, I was able to help another group understand topic A and the differences between Hamilton and Jefferson regarding the National Bank.

What I enjoy about the flipped, small group discussions is my ability to move around the room, working with each group and be responsive to each group's needs. This has reinvigorated me as an instructor because I am able to have a more direct, personal connection with my students. As noted earlier, some students are reluctant to speak in large groups but, when they are in small groups of their peers, they are more comfortable and willing to share their ideas. I am able to get instant feedback on their comprehension of the material and redirect as needed. Then, when I move the class from small group to large group discussions, students that have shared their ideas in the small group are more likely to feel confident and express those ideas again in the large group setting.

One student in my class was reluctant to speak during class discussions. I asked her, privately, why she did not participate in class discussion. Her answer was that she needed more time than others to process the question, and she also was unsure of her answer and did not want to speak publicly in that situation. When students are allowed to work in cooperative groups of their choosing, they are able to move at their own pace and feel more at ease in speaking and asking questions. After I had the students work in small, cooperative groups and then return for a large group discussion, the student mentioned above began to participate and has continued to participate. Her level of comfort with the material is important, but more importantly, her level of comfort with her classmates has made her more willing to speak.

FLIPPED GRADING

I teach an advanced placement U.S. history course and a key component is essay writing. Over the course of the year, I will grade over a thousand essays, and giving my students timely, detailed feedback is essential to improvement. In May, students have to write three essays in a timed format and because a majority of my students are only sophomores, this has become a difficult task for them in this college-level course. I have encouraged my students to come in for individual meetings to go over their essays and explain my comments on their papers but, due to numerous reasons, they usually do not.

I flipped my essay grading by having my student aides take pictures of the essays from each period with my iPad. I then use the pictures of the essays as the background in Educreations, and from there I evaluate the essays both with a pen and through audible narration of my thoughts on their work. To make the process of using Educreations to flip the grading of essays more efficient, I had students print their full name and email address on a 3x5 notecard. When I completed the evaluation, I simply had my aides match up the student's name/email listed on the note card with the name I saved the Educreations feedback under.

Flipping the essay evaluation has been helpful for numerous reasons. For one, I am able to transport over 50 essays in my iPad without carrying a huge stack of paper essays with me. The portability of these essays on my iPad has reduced my stress and saved on paper and ink. Now, when I leave my classroom and head down to study hall, I bring my iPad and grade without the paper bulk. When I go home at night, I am able to again carry these essays with ease.

Another benefit of flipped essays is the virtual meeting with my students via Educreations (in Educreations the project you make and share is called a lesson). Students are able to access their essay, play my comments, and hear an explanation of my thoughts instead of merely reading my handwritten comments and trying to understand their meaning. Students enjoy being able to replay the "lesson" and review their work. Parents have also made comments about watching the videos and the benefit they bring their child. I am able to speak my thoughts more rapidly than write them out, thereby saving me more time.

My students are involved in numerous after-school activities and when meeting in person is not feasible, a flipped evaluation bridges the gap. My students have commented on enjoying the narrated essay evaluations and feel that they have a deeper understanding of the grade they earned and ways to improve their writing beyond what a traditional evaluation can provide. Students have felt comfortable enough with the process to pass on their flipped essays to classmates so that they can learn from the work of others. In a traditional essay, I would have to pass the one essay around the room for students to look at or make copies of the essay. Now, I can take a picture of an exemplary essay and send it out as an email for students to look at whenever it is convenient for them. My students enjoy reading other students' work as it gives them new ideas on how to explain their thoughts and receive feedback from their peers.

As an added bonus, in a time when schools are facing ever diminishing budgets and resources, flipped evaluations help to cut down on paper and ink usage. When I evaluate these essays, there is no additional rubric to print, I do not have to make copies of students' work as a class set for all to see simultaneously, I do not use actual ink, and the essays do not take up space other than my inbox.

Flipped Learning Opportunity (previously known as homework)

As a teacher of history, I, like so many other teachers, have struggled to get my students to read their text and go beyond it in search of a deeper understanding of the content and to make a personal connection to their learning. I wanted to find a way to achieve this goal, and flipping parts of my class gave me the desired effect. As I mentioned earlier, flipping has no exact guide or plan, and *that* is the beauty of flipping.

I decided that I was going to flip my U.S. History course three weeks into the new semester of a year-long course. We had been using a practice of me introducing a section or two of a chapter in class and having the students read that night, then complete a few names/terms questions and a short paragraph question or two, due the next day. I would start off the next day walking around the room checking off their work, and then we would have a class discussion of the previous night's homework. After discussion, the students took notes that I created off of the SMART Board.

I knew they were learning, and we had some quality discussions, but deep down I knew they could learn more! I was getting frustrated that my students completed the work but rarely did they actually read and have any depth to their answers. In a perfect world, the students would read all of the text material first, complete their work and then come to class ready to participate. This simply was not happening. I decided to make a change and flipping was the answer.

I began the process of flipping by first taking time to think over the changes I wanted to see. I wanted my students to read the book because history is content-heavy, so I started giving my students time to read in class. This may seem to be the opposite of flipping or returning to the way history was taught years ago, but the students were not reading at home so I needed to free up time for them to read in school. I still took time to introduce the chapter, but then I gave them a good amount of time each day to read. After reading, we took time to "huddle" and the students discussed what we read with anyone they chose. I found this helped the students to be ready to discuss in our large group discussions. The notes I used to put up in class came down and the students took their own notes based on whatever they thought was important. They were now in control of their own learning. I wanted my students to be more responsible for their learning, and I started to see it happening. Where the flipping really came into place was in fulfilling my earlier hope. My students now possessed a deeper understanding of the content. When we had discussions, my students truly understood the material and could explain and synthesize what they learned.

Another way I used Flipping to better instruction and increase student choice was when I flipped the idea of homework and turned it into a "learning opportunity." When we cover a chapter I always encouraged my students to go beyond the text and "dig deeper" to learn. Again, this simply never happened. I flipped the concept of homework assignments and told my students that they were to go learn about something from the chapter and present the learning to me using some form of technology. In the past, when we would study an event or time period, I would introduce the chapter, one section at a time and explain interesting details about the events. In the flipped classroom, the introduction to the chapter and subsections is quicker and instead of telling the students all of the information, I attempt to create information gaps where they want to learn more.

When I covered the 1920's in years past I would explain Babe Ruth's impact on baseball and sports nationwide, explain the roots behind the Prohibition movement and key figures as interesting as Al Capone, explain President Coolidge's foreign and domestic policies, and play some examples of Jazz music to expose students to the genre. When we studied the 1920's in the flipped classroom, students were still introduced to the key ideas, but I left information gaps and challenged the students to learn more about each topic. In that lesson students produced projects on Babe Ruth, Prohibition, President Coolidge and Jazz music, or whatever they were interested in learning more about at a deeper level.

The flipped class learning opportunity shifted the focus away from teacher-driven material to student-driven choices, all while maintaining the core focus of the class content. Students diverged from the main topics and covered topics about the flappers, organized crime, automobiles of the time period and more. The students were excited to learn more about each chapter because they were able to make choices in their area of interest in each chapter. Our discussions regarding our research and projects deepened the understanding for everyone, including me. I was learning new information from my students and our learning community was truly taking form.

In our flipped classroom the by-product of passing the locus of control to the students has been improved participation in small group discussions, improved participation in large group discussions (even previously shy students have begun to participate), improved depth to our discussions, improved quiz and test scores and best of all, an increased excitement about their learning and a desire to learn more. Students enjoy having time to work in class on their reading and then discussing their findings with their classmates and friends. Students have told me that they feel more comfortable discussing the material with others because they have time to read the material. The students feel more comfortable discussing the reading material with their classmates in small groups first, before discussing with the entire class. The main way that this material has changed instruction and learning is that in the past, students had homework that brought all of them to a predetermined ending, and now the students have the opportunity to choose their own ending.

My favorite part of this new learning opportunity is student reflection of what they learned. As part of the requirement for their learning opportunity, students must cite where they found their information and then have a reflection on their learning. In these reflections, students have explained how they learned something new, had a change of heart or a change in perception of a topic. Sometimes the reflections have explained how students are angry after they learn more about a sensitive topic from the past. I could read and feel their true, pure emotions, thoughts and ideas on a topic. Due to the fact that they chose the topic of their learning opportunity (within the chapter) and the format in which they presented their learning, the students felt they were in control. Very often, I will have students tell me how their research for their learning opportunity led them to new knowledge, but then they continued on searching for more and more information. This lead them to off-shoots of the topic and having the overall depth of understanding I had always been striving to help them achieve.

As we continue to pursue these learning opportunities, I continue to make slight adjustments to them. I believe a conceptual part of flipping your courses is to understand that your lessons are never truly "done." Lessons continue to take on new shapes and direction as provided by the technology and the students' choices in our classrooms. The most recent addition to our learning opportunities has been having the students publish their work by posting it to Edmodo. I had my students create technology projects for their learning opportunities for four chapters before we began posting to Edmodo. I wanted them to feel a sense of safety and have some practice with different forms and options for technology before they presented their projects to the world. One condition of posting their work to Edmodo was that all students must view and post a detailed comment to at least three projects made by other students. The students enjoy the sense of community as they are able to view and comment on the project of any student, regardless of the hour. In a traditional class, students would bring in a poster or project, stand in front of the class and present their work. If you have a class of any substantial size, this may take several days for all students to present. In a flipped class, the students post their work and others are able to view it on their own schedule and leave comments for all to see. In a traditional class, if you want to showcase student work, you have to tape it to the wall and then take it down at some point. In a flipped class, student work is always available for others to view and appreciate.

FLIPPED PROJECT INTRODUCTIONS

In prior years of teaching, I would introduce a project to my classes, typically one per quarter in the traditional format. I would stand in front of the class, pass out a rubric and then begin to explain the various parts of the project and how to complete the task. I would keep exemplars of prior projects, both good and those that needed corrections, to help students understand the project. Introducing the project in this manner would take nearly the entire hour, leaving little time for students to begin thinking, planning and working on the project.

Flipping the project introduction provided the perfect resolution. In my flipped project introduction, I use either the Educreations or Doceri on my iPad and set the rubric as the background. I narrate over the rubric, still covering all of the key points. I have taken pictures of past projects, again using my iPad and setting them as the background on additional slides for my flipped project introduction. The key difference is when the presentation takes place. In a flipped class, I have made the project video and loaded it to my Edmodo page prior to the project introduction date. My students view the project video on their own time, prior to the project day. I start off class asking a few, simple comprehension questions regarding the content of the video, and then I ask if they have any questions about the project.

Now a project introduction and explanation that typically took the entire hour is covered in ten minutes, and my students have time to actually work on the project in class on day one. As the students begin their work I am able to walk around the room and assist with students' individual needs and questions. One professional benefit of flipping my project introductions has been that I am not presenting the same information five times in a row on the same day; my day has become more interesting and fluid in my response to student needs. Another benefit is that the project introduction is curated for future years to my Edmodo page so that the process is even less work in year two. As for my students, they may watch the video multiple times making sure they understand each portion of the project. They can watch the video at a later date if they have forgotten some facet of the project. If students are sick, they can still watch the video from home and not feel as if they are left behind the rest of the class. In the flipped classroom, my students post questions about the project to our Edmodo group and either classmates or I answer them.

To me, the best part of flipping is the increased amount of class time that is dedicated to more complex work while the set-up is carried out prior to class. The classes across different hours feel connected to each other as they are able to post questions and receive answers from anyone, often times helping them to make new friends. There has become a real sense of community as a result of a virtual classroom where we are able to share and exchange ideas, opinions, questions, and answers.

FLIPPING IN THE FUTURE

I am excited when I think about other ways I can use flipping to enhance instruction, and to be honest, make my life easier. Over the years, I have toyed with the idea of making a video for parents to watch about how my classes operate. In the past, others would have thought the idea was crazy or lazy, or just plain stupid. Now with flipping becoming more common, I plan on making a video presentation to help parents become more informed and hopefully, even more involved in our classroom. I could make another video prior to conferences to expedite the process and again, free up more face-to-face time for deeper questions regarding their child and our class. I will continue to find new ways to flip my classroom. This process has helped to reinvigorate me as a professional and has provided great benefits to my students.

THE IMPACT OF FLIPPING

Flipping my classroom has led to a change for both my day to day instruction and my thought process for delivering content. Flipping does not have to be an intimidating and overwhelming, all-or-nothing process, but rather a process of making flipping work to your advantage as you see fit, as a professional. If you are hesitant about flipping, start with some project, topic, chapter or section that is either your favorite or least favorite and find a way to make it better for you by flipping some aspect. The impact of flipping on my students has been very positive. Students have told me they enjoy the freedom to work at their own pace, choose their own topics of interest, communicate with other students across different class periods and receive help any time they have questions.

As for me, I have enjoyed more one-on-one or small group discussions with my students as I now am up in front of the class less and in the trenches more. Flipping my classroom has had an unexpected impact in that flipping my classroom has led to me finding ways to flip other aspects of my life. As a basketball coach since 1999, I have found new ways to flip coaching from creating virtual playbooks and instructional videos, to creating an Edmodo page for my players and other coaches to watch videos and learn our plays as well as ask questions of me or others. In my personal life, I have used concepts created in the classroom due to flipping, and incorporated them into ways that I communicate with my family members. The impact of starting or increasing the amount you flip your classroom can have a large impact on your everyday life. The only limits are the ones you create.

Kenny Bosch *has been an educator for 15 years and has taught World History, U.S. History and A.P. U.S. History. Over the past two years he has been an educational technology consultant and has presented at local seminars and workshops. Kenny was named 2013 "Outstanding Educator" by Lawrence University for his ability to connect with and inspire students. He can be found on Twitter @kennybosch and at kennybosch.blogspot.com.*

Elementary Flipping
Todd Nesloney

I guess the best way to start is to explain WHY I chose to flip my classroom. I am a teacher in Texas, where Standardized Testing has a huge importance in education. Often it almost feels as if your job depends on how your students score. So like most teachers, I was teaching a test. After about five years of doing that I began to resent my job. I didn't like what I was doing, it wasn't fun, and I felt like I could be teaching my students so much better. I also began to feel like I wasn't really meeting the needs of my students. Sure my students were still scoring well on a test, but I wasn't teaching them skills that could carry on from year to year; I was just preparing them for a grade-level test. I also couldn't find the time to teach creatively or passionately.

WHEN EVERYTHING CHANGED

Then one day I heard about a webinar (from my co-worker Stacey Huffine) about the Flipped Classroom that Crystal Kirch and Sophia.org were doing. I signed up, and after watching for over an hour I fell in love with this different concept of how I could be teaching my fifth graders! I went to Sophia, took their free online Flipped Class Certification program that they have with Capella University, and began planning how I was going to make this work!

I knew it would be difficult because I work in a very rural and low socioeconomic status school. We have 66% of our students on a free-and-reduced lunch program, and I have almost 50% of my students that either don't have internet at home or only have dial-up (which I didn't even know still existed!) So I knew that convincing those around me to allow me to do the Flipped Classroom model would be an uphill battle.

At the end of the school year, after getting Flip Class Certified, I went to my principal with my idea. We sat down and went through all the pros and cons and how I could make things work for every student.

We discussed students who wouldn't have internet, parents who might not be fully on board, if we were prepared as a school for this, and more. After discussing the issues and figuring out some sort of solution to every problem, my principal was totally on board. That is one huge difference maker for sure when your administration supports some crazy new idea; and my principal, Claudia Mordecai, always does! After speaking with my principal I also went to my District Technologist (Rosa Ojeda) and my Assistant Superintendent (Kevin Moran) to explain to them what I was doing. Since I was going to be the first person in my district transforming my classroom I wanted to make sure I was keeping everyone in the loop.

MEET THE PARENTS

After getting everyone on board, I spent the summer reading about Flipped Classroom through different articles and talking to as many educators as I could, on Twitter, who were already flipping their classes. When August came around, I felt like I was ready for Meet-the-Teacher night. I borrowed Crystal Kirch's (@CrystalKirch) Parent Information Packets (you can find more info at flippingwithkirch.blogspot.com) and changed some of the wording to fit my school and my students and school environment. I was ready to go and I spent quite a bit of time explaining to parents how different things were going to be. Many seemed excited but I could tell there was still quite a bit of nervousness. For many parents, this was the first time their child was going to truly begin using technology in and out of the classroom for education purposes. Sure the kids had used computers before, but sadly that was about it and parents were nervous about that. What I came to found out later though was that parents were actually much more concerned with themselves not knowing how to use or understand the technology, rather than being nervous about their child using the technology. The only other major concern that was expressed from parents was the confusion over what exactly my job was going to be during class, if the majority of the instruction was going to be done via video at home. I discuss later in this chapter how exactly I relieved those concerns, but to share quickly now, I just completely opened up every aspect of my room to parents and guests.

I do have to admit that many of the tools I used and letters I sent home at the beginning of the year were not of my own creation. So, borrowing from other experienced flip class teachers is definitely a huge part in making the transition a little easier on yourself. In addition to the authors of this book, a few other amazing Flipped Classroom teachers are John Fritzky (@JohnFritzky), Delia Bush (@DeliaBush) and Jonathan Bergmann (@jonbergmann).

FILLING THE TOOLBOX

Once school began I had to do a lot of "training" with my students before we actually started flipping. The entire first week of school was just spent doing team building activities and learning the many technology tools that we were going to be using that year. I wanted to make sure I built a firm foundation in my students with the technology and emotionally. I didn't want their "uncomfortableness" with the technology to hinder what I had planned with the Flipped Classroom. I also wanted to make sure that I was building relationships with my students. The flipped classroom idea is awesome, and I am so glad I did it, but building those relationships with students from day one really does make all the difference. My students quickly learned that I care about them, I fight for them, and that no matter I'm here for them and am looking out for their best interest. So besides doing different activities to build camaraderie we spent the first week setting up accounts and learning how to use the many different tools that were going to help make our flipped classroom a success.

- **Edmodo**: This was the "central hub" of our class. On Edmodo I put all links to everything and everywhere. The students knew that to communicate with me this was the place to go. Because Edmodo looks so similar to Facebook many students (especially elementary-aged students) LOVE using Edmodo. It really has become our online classroom environment.
- **YouTube:** Students know what YouTube is but they don't always understand how to correctly navigate YouTube. So I spent a little bit of time telling them exactly how to find my videos, even though YouTube is still blocked within our district. Students are using YouTube at home, so why shouldn't I teach them how to navigate what could become a very dangerous terrain!
- **Sophia**: Sophia was our main hub for the flipped classroom. This is where I uploaded videos, put their forms, and more. As the year progressed Sophia updated their site more and more and now they not only offer quizzes to go along with videos but also

analytics. This will become more of our classroom hub in years to come.

- **Remind101**: I had to explain exactly what Remind101 was and how important and easy it was for their parents to sign up so I could communicate with them effortlessly. This was by far the parents' favorite tool because almost every parent in my classroom carries around a cell phone with them!
- **Google Accounts**: This took the most training but was by far the most beneficial. Much of what we do in my class is presentations and having Google accounts really allows seamless sharing and collaborating for students. They now essentially have virtual portfolios of all their work from this school year that they can access on any computer with an internet connection. But this was all so foreign to the students that this by far took the most time to train the students on.
- **iTunesU App**: this was a great resource for us to use in class because students could use the Wi-Fi at school to download videos onto their iOS devices to later watch at home with no internet access required!

The second week of school we jumped right into Flipping. I started the year using Screencast-O-Matic to create all of my videos. I used that program for several reasons. First, it was just quick and easy to pull up and start recording. And secondly, after I was done recording it allowed me to directly upload to YouTube! Currently, I like to use TechSmith's Camtasia and SnagIt. These tools have some amazing editing features and allow you to create some pretty awesome videos. Now for those of you reading that may not be aware of how screencasting works or what exactly it is, let me explain. I start one of the programs I mentioned before and it immediately starts recording my screen. Therefore anything that appears on my computer screen is being recorded. My face is never shown (unless I turn my camera on) but my voice is heard the whole time.

Since this was my first year flipping my classroom, I didn't have any videos made coming into this school year. I would make about 2-3 videos at a time up on my SMART Board. I would show up to school a little early, turn on Screencast-O-Matic or Camtasia and record my lessons standing up at the SMART Board as if I were teaching my class at that moment. I know some teachers can record lessons on their laptops or from home, but I just couldn't do that. It wasn't my style. I also never use lessons recorded by other educators. My reasoning behind that is that I want my students to hear the way I teach it, so when I do things or say things in class there will already be some familiarity. I tend to be a very charismatic teacher, so with the whole shift in learning, it really made my students much more comfortable knowing they were still going to be learning from my voice even though it was through a video and that they weren't going to have some 'stranger' talking to them at home and then me leading them in class. So yes, your first year flipping your classroom is a lot of front-loading, but in the end it's totally worth it!

THE FUN BEGINS!

So the second week of school I assigned my first video for homework! Since not all of my students have internet at home, here was my plan of action for getting them to watch videos:

1. If they have internet at home, they watch the video on YouTube, Sophia, Edmodo, or the iTunesU app.
2. If they have a computer but no internet, they bring a flash drive and I'll put the videos on there.
3. If they don't have a computer but have something that can play a DVD, I would burn the videos to a rewritable DVD for them.
4. If they don't have a DVD player they had several options:
    a. show up to school early
    b. stay after school
    c. come watch during recess/lunch
    d. check out an iPod Nano from the library and watch the video on there.

When I assigned a video I didn't just require them to watch the video. I also required them to fill out a WSQ (another Crystal Kirch creation) in their math notebook. What is a WSQ? The "W" stands for "Watch". When and where did you watch the video? The "S" stands for "Summary". Write a summary of the video. And the "Q" stands for "Question". What is one question you have from the video? And if you don't have a question, think of a question someone else might have or create a question you could see on a test.

When the students would come to class the next day I would split them into groups of three or four to discuss their WSQs during the first ten minutes of class. This had a dual purpose. Because we were discussing the WSQs for the first ten minutes and because the videos were never longer than ten minutes, if a student showed up to class unprepared they had to go sit at a desktop computer in the back of the room and watch their video while the rest of us discussed our WSQs (If you don't have a computer in your room, bring your laptop from home or check out a few laptops from your computer lab; if you are committed to flipping, you'll figure out a way to make it work!) The students did not have to watch a video every day, but when I did assign a video to watch at home, they had to watch it that evening and be prepared the next day to discuss in class. Often we would plan about two weeks in advance on their calendars of certain dates they had to have particular videos watched (that way they could watch some early, if they so chose).

Then Came Project-Based Learning

When I first started flipping my classroom, I had planned on doing it the very traditional way. What is that? That is where the students watch the videos at home and come to class to do the work they normally would have done for homework (worksheets, packets, etc.). After doing that for a week, I realized that I still wasn't having fun and the students were still learning the same way as before! What I mean is that, the entire reason for me deciding to "flip" was that I wanted to teach my students in a much more meaningful way: a way that didn't require me to shove worksheets down their throats or continually teach test strategies. But what I found was that, even though I was doing a flipped model, and the students were gaining knowledge from home, during class I was still teaching worksheet after worksheet after worksheet. What's the fun in that? To me, that just ruined the entire flipped classroom experience. School needs to be about inquiry, creativity, and fun, and that's why my class transformed from a traditional Flipped Classroom into a blended classroom which I call a Flipped PBL Class (PBL stands for Project-based Learning).

Since we moved to a PBL class my second week, I had a great idea for those students who were not watching their videos. The first video I assigned I had 27 of my 75 students not watch the video. As I stated above, I made them watch the video in the back of the room while the rest of us discussed our WSQs. Then, while the rest of the students were able to begin a project-based learning activity for that day, those students who did not watch the video had to stay at the back of the room and work on a packet of worksheets that I had given them dealing with the same concept we were covering through a project. (The students who had to work on worksheets at the back of the room were not left to their own devices. I still interacted with them and answered any questions they may have had, they just didn't get to join in on the projects for that day.)

To say this worked is an understatement. The first video, 27 students didn't watch. After employing this consequence, the second video had three students who didn't watch. It worked wonders. The students were so hungry for a new way of learning, and project-based learning really fed that hunger. And when they had to miss doing a project because they didn't watch their Flip Class video, they were very upset. I continued this throughout the year and I never had more than six or seven students who didn't watch a video, but was surprising to me is that it was never the same six or seven students. Again, I was not assigning videos every night. Many times it would be two or three videos a week, max. Sometimes it was only one video a week. It really depended on the concept being covered and how long our projects were taking. Either way my students were in no way bogged down by having to watch videos.

How did my project-based learning classroom look? Well, what I did was find many different project ideas. I would give my students a starting a point, some of the materials needed, and then a general idea of what I expected as a final product. I provided hardly any of the in-between steps. Now this was the most difficult part by far. My students had become so accustomed to having their hands held the entire time through any activity that breaking them out of that mold was unbelievably difficult. But I committed myself to the process and stuck with it even when it felt like I was banging my head against a wall and getting nowhere. Eventually though the students began to slowly break out of their pre-designed boxes. How? I built a classroom of trust and security. I let my students know that the one thing they should never be afraid of is failure. Sometimes the times we learn the most are the times that we fail, fall, and figure out how to get back up. I explain to them that I make mistakes all the time and it's how I deal with those mistakes that make me the person I am today.

But the other big part of my classroom is my "3 Question Rule". Every single project that we begin, I allow each project group to ask me a maximum of three questions throughout the process....and yes asking to go to the bathroom counts as a question! Putting this "rule" in place was very eye-opening in getting the students to rely more on their peers and figuring out things on their own instead of always running to the teacher to do every single step. I would say that implementing this "3 Question Rule" was a definite game changer in my quest to get my students to think and problem-solve.

Many of the questions I get from people about my classroom tend to stem from my project-based learning side as well. People always want to know where I get my ideas. I will say that Twitter is my go-to place for ideas. I tweet out for ideas all the time to my PLN (Personal Learning Network) and include different hashtags like #21stedchat, #edchat, #edtech, #flipclass, #pblchat, and more. There are so many amazing teachers online that I'm never above asking for help with ideas!

The other place I get a lot of my ideas from is Pinterest or EduClipper. I just scroll through the education page and see different things that stir ideas and creativity within me and take that idea and run with it. So, Pinterest is a definite great springboard from PBL ideas. We've done projects about making lemonade, math fair, student-lead EdCamp, creating board games, planning a party with a budget, building bridges, building roller coasters, and so much more (you can check out detailed information about all our projects through the year at my blog: nesloneyflipped.blogspot.com)

SWELLING WITH PRIDE

I will say though that my favorite project this year was the Math Fair. We've all heard of science fairs and I thought, "Why can't we do a math fair?" Students had a month and a half to work on this project (*all* at home). I wanted to do a project that my students would have a blast doing, and I thought, what better way to do that then bring in their passions? So that's exactly what I did. I allowed the students to pick any topic they wanted. Yes, *anything* they were passionate about. They had two weeks to "submit" their topic to me electronically via Google Docs (no two students could have the same topic). After having their topic approved, the students were allowed to begin creating. They had to create some sort of visual and a 2-3 minute presentation that explained at least six ways that math was involved in their passion. It took a while for my students to warm up to this project. They honestly couldn't believe that I was allowing them to choose absolutely anything they wanted to. But after they realized I was serious, the ideas just started rolling in. Students chose everything from barrel racing, zookeeper, karate, ballet, basketball, macaroni and cheese, Jack in the Box, Temple Run, Angry Birds, Sky Diving, and so much more! They were inspired and they had a blast because I didn't pigeon-hole them. I allowed them to show me what they loved and to find ways that their passion incorporated my subject area.

At the end of the month and a half time period, the students practiced their presentations in front of their peers. I did that because I realized students don't know how to present in front of others. So they each presented in front of their classmates and we all provide some constructive criticism for each student. Then on a Thursday evening from 6:00-7:30, they presented their projects for the public. This Math Fair was mandatory for my students. This was actually the first after-school thing that my school had ever done that was mandatory. And to say I was scared to make it mandatory is an understatement. I was sure I would get tons of parents calling me explaining one reason or another that their child couldn't attend.

But when the Math Fair arrived, I had 73 of my 75 students attend, and better yet we had over 250 adults attend!! Oh and by the way, not ONE parent called to complain about having to be there. The number of adults in attendance was beyond believable. As I've said before we are a very rural school and to get parents to return to the school after hours is extremely difficult. But this event meant so much to these students, because they were so proud of their work, that every child *wanted* to be there, and the parents wanted to see what all the hullabaloo was about! In all actuality, we have never had that many parents attend anything during after school hours. But then we all got to experience my students' presentations. And wow, they blew me out of the water. I was in tears most of the evening in awe of their presentations and passion behind what they did. I can honestly say that was one of the major highlights of my educational career. I was able to see the growth that the Flipped Classroom and PBL built in my students, and I got to see them bloom to their potential. I have never been more proud of any student then I was that night. I will never forget the overwhelming emotion that I was feeling and that was clear on every adult's face in attendance that night. Had I not decided to Flip my classroom and go completely project-based, my students would have never developed the deeper thinking skills and creativity necessary to pull this off! To this day I still have students and parents talking about how much fun the math fair was.

THERE ARE CHALLENGES

The most difficult aspect of PBL though is grading. It is very difficult for me to get grades from projects because I do not accept a project until it is done correctly. That means that some students have to complete a project four or five times before they do it right. I don't feel it's fair to give them a grade based on their first submission. I'm much more concerned about mastery of a concept rather than just a letter grade. So I make sure to give vocabulary quizzes, fast fact quizzes, and random 3-5 question quizzes so I can get grades to keep my administration happy. I've debated over and over again whether or not I want to include in-depth rubrics, and I think the final decision I've come to as of now is I still *don't* want to do that. Why would I not include detailed rubrics? My whole reasoning for doing PBL was to inspire creativity and innovation, and sometimes I feel like rubrics still keep them in a box. I will continue to use some form of criteria to keep them on track, but I don't think I'm ever going to provide a detailed rubric for my students. That's why I am there in class. By closely observing and participating in my student's learning I can steer them to the right path without explaining every step along the way.

IT WORKS!

Finally, by using a Flipped PBL model, I made the conscious decision NOT teach any test-formatted questions from October to April (when our state exam is). I did not teach even ONE test-formatted question that entire time period.

I'm often asked is there any research or anything that proves what you're doing works? My answer to that is that my students are my proof. State Testing is very important in Texas and especially in my district, which is a recognized school district. We've always had decent to great scores on our state assessment. As I stated above, I set out to prove this year that you could have students be successful on a state exam without ever needing to even mention or "teach a test". I hated test-formatted questions and I wanted to prove I could prepare my students through actual hands on learning. My district did get a little "nervous" and asked me to teach test-formatted questions the week before my exam, but other than that our class was completely Flipped PBL with no test formatted questions.

I'm so proud to say that this year I had 96% of my students pass their state math exam. That is higher than I have ever achieved with my students. Not only that but my students also scored a minimum of 9% higher than the other five elementary schools in my district and 21% higher than the state average! So to me that is the proof that the Flipped PBL Model works! My students are deeper thinkers, they have amazing conversations about what we're learning, and they're having fun. What more could I ask for as a teacher?

CLOSING OUT THE SCHOOL YEAR

The final thing I did this year that was beneficial for me, was giving my students a detailed survey to fill out about their experiences this year. The overwhelming response was that if they could go back in time and start this year over again they *would* continue with Flipped Class and Project-based Learning. In fact, many expressed their concern about moving on to the next grade level and having teachers who don't teach like that. The students also appreciated the use of technology. They said it "brought the learning to them" and "let them use what they like in class" and "made learning fun". But I think the most powerful responses came from the question I asked them about using five words to describe their experience with the Flipped Class and PBL this year. A few of the words used were: *awesome, wonderful, always changing, exciting, interesting, different, creative, entertaining, extraordinary, technology, cool, active, social, educational, fantastic,* and *challenging.* I think that speaks volumes. (You can check out the survey responses by looking here: bit.ly/flipping57)

I also chose nine students to interview about their year. I purposely chose students who were from all walks-of-life and ability levels. Their answers were very eye-opening for me and encouraging at the same time. You can check out their interview at bit.ly/flipping58.

Flipping the classroom is not easy. Project-based learning is not easy. But as we've all heard before: nothing easy was ever worth fighting for. I am beyond proud of my students and their growth and attribute that mainly to the transformation that happened because I chose to move to a Flipped PBL model classroom. So what are you waiting for? Get your feet wet or just jump right in, but don't ever be afraid to try something new and see where it takes you and your students!

Todd Nesloney is a 5th grade teacher at Fields Store Elementary in Waller, TX. He was selected as one of the National School Board Association's "20 to Watch" for 2013. He is also a SMART Exemplary Educator, Discovery STAR Educator, Part of the Remind101 Teacher Advisory Board, a Flipped Classroom Certification Instructor for Sophia.org and a co-founder of the The3TechNinjas.org. In addition to being a part of this Flipped Classroom book, Todd has also written and released his first Children's Book called "Spruce & Lucy".

Middle School Flipping
Nichole Carter

Why did I Flip?

About March or April of 2012 my administrator came to meet with each individual department to talk about big changes for the following year. What was that big change? Going to a full STEM model, across all curriculums, throughout the building. At first I was overwhelmed; teach science in an English class, how will that work? I was fairly quiet during this meeting, which is unusual for me. I think at the time I just didn't quite know how to wrap my head around it, and scary terms were being tossed about—things like, "You might have to lose a novel to integrate it all." Lose a novel? The only place they read literature at all is in the English class. No, that just wouldn't do. I had to find a way to keep my curriculum while adding these other components to satisfy my admin's request for full STEM implementation. Now, I am not averse to social media outlets for teachers, in fact I love them, and I did remember seeing the concept of "flipping" bandied about by people here and there. But it wasn't until I was faced with what seemed like an impossible situation that I realized: flipping could work.

Through "flipping" I have been able to maintain all of my traditional units, at the same pacing as previous years, as well as adding in STEM related content and lots of collaborative in-class work. I feel as if I am closer than ever to a truly differentiated classroom that allows for collaboration and students to move and excel at their own pace. I feel like flipping is the major reason that I can attain that. While I am making sure to provide articles and research opportunities that touch on the same concepts my students are learning in their science classrooms, I feel like flipping allows for so much more in the STEM construct. I clearly have the "T" in STEM covered both in and out of the classroom, and while I can't say that it is super easy to add engineering into the English classroom, I do believe allowing the students to create and work in groups on end-of-the-unit PBL opportunities also covers more bases with STEM. Without removing

245

those lecture pieces from the basic construct of a teacher-centered classroom structure, I never would be able to manage *all* these things.

> *"It (Flipped Classroom Model) is helpful in the sense that we get to learn the material in the comfort of our home, plus, if we have any questions we can ask at the end of the video diaries, or ask you the next day in class. Another advantage is we have more time to practice the skill in class, instead of going through a boring lesson."*
> —*8th Grade Student Answer to "What is the most helpful part of the "flipped classroom" in your own words?" Student Feedback Survey (February 2013)*

HOW HAVE I FLIPPED?

During the summer I did a lot of research on the topic, and from what I could gather, there were not a lot of individuals in English, or more importantly middle school English. So I started shopping around for anyone or someone that could be a wealth of information and more importantly didn't mind—in fact, encouraged—people using what they had developed thus far. Of course, I am talking about the incomparable Crystal Kirch. It didn't matter that she taught math, and it didn't matter that she taught high school; instead, what mattered was that the concepts were sound. They could work for any class. I went ahead and used her concept of the WSQ (pronounced wisk) which stands for "watch and take notes, summarize, and question". Otherwise, there wasn't a lot of guidance or pre-made videos for my particular units or mastery tests, so I needed to create the videos on my own. I found this to be easier in the long run because the videos were tailored made to exactly what I wanted covered.

I started making videos by using Prezi for the first month and recording my voice over the top of the Prezi via Screencast-O-Matic. This process is called screen capture or screen-casting, the act of recording your computer screen. This can also include audio, and even the use of a video of your face to go along with the audio. I have asked my students if they are fine with my disembodied voice, and so far they seem to like the end product just fine. At the beginning I was using the free service for Prezi and Screencast-O-Matic, and then I decided to upgrade Screencast-O-Matic for a yearly price of $19.00. I am not entirely sure the upgrade was necessary as I think I could have gotten by with just the basic free service. Some people have also talked about using Jing, and Camtasia. I have not tried the others as I have been happy with using Screencast-O-Matic, and I don't see a need to change at the current moment.

By using Screencast-O-Matic, I was able easily to upload straight to my YouTube channel—again, free!—as well as save an AVI file straight to my computer. The AVI file was important because I did have three students that did not have access at all, due to living in a rural area where cable internet isn't accessible (or in the case of one student their internet wasn't fast enough to support streaming the video.) For those three students, they would bring me a thumb drive, and I would load the videos on the thumb drive for the week and they were all set. So I was able to solve the problem for those students of non-access by a fairly easy fix. I would have a few students come in after school to use the iPads in my room, some would use our after school program to access the internet, and some even went to the public library. They had the will to watch the videos, and they found a way!

The WSQ

The WSQ concept was introduced to the students at the beginning of the school year. In class, we walked through all three concepts, and for the first three weeks I used guided note packets for each week due on Friday. This process, as with all teaching, is evolving as I go. I went over my expectations for summary, and it also helped that our first unit was explanatory writing with an emphasis in summary of nonfiction. So they repeatedly worked on what a summary is and should look like. I would check in class the day after homework was assigned to see who finished it; this allowed me to have one-on-one conversations at the beginning on who was having issues accessing the content. Simple questions like, "Why didn't you do your homework?" or, "When can you get it done? Can you stay after school?" can work wonders on middle school student motivation. Allowing for those students that have problems accessing the internet at home for whatever reason a way to access is vital for this system to work. I will talk about strategies for this later, but you cannot discount the power of simple face-to-face communication and relaying the importance of watching the homework and following through. I think one of the biggest benefits of flipping is switching a lot of the onus onto the students, empowering them to be in charge of and responsible for their own learning; for middle-schoolers this does take a bit of training.

My district put out a curriculum framework that they wanted us to follow and, lo and behold, three of the top things on this list were notes, summary, and higher-order thinking skills. Well, obviously the students are being asked to take notes as they watch the video. From the beginning, I have used a clipart picture of a pencil to indicate when I want them to take notes. So, any time they see that pencil they know they need to pause the video, if needed, and write down what is on the screen. This has worked phenomenally well. In fact, I had a student teacher for the month of December and for the first few videos that she attempted, she did not use the pencil and the students were a little beside themselves, they really liked that simple indicator. After the first couple of weeks, I started to notice their skills and attention on the summaries were slipping. So I did have to go back and do some re-teaching on summary, and what my nightly expectations were for that until that skill was mastered. Really their entire homework, including the question, is a great formative assessment.

I have also stressed the importance of asking the question at the end of the night's homework, and not just any question but a "HOT" question (higher-order thinking). They were given question starters, and I had an anchor poster hanging in my room for a long time to remind them about using higher-order thinking skills. They must ask a question even if they are not confused or have an actual question: they can ask a question that they already know the answer to. Either way, it still is forcing them to analyze the information from that night's video which is really the reason we have them do it anyway. At the beginning of the year I tried to have class discussions on their questions and it was difficult to facilitate that, while at the same time trying to check their homework. They have recently asked, or given feedback, that this discussion time would be helpful for them. Towards the middle of the year, they obviously feel comfortable enough with each other and this process that the discussions go very well and are in fact helpful. This can be done in a number of ways; one of their favorites is picking the best question from their table group and writing it on a whiteboard for me to read and answer to the class as a whole. The whiteboards I use are locker whiteboards that can be bought at the dollar store, with an attached marker and eraser. For a mere ten dollars I was set. Obviously these can be used for many other activities, but they work amazingly for this activity. Another option would be to have the students work in their table group to write a group summary of the previous night's question. They could write that out and turn it in, they could write it on the whiteboard and read it to the class, or they could even post it to a social networking platform like Edmodo. Regardless, giving them 5-10 minutes in class to reflect has given me more information on what they are still struggling with on the concepts.

PROGRESS AND CHANGE

I think one of the biggest skills as an educator is the ability to reflect, not just the monitoring or adjusting as the day goes on, but the true skill of trying as objectively as possible to look at your work and figure out how to make it better. From the very beginning as a teacher, I have been working on this. I first started out with a regular journal and an alert on my desktop calendar to write in the journal at the end of every day. It has obviously evolved since then, and I would say a large part of that was due to the big push about five years ago to data-driven instruction and planning. As the pendulum swung in this direction, however, I found that data-driven instruction and reflection was unavoidable, and quite frankly now I can't imagine teaching without it. The reason I bring all this up is because the way I started flipping with my middle school classroom at the beginning of the year was vastly different from what it looked like at semester change. I was evolving, due to student feedback, my own concerns, and more education at the hands of any free webinar I could get my hands on!

I began to realize that while Prezi looked great, it was a lot more time consuming for me to construct, as well as there seemed to be some limitations for access for the students both in the building and at home. I started to fall back on what I was more familiar with, PowerPoint. I would suggest that if you decided to go the route of making your own material, use what you are comfortable with, and what you can use to create something quickly. Because let's face it, if this is too difficult and time consuming, the odds of you being able to stick to it drop considerably.

I also noticed that while the packets for the week were fantastic, especially at the beginning while teaching the concepts of the WSQ, I found it incredibly difficult to create them in addition to make the videos for the week. I also found it hard to grade them, and get them back to the students in a timely manner so that they could use those notes on their tests and work in class. The last part I found, as the year progressed, was incredibly important. We are a proficiency- or mastery-based school, and as such most of the time we are working towards that big summative assessment at the end of the unit. Those notes came in handy, and the kids wanted to use them! Far be it for me to keep those from them, simply because I couldn't get them graded quickly enough.

It also became apparent quickly that the social networking platform that I was using to get the videos and information to the students was severely lacking in its transparency for the parents. I also noticed that I didn't have the kind of organizational options that I would like to have. Something had to be done to address all of these problems. I think if I am not being consistently hard on myself, and thinking *how can I make this better?*, than it would have been easy to stick with what I was doing. However, it was difficult on me to keep up. I wanted to be as easy and clear for the students and the parents as possible.

Technology

Obviously I feel like engaging the students with technology both inside the classroom and outside the classroom, but using the technology judiciously and with the caveat that it was a tool not the end-all-be-all, has worked incredibly well. Outside of class we are using social networking sites to keep connected and informed, in addition to accessing our flipped videos. After the semester change, I started using Google Forms to aid in the collection of the students homework, and to ease my burden on grading. I have also used Google Sites to create a website to house and organize all the units and videos. I believe once our school goes through our digital conversion and officially goes 1:1 that this will be incredibly helpful. By offering a "viewing party" after school I am attempting to level the playing field for those that don't always have access at home. Most students are engaged with the technology and just eat it up. I do have a few per class period, however, that don't like using technology all the time so it is good to have a balance.

Why is Flipping Practical at Mid-Level?
STEM/PBL

Flipping has allowed more time for me to create more authentic project-based learning summative assessments at the end of our units. As I have stated before, my school has switched to full STEM implementation, and we are pushing for next generation assessments in the next two years. Flipping has allowed me to find time to go from a one-week summative assessment, like an essay, to a full real-world problem, three-week PBL, as was the case in my first writing unit, explanatory writing. In previous years I would use a state-provided writing prompt and allow the kids a week to write to this arbitrary concept, they would go through the whole writing process and in the end turn in an essay that was altogether fairly uninspiring for both student and teacher. This year we created a PBL around the concept of *what do you want to do when you graduate from high school and what do you need to get there?* The students had to do interest surveys, from there look at careers that fit those interests, then start looking at high school classes to support their goals, and colleges that provide majors in those areas. Many of these concepts were brand new for my students! You mean I don't get to go the school just because I like their sports program? It was a revelation. I was able to get in contact with our own school counselor as well as the high school counseling program, they were majorly on board and helpful. The students had to look at a real high school transcript, and start looking at graduation requirements. In a previous teaching model in order to do this three-week long project, I would have had to give up something else, like a novel. Instead I am staying on track with previous years, and I fully expect that in the years to come I will have to create *more* content to keep up with my students that are moving at a faster pace. At this point though, it is important that I stay on track, as the other members of my department are not flipping and we are supposed to be as aligned as possible, giving our assessments at roughly the same time.

Collaboration

I have also noticed that I have more time in class to have the kids work on collaborative group projects, and activities that I normally wouldn't have been able to find the time for. I almost feel like it is my duty as a flipped instructor to find this time. It isn't a case where I can take advantage of the time for grading and allow the students "free" time in class. With fifty minute class periods, my class time is precious and valuable and I have to find ways to keep them going and engaged.

Note-taking Skills

Also at the middle school level students are still learning what it means to be a student that travels from class to class, what it means to take notes, and what it means to self-advocate and communicate with the teacher. They are still learning to be students and haven't been tracked into leveled classes or AP courses, etc. The ability to pause the video and actively learn how to take notes, while being in charge of the pause button and allowed to go at their own pace, is still a super valuable skill. Over the course of the school year they will get better at being a successful student. They will move through the homework more quickly, and they will actually begin to realize how to write shorthand notes that focus on the key details. Prior to this method, I didn't lecture in class that much, but when I did I noticed that I would have to pause in my lecture to wait for students to catch up. They truly were developmentally not at the point yet, or hadn't had enough practice, where they could breeze through a lecture taking down notes as one might expect from a high school or college student. And why should we have that expectation at this age? The simple ability to learn at their own pace, have the ability to re-watch, and start to take real ownership of their education is vital for this age group.

Depth of Content

Flipping allows you to go more in-depth on topics that you didn't have time for before. For my grade-level and content area, we are beginning to go over some really abstract concepts. Things are no longer just black and white; we have now introduced shades of gray. The ability to chunk the information into more manageable parts by each video allows you to give more information to the students. I try to keep the videos to 2-3 per week, sometimes there isn't enough content to do three, but I usually can find enough for two videos. So for example as we start a novel in class I now have time to go over author's background, key points and specific things to look for as we read. These things are talked about in class but in more detail through the video homework. I also have time to review what we read or will be reading for that week, and focus on different literary devices as seen and applied to examples from the text. Then the next day as a class, we can have a great in-depth discussion about those concepts for about ten minutes or so before diving back into the book and doing other projects.

If there isn't enough regular core work that needs to be done, I have found that videos working on grammar or other issues I am noticing in their summative assessments that need to be addressed can be done when there is "extra" time. For example, my students turned in a literature test that consistently showed students not capitalizing proper nouns, so a video on capitalization rules or more specifically on identifying proper nouns and their significance was created. By keeping to the two to three videos a week though it keeps the students in the homework routine and you see a much more consistent turn in rate.

HOW TO FLIP MIDDLE-LEVEL ENGLISH

As I stated previously, prior to using the flipped model I didn't actually lecture that much, so I found that I was adapting different activities and pieces that I used to use in the classroom for the videos. For the most part our class alternates from writing to literature. We have a small unit on persuasive speaking in the middle of the year, but for the most part we move from writing to reading and back again.

Writing

We begin the year, as most do I imagine, with explanatory, move to persuasive, and spend smaller chunks of time on narrative writing. As we move through the different genres, I usually do a video that discusses the nuances, how to write the different parts, and expectations based on the genre. I try to build on the topics so as not to completely become repetitive. For instance in the explanatory introduction video we went over some more basic concepts for thesis statements since it was the beginning of the year. Then for the persuasive introduction video, the thesis sentence examples were more complex in structure and internal punctuation, as well as more suited to the persuasive genre. So you can work in some basic yearly scaffolding.

Literature

At the beginning of the year we focused heavily on ways to be active readers, to focus on some close reading strategies: how to summarize, highlight and annotate a text. Then depending on the unit, and the common core standards we were addressing, the videos would be highlighting those reading and literature components. So for the historical fiction unit, we would learn about that genre and historical context, and then dive into CCSS 8.RL.1 learning inference, textual support, theme and author's purpose. Each video concept would move them through the understanding of those concepts, and the expectations for the final summative assessment. We would read and discuss the literature selections in class, as well as take the assessments. I saw a greater focus in my direct instruction through the videos as well as in the answers on their summative assessment. Going back to what I discussed earlier about how I was able to go deeper into the content than before, and in the end be clearer.

Mastery/Proficiency Model

Standards design and the common core are perfect for the flipped model, but that isn't to say that the flipped model works for everyone. By flipping I have found that I am able to gather data quickly, not just on the in-class summative assessments but each digital homework submission now becomes a way to gather formative assessment data. What are they getting, and not getting? I can clearly see through their summaries, their HOT questions, and their small quizzes on each concept what is getting through to them. I am able to track the analytical data on who is watching what video, and for how long. I am able to view this data as my students sign on to Sophia.org. I am able to see how many views my videos have, while not necessarily showing me which students are accessing the videos multiple times, I can at least tell that if I have over 200 views on a video, it is a concept that my students went back to review. All of this guides my instruction as we move forward. At this point it still is a class that largely moves from one unit of study to another together. I haven't switched to a fully student-centered and self-paced classroom. So the data collection does help me to know if I can move on.

PRACTICAL CONSIDERATIONS

Keep videos short!

I think for younger students, you have to remember to keep the video short. Very rarely to I have a video that goes 15 minutes. I honestly try to keep them around 10 minutes in length. You have to remember there will be a lot of pausing, and if you include some application of knowledge or activities with your video even a 10 minute video could in reality take 20-30 minutes to complete.

Lots of practice on protocol and re-teaching of your expectations.

At the beginning of the year, the guided note packets work great at getting the students to understand the concepts you think are important: key ideas and what to focus on. As well as showing them the components you are looking for. If you are a Cornell style note-taker and you want your students to do that, too, then start with some packets that reinforce those ideas.

Likewise prior to ever assigning a video, go over—via a projector in your room—how to access the links. Walk the students through a video, doing it together in class. Show them the importance of the pause button. Perhaps even let a student come up and demonstrate instead of you. I am lucky enough to have a SMART Board in my room, so it is very convenient and easy to have a student come up, stand next to the board, and pause when the student feels like it is a good time for them to pause and take down more notes.

Middle school students learn your expectations the best through repetition, practice and a lot of modeling. Especially if some of that modeling is done via peer examples. I can safely say that now, mid-year, students are writing fairly consistent, in-depth summaries, and thought-provoking questions. They have really started to be more critical about what they write down in the form of notes as well instead of believing they have to write every...single...word on the page!

It's ok to have high expectations, just be consistent-stay consistent.

I have 2-3 videos a week; it is a routine. When my student teacher broke from this routine and had either no video or only one video, my turn-in rate started to slip. My school operates on a mastery grading system where 90% of their grade is based on their summative assessments and only 10% for everything else (including their homework), so I am already fighting an uphill battle on many levels for homework completion and turn in. It seems like the students do homework when influenced by their peers, their parents, and lastly by their teacher. So, to create an environment where the students want to do the homework and by simply doing it, can influence the peers around them to complete it as well, is highly recommended.

Have some interventions in place.

One fairly successful intervention I have used is one day a week to have a "viewing party" where I am available after school, and the students can use the classroom computers or iPads to view videos. Sometimes I offer a snack, sometimes I don't. I can see anywhere from 15-20 students coming in on a regular basis for varying lengths of time to catch up on their work. In a district where there might not be as much digital access as one would hope, having times available for them to access the content from school as an option is huge.

I do have iPads in the classroom, so when the content is really important to a discussion we need to have in class, or needed prior to taking a summative assessment, I will have a different activity planned for those that finished their homework while the other students watch the video or go through the slides. Those that did that night's homework might watch a short video clip, and we will have a discussion or a timed write or any other varying type of activity that pertains to the current topic.

(I would think that as this process changes next year, and I have kids moving farther and farther ahead of other students, that the old idea of trying to keep them all moving at the same pace and on the same homework will have to change. This concept will be thrown out in place of something else, but for now this has worked well.)

I will also walk around the class as they are doing a daily vocab activity and check their notes, and if the video had any practice/application pieces, I will look to see that they did it, and then we will have an activity to discuss those answers. Staying on top of the notes and holding them accountable for doing them in a timely manner has also helped with turn in. It is during this time that I can have a simple conversation with the student that is falling behind and ask when they will be completing it, why they haven't yet, etc. It seems that just that simple interaction is enough to stick in the minds of most students and remind them to get on it.

Occasionally I will hand out a little "ticket stub" print-out with the missing work. Usually there are about 4-8 concepts per unit, so it is fairly easy to pick out those students that have missed three or more concepts and quickly give them a reminder slip.

Last resort would be to use our teleparent system that sends out automated calls. I have only done this once this year. Most of the time the above interventions are enough to have the majority of my students completing the homework, even if it only accounts for 10% of their grade.

Maintain contact and engagement via social network platforms.

Using platforms like Edmodo, Twitter or Remind101, and Instagram keeps the kids informed—on their level—as well as engaged in what is happening. My students do want badges (like digital stickers) on Edmodo. They might be teenagers, but they go crazy for this stuff! They have said repeatedly that a reminder later in the evening for homework is helpful, so I have set up a reminder on my phone for 5:30pm and regularly tweet out the link for the night's homework. I have started a private class Instagram, thanks to attending a webinar hosted by Todd Nesloney who happened to mention this very thing. It's great because the kids and parents get to see themselves learning and yet having fun. More importantly my class, and its content, is consistently in front of them, in their face, and impossible to ignore.

Set up a class schedule or management system ahead of time and train the students around those parameters.

This is especially important as the students start to pull away and move in their own directions and pacing. The classroom can get chaotic; this is hard for teachers—a total pedagogical shift, so having a semblance of routine will help with monitoring progress.

As my students walk in they have a quick vocab warm-up, which takes less than five minutes. We usually reserve the next 15 minutes or so for a Q&A discussion on the previous night's video homework. If there wasn't homework, we will do a mini-lesson activity based on the day of the week. Finally, we end the class with guided and/or independent practice for the last 30 minutes.

Bottom line: as things change, I try to change with them in a way that is engaging and a "best practice" for the students. I think it helps with this age group to take an interest in what methods they are using to communicate, and be engaged and adapt them to meet your educational classroom needs.

COLLABORATION IS KEY

In house I have both CIT, or continuous improvement time, and data teams that meet during our late start Wednesdays. We have a little over an hour to get together. This has been invaluable time to collaborate with my department team members to analyze our data on summative assessments and homework completion. Occasionally this year we have also held conference-style breakout sessions where members of our own staff presented content, and we were able to pick and choose which to attend that would benefit our classroom the most. By utilizing digital submissions, going to the flipped model has made data collection and analysis easier than ever before. I am able to quickly see how many students did the previous night's homework, which in turn guides my interventions. I am able quickly to see what they are understanding or not, based on their summaries and HOT questions.

As far as developing a PLN, or professional learning network, I use Edmodo to get more specific answers to questions. I have tried a few times on Twitter to get responses, but it doesn't seem to work that way for me. So when I have a problem and want a definite answer or direction, I turn to Edmodo to find it. I use Twitter to get information and help stay on top of the current trends. People are constantly tweeting informative articles and blog posts that are at once inspiring and helpful. I have also connected through Sophia.org and the Flipped Learning Network. The people online following through with the same things you are trying to achieve are always more than willing to offer up their ideas; they are extremely supportive.

I would also recommend signing up for as many free online webinars that pertain to flipping, using technology in education, or current practices. As long as I can try to attend, I am signing up. I have found a wealth of information through this avenue and it's one that many people, at least at my school, are not yet taking full advantage of. I totally understand this; where do you find the time? Often these webinars are set for EST and they often don't match up for me out here in Oregon, so accessing *archived* webinars are also high on the to do list for me. Many of the same websites I have already listed offer webinars on a fairly consistent basis.

RESULTS

How to Learn from My Mistakes

If you can become a bit more digital, while it might take a little bit of time upfront to create a template, it will save you loads of time in the long run. So my first goal was to do something else to make the WSQ easier to grade, and less work on my end. Who knows? Maybe next year when things are easier, I will once again attempt the weekly packet. Some students said they really missed them, but overall most students said it didn't matter one way or the other, packet vs. spiral journal for notes. They above all just wanted access to those notes for tests. I had a section of time where I had a student teacher doing her practicum for a month; this was right before winter break. So as I transitioned back into the classroom at the start of the New Year, I rolled out the new features. These were major changes that have since made my life so much easier.

The Changes

Original	New Year Roll Out
Weekly WSQ and Guided Notes Packet	· Changed to student created notes in a notes spiral · Digital submission of summary and HOT question on Google Form embedded in the daily tutorials
YouTube Channel and Link up with Edmodo	Embedding YouTube video and Google WSQ form into Sophia.org tutorial and playlist. Still using Edmodo to distribute the daily video link.
Edmodo for video storage	BlogSpot website · All units have their own page · All units have a video playlist on Sophia.org which is embedded to the correct page · Each page has a breakdown of the videos and weeks associated with it and any additional handouts and worksheets needed · Also has a spot for student created content *This was perhaps the most important part of the new roll out because it gave me a clear spot to point out to parents who wanted to help their student at home get caught up on their work

Improved Scores

Last year, we were using iPads two times a week, using Edmodo, and Twitter to stay updated. As I noticed last year, the technology components kept the kids engaged. That hasn't changed. I have noticed that I have a higher turn in rate of big summative assessment essays this year compared to last year. The students seem to be able to construct the essays in class, re-watch concepts that they are struggling with, and turn it in. I have also noticed a higher rate of students passing these essays, as graded by the state of Oregon writing rubric.

This year after the first round of state testing in the area of reading, I have a higher percentage of students passing compared to the same time last year. I also have a two point average gain on their scale score compared to last year at the same time. I also have 92% of my students meeting or exceeding the test standards. Even though at the end of the year, my scale score has remained the same as the previous year, I have more students in total this year and a smaller percentage of students not meeting.

As far as homework turn in last year I was seeing about a 50-60% turn in, and this was just normal style homework, worksheets pertaining to the content matter, or work on essays that we were doing in class but that they might not have finished, etc. I did not do a lot of interventions as they pertained to homework, I did interventions for summative assessments, but the homework didn't take on as high of a level of importance as it does this year. So this year on a regular basis I am seeing 80-90% turn in rate, but I am doing a lot of interventions on a weekly basis. One of those interventions, the after school "viewing party" allows me to see about 20% of my students on a weekly basis after school, which was not nearly as high or consistent last year.

Student & Parent Feedback

In February 2013, I did a survey of my students and found some very interesting results:

1. When asked if the student watched the video on time at night 76% answered that they did, 19% said sometimes, and the others said it depended on the night.
2. 78% said that they were putting in a good amount of effort at home.
3. 93% of my students felt that after watching all the concepts on the videos and doing a walkthrough of the test in class were confident in their ability to take their first attempt.
4. 98% felt like they were putting in a good amount of effort in class, so a slight improvement from the "at home" work ethic.
5. 93% of the students felt that the videos, notes, and in class activities were the most important and helpful part of the flipped classroom model.

And in their own words, the most important and helpful part of the flipped classroom model:

> "That if I miss a topic or important detail I can easily get the information."

> "Since the homework is quick I have time to do other things. I still learn a lot though. And because we do most of the learning at home there is time to do fun activities in class."

> "I think that working with other people encourages us to really dig deep into the topic we are on."

> "I think we cover more material (or have the potential to cover more material) throughout the school year with flipped learning. Not only do we have the opportunity to participate in more interactive, interesting lessons and activities during class, but we can listen to the lectures at home in a more comfortable environment, which makes it easier to process and actually follow the lecture/lesson. I personally like the fact that we can learn in our pajamas, and lie sprawled across a relaxing bed, all the while improving our knowledge in the different areas of language arts. I unfortunately have not been able to enjoy this very often, as I have a major procrastination issues when it comes to homework..."

> "The video is extremely helpful for me because I learn by listening and images."

> "The most helpful part is being be able to re-watch the videos if we're still confused."

Parent Feedback

In April we had our Spring Parent/Teacher Conferences, and I was able to ask the parents for some feedback on the flipped model as they were waiting in line to talk with me. Here are some of their comments:

1. What have you noticed at home with your student and watching the video homework?
   a. "It is great that she will have a better opportunity to discuss the theory or the concepts in class w/the instructor. This way they don't have to waste time (so little they've got)."
   b. "She jumps on it right away."
   c. "Homework is not an issue, where in other cases can be a challenge—especially if he is stuck on a topic or problem. Watching YouTube videos with the academic content and taking notes during the process is a great use of time."
   d. "I have noticed my student enjoys the homework, does the homework several times a week, and I feel like it is a positive and exciting change to homework."
2. Do you have any questions or concerns or any feedback on what you have noticed from your students this year using this model?
   a. "I think it's great as it is the model of the future."
   b. "The technology glitches can be very frustrating, sometimes." *(Because I have students using all sorts of different devices I have noticed that sometimes certain devices will not submit the digital Google Form- this is what this parent is referring to.)*
   c. "It has been good for me to hear the information that is being given for the class so that I know what is expected and can help with the homework. I love this class model!"

All of the projects and work this year take a significant amount of time, time that is fought for throughout the year so that we can cover the standards needed. There is no way all of this work would be possible if not for removing a lot of the direct instruction from the classroom through the flipped classroom model. By taking the time to teach through a video how to build the expository essay, we could take the time in class to research and construct those essays with their teacher right there with them every step of the way. By teaching the actual steps of how to write an opening statement, the four-step rebuttal process, and writing a closing statement through the videos we were able to perform the debates in class to the delight and heated arguments of the students. Overall I am extremely pleased with the results that I am seeing this year, and since our district is moving to a digital conversion for next year, I believe that all the hard work I have put in this year with flipping will make the transition that much easier for me! I hope to see the differentiation ramped up, as well as more content being developed for the end of the year. Overall it is very exciting, and I can't wait for what next year has in store.

__Nichole Carter__ has been teaching for ten years at Neil Armstrong Middle School in Forest Grove, Oregon. For the 2012-2013 school year she primarily taught honors language arts with one section of speech and debate. Next year she will be taking on two sections of honors and two sections of regular language arts, as well as a new role of tech coach. Find her on Twitter @mrscarterhla, or email her at mrscarterhla@gmail.com. You can also find her resources on her YouTube channel (bit.ly/flipping59) and her Google Site with videos and handouts (bit.ly/flipping61).

World Languages
Heather Witten

When I began teaching Spanish, I was so nervous. I clung to my textbook and listened to every word my mentor teacher said. The next few years, I continued to grow and be more comfortable in my role as teacher and as that happened, gained confidence and started being more creative with my assignments and assessments. I moved from teaching Spanish I and II to Spanish III and IV and then, AP Spanish. It was when I went to the workshop to prepare for teaching AP Spanish that I realized I still had so far to come as a Spanish teacher.

I needed to cover not only more content and culture in class, but give the students more opportunities to practice Spanish in real world situations. Only when I did that would students be able to increase their knowledge and fluency to truly be successful. In order to do that, I needed to change my objectives for all levels of Spanish, rework my curriculum, and find a way to do more in the time I had with my students in class. After some investigating and reading an article from the Wall Street Journal about the flipped class, I knew that I had to learn more.

I attended the Flipped class conference in 2011 led by Jon Bergman and Aaron Sams in Woodland Park, CO. It was a small conference, but full of educators that had come to the same conclusion that I had –something had to be changed in the traditional classroom so that we, as teachers, could better educate our students. I attended every session I could, found the two other language teachers at the conference, and brainstormed how we could make this new structure work in the classroom. I left that conference feeling excited about all of the changes that I could make to improve my classroom.

Although the flipped class is widely publicized in Math and Science, I think that it is perfect for World Language classes. One of my goals as a teacher is to keep striving for 90% of class in the target language as recommended by American Council on the Teaching of Foreign

Languages (ACTFL). Implementing the flipped class has helped me get closer to reaching that goal. Before my class was flipped, I was so focused on teaching grammar, and too much time was spent speaking English explaining difficult grammar concepts. With the flipped class, I have moved my formal lectures out of regular class time. I make videos that cover grammar basics, some culture, and vocabulary practice that students can watch on their own time, at their own pace, as often as needed. I am able to give explanations in English with many examples in both Spanish and English to help the students grasp the concepts. Then, we can spend the time in class practicing their new skills and vocabulary with skits, conversations, presentations, and projects which really spark the students' interest. Since I flipped my class, I am able to better model my expectation of communicating in Spanish throughout class, and my students are focused on tasks that help them communicate in Spanish more often without my constant reminding. This has helped me get closer to my 90% goal than I have ever been before.

First Steps

The first piece of advice that I give all teachers interested in flipping is to choose one level at a time. Moving from a traditional to a flipped class takes a large amount of up-front preparation time, and trying to make the change with one class is difficult, but multiple classes could drive a teacher crazy! Which class you choose is based on your personal preference. I chose to begin with my Spanish III class, because the majority of my students are in Spanish III and because I thought that Juniors and Seniors would be a little more tolerant with any hiccups that might arise. However, I know that some teachers are looking for ways to better handle classes where they have two levels of a language at the same time, such as a Spanish III/IV combination class. Choosing which class to begin with should be based on what you feel would be best for your students in your school. There is no one right answer.

Second, teachers should concentrate on how you can give students an opportunity to do more meaningful practice with the target language rather than teaching more content. For me, the goal was to find a way to do more speaking and listening practice. I always felt that these activities were always pushed to the side for "next time" because we were so busy focusing on grammar in class, but too often, "next time" never came, and my students did not get the practice that they needed and wanted. Now, since I do not formally lecture in class every day, students have more time to engage in listening and speaking practice with activities such as conversation, skits, videos, presentations, and projects. The students love these projects, and I can tell because this is where I see their best work. The students really come alive when they are given a chance to perform and demonstrate their knowledge. Not only that, but they start to look forward to the next project and look forward to what the new units will be. They often don't even realize how excited they are to continue learning, but I do and that is when I know the class is really moving in the right direction.

What is your class going to look like if you are no longer lecturing? The flipped classroom requires teachers to stop being the focus of their classroom, and instead makes the students the primary focus. This can be hard; I confess that it was a hard change for me. I am a control freak; I love teaching in front of the class and being in control of the class at all times. But, it is a necessary change because a student-driven class leads to more student success. Especially in the World Language class, students need to be the star of the show. Obviously we as teachers can speak the target language, so we need to step aside and let the students practice. This is not any easy task since as we all know, many students are so afraid of making mistakes and appearing foolish in front of their peers, that instead of trying to participate, they all suddenly become mute.

To minimize this fear and hesitation, I have worked to structure my class so that students can work individually, in pairs, or in small groups, whichever they find more comfortable. This allows students to be less afraid of making mistakes because they are with their peers. It also allows students to help their friends in a more relaxed environment than when they have to talk to me. I then spend the class moving from group to group; offering suggestions, asking higher-level thinking questions, correcting practice assignments, pushing students to move beyond what is easy to be able to improve their fluency, and generally monitoring what everyone is doing. I guide their learning by reinforcing good work and encouraging them to continue putting forth good effort. Since the students are working together they can fill in the gaps in each other's knowledge, and this allows me to spend time with students that are really struggling and need my help.

COMMUNICATION

Clearly, before you start any type of new program, you need to have a conversation with your administration. Although you may not have everything worked out, you need their support before you invest time into flipping your class. This is a very different class format, and it would not be unusual for students to complain to parents, and then for parents to bring their concerns to admin. You need to make sure that administration understands not only what the flipped class is, but why you are choosing to implement it in your classroom and how it is going to improve student fluency.

When I began flipping my Spanish class, I made sure to keep administration informed of what I was planning. I met with them and explained the flip class and how I was planning to implement it in my classroom. I also gave them copies of information that I sent home to parents and students before the school year started which outlined the new class format and encouraged them to communicate any concerns with me. By keeping administration in the loop, they were fully prepared to answer any questions that parents or students had. Having administration approval and support from the beginning makes it much easier if a student or parent has a concern down the line.

Parent communication is key to success as well. Before the school year begins, I send all of my parents a video about how the flipped class works and encourage them to ask questions before or at any time during the school year. I know that as a parent myself, having some knowledge about the class structure makes it easier to understand my child when he complains. I have found that by doing this, I have headed off many questions like *"Why aren't you teaching my child?"* or *"What are you doing in class?"* or my favorite, *"If my student is just watching videos, why don't I just buy them that program on TV?"* Many parents have actually approached me and told me how much they like the flipped class because they can learn along with their student, and that it gives their student, who needs more time to process new information, the opportunity to go back and listen to the lectures again and again until she understands. At fall conferences during my first year of flipping, one parent said, "Tara has a hard time keeping up with teacher lectures, and your videos have made a real difference for her. She watches them multiple times and uses them to help her study as well."

Student communication has also increased since I began the flipped classroom during and after class. I believe that there are a few reasons for this. With the flipped classroom, I am able to spend more time with students one-on-one and therefore they are more comfortable coming to me with questions. Not only do I get specific content questions, but other questions such as *"How can I improve my listening?"* or *"I really struggle remembering vocabulary, what can I do?"* Many of these questions lead to bigger discussions about how students study and offering advice on other methods or techniques which help students be more successful in all of their classes, not just mine.

Additionally, since much of the curriculum is online for students, I receive emails from students that are working on assignments outside of class. They don't want to wait for me to clarify for them during class, they want answers right away. Usually, I can answer these questions with a quick note, but occasionally, with more complicated questions, or questions that I am hearing from multiple students, I will address them in class. Students emailing me is a fantastic way for me to give them what they need when they need it. I now actively encourage students to email me with questions or concerns, which is especially helpful when I am unable to be in class. It allows me to help keep students on track and working at their pace with only a small additional time commitment from me.

PLANNING AND IMPLEMENTATION

In order to structure the class to focus more on the students, I have had to plan more than ever before. Honestly, planning a thematic unit with the flipped class model takes me at least three times as long as it used to with the traditional model. Finding quality, authentic resources can be challenging and time-consuming, but to give the students a rounded exposure to the different cultures, this is a necessary task. To ensure I am meeting my class and unit goals, I plan entire units at once. So, there is quite a bit of work up front, but on the flip side, I am never scrambling at the copy machine before class. I walk into my class ready to help my students and facilitate their learning.

With the flipped class model, achieving student growth on the ACTFL scale is much more attainable with clear objectives. Because the flipped class gives students more freedom to work on things they need to spend more time on, class and unit objectives must be clear and measurable to keep the individual students and the class on track. When World Language teachers create objectives, we need to consider not only content, but that all of the modes of communication are being practiced and assessed frequently. To do this, objectives should be created for the year as well as unit by unit and need to be not only given to the students, but reinforced in the classroom as well.

An example of a yearly goal for my Spanish III class is:
- Students will increase their listening comprehension to move up at least one level on the ACTFL proficiency scale from their beginning of the year assessment.

With unit objectives to help meet that yearly goal such as:
- Students will listen to native speakers in real-life situations and demonstrate comprehension of the listening selection
- Students will listen to the first minute of a conversation between native speakers and be able to logically complete the conversation with a partner.

The key is to always keep the yearly objectives in mind when creating the unit goals. Then you will be able to best use your class time and curriculum to increase student fluency. Class will then be able to stay focused even with students being given more freedom and choices that the flipped class allows. The creation of these clear objectives has also eliminated the "*Why do we have to do this?*" conversation with my students, or the "*Videos aren't really important.*" They can see that they need to learn the grammar and vocabulary to effectively do listening and practice, and learn all of that to be able to do well on assessments.

Currently, I do three full units per semester. Each unit is five weeks long and contains two to three grammar concepts. Students receive a packet at the beginning of each unit which begins with a Unit Outline, containing the objectives for the unit as well as a calendar for when assignments, quizzes and projects are due. The packet also contains vocabulary for the unit as well as short practice grammar exercises, discussion questions, interpretive listening and reading assignments, and project assignments and rubrics. The students are free to work on whatever assignment in the unit they choose, but I do quiz everyone on the same day, and projects and final assessments are all due at the same time. Therefore, students are usually not more than a day ahead or a day behind each other. Each semester, the three objectives and units focus on a specific mode of communication. So, the first unit may be presentational (oral), the second interpersonal (conversation), and the third presentational (written).

Quality objectives are essential to any class, but in the flipped class they make all the difference. For example, by giving the students the assignments and expectations for the unit at its onset, the students become responsible for getting things completed on time. They do not need to rely on catching up with me to get information or assignments which helps keep the students focused, even if I am not there. Substitutes love my class since students always know what they need to do, and I don't feel so guilty if I have to be absent. I never have to leave sub plans that are not the best use of my class time like I had to when I used the traditional teaching method – students can continue working without me in the classroom. The students like the flip format because if they know that they are going to miss class for a basketball game, they can work ahead and not have to worry about doing make-up work, and if they have a mind-melting test in Calculus before my class, they can choose an easier assignment to keep them on track.

The best part is that since the objectives are clear, giving students more choice with assignments is easy because they understand what they need to achieve. I love giving summative assessments for students where they have as many choices as possible from their specific topic, to a group or individual project, to a formal presentation, or a more informal debate. As long as my students can demonstrate they have mastered the material and are increasing their fluency as we progress for the year, they can choose the specifics.

For example, when we learn about the subjunctive, students are tasked to create a skit, song, or game in which they are expected to teach the concept to their fellow students in a creative and fun way. They may work together or individually and can choose any of the rules for the subjunctive to include that they would like. They can use an existing song or game and modify it, or create their skit, song or game. They all have a good time with the presentations, and since they are interactive for the entire class, everyone is participating and learning. *A side note here – Each unit requires a different type of assessment (i.e. presentational or interpersonal, written or oral) so I can ensure that they are continuing to increase fluency in all types of communication.

TECHNOLOGY INTEGRATION

Incorporating technology effectively in class has its challenges. Often, the technology in school is not all we hope that it would be. Websites we want to use and share can be blocked, and many of us have students with minimal or no access to technology at home. Every situation is different, and teachers need to think about the challenges in their classroom when adding technology components to the classroom. Just remember that technology challenges can usually be overcome with good planning. I am not in a 1:1 school, and in my class we use a combination of donated technology and the technology the students bring to class.

I had one student, Barbara M., who had access to a computer at home but no Internet access. Therefore, I made *.wmv files of all of my videos and gave them to her on a flash drive. There have been a few other students that have encountered temporary loss of Internet, and the best way I have found is to make sure that those students get the first opportunity to work with the technology in the classroom, or a pass to use the library.

Videos for grammar and culture, as well as listening selections, are almost exclusively online which allow me to incorporate a greater breadth of authentic materials in my class. Additionally, I use an online journaling and Google Voice for weekly speaking and writing formative assessments. There are so many great resources available, but I try to choose two or three good ones to keep things as simple as possible for my students. My goal is to choose the best ones that will help my students achieve their goals and enable students to access them in one central location. However, I do provide links to other resources that I believe students can use to supplement the ones that I use for class.

At the onset of the flipped classroom, I instructed all of my students that it was their responsibility to let me know if there was problem with the technology right away, and we would work it out. This helps students take charge of their learning and be an effective advocate for themselves. However, I do try to probe students if suddenly they are not completing their online assignments. For example, I had a student, Jordan B., who had been faithful about doing all of his assignments, and then did not do any of them for three weeks in a row. Jordan is a quiet young man, and did not want to tell me why these assignments were not being completed. Finally, I had a one-on-one chat with him and found out his parents had forbidden him Internet or phone access for the last three weeks. So, we worked out a deal so that he would have first access to the tablet and could use a classmate's phone during class to get these assignments completed. Good relationships with the students encourage communication which is critical in resolving any technology issues quickly with minimal impact to the learning.

MEANINGFUL VIDEOS

I have always found that having to explain difficult grammar concepts in the target language is nearly impossible. No matter how hard I tried, the grammar lectures ended up moving to English, and then the focus of maintaining the target language became harder and harder. So, the first thing I did when I flipped my class was to move the grammar lectures to video so that students could do them in their own time. I have used a variety of formats to create the videos, but my advice in your first year is to keep it simple and make them meaningful. My grammar videos have evolved more and more into stories to keep the students engaged. For example, my video about *por and para* (bit.ly/flipping69) tells a story of a dad going to buy shoes for his son, making sure to point how these two small words can drastically change the context of the story if you use them incorrectly. Students will remember the concepts better when they are used in context as opposed to lists of rules and random example sentences. The best part is that since it is a video, you can do as many takes and tons of editing to make it prefect, which is something we can't do when we lecture in front of the class.

In my video for writing a letter, I describe how to write formal and informal letters (bit.ly/flipping70). The story line of the video is a love story where a boy writes a love letter to his girlfriend and then later writes a letter asking her father for permission to ask her to marry him. On many occasions, when we work on letters, I have heard the students comment, "That is a letter like that boy writes to his girlfriend, so use ...." or "Writing to a person in the government is like asking permission to marry someone, so we must have to use....".

Besides grammar videos, I have also created videos for the students to practice vocabulary. These are simple videos with picture clues and fill in the blank sentences so that the students have another way to practice, and they also function as listening practice as well. I make these mandatory in the first unit, but they are voluntary after that because I want to give students the freedom to choose the way to study that works best for them. Last year, I introduced some cultural videos on concepts such as how to write a letter and how to talk on the phone and leave voicemail messages (bit.ly/flipping71). These are small cultural elements that are so important, but I had been overlooking in class because I ran out of time with the traditional format. I am glad that now I am able to always make sure my students learn and understand these important cultural cues because I have made them an available as a video, so they are never a "next time" activity. They are a meaningful part of the class.

PRACTICING IN THE TARGET LANGUAGE

Students want to learn how to speak in the target language. They want to be able to talk to a waiter in a Mexican restaurant, or a pretty girl when they are on vacation in a foreign country. I have never met a student that comes to class dying to learn grammar. There are so many fun and engaging activities that can be done in the classroom with the additional class time. I had notebooks full of great ideas from conferences that I had never been able to use in the traditional classroom and with the flipped class, I could use them all. Now, the students and I are happy because they are practicing more Spanish in class, increasing their fluency, and having fun. The trick is to stay focused on the class objectives while creating fun and meaningful assignments and projects for the students which encourage them to stay in the target language.

In my Spanish III class, our first unit is Challenges in Teen Life. This is one of my favorite units, and one of the students' favorites as well. The focus is all on teens, their problems and struggles, and how they compare to the teens in other countries. After some vocabulary acquisition, the students work on their conversation skills with topics they can relate to such as allowance, divorce, jobs, stress, suicide, depression, drinking and drugs. We watch a video about

Gang Stigmata in Honduras and have some great discussions about tattoos, gangs, violence, and peer pressure. Their final assessment for this unit is to create a campaign to help teens with a common problem, such as teen drinking. Students work in groups and choose any teen problem that they wish. They have to present their campaign, and it can be in any format. Some students have created posters to represent billboards, others created Power Point presentations, and others created video public service announcements. I leave the details as open as possible so that students can utilize their individual talents to really get excited about the projects. The students use some class time to work on the projects and all must do a practice run through before presenting. This year, after the presentations were complete, one of my students came to me after class and said, "This is the best Spanish project ever. I learned so much." What more can any teacher hope for?

For me, one of the hardest parts of teaching the higher levels of Spanish is to find time to revisit some of the themes and vocabulary from Spanish I and II that are so relevant to daily life. Last year we added a cross-level project where the Spanish III students set up booths in a "market" and the Spanish I students came and shopped. This project served not only as a great speaking opportunity for both levels, but also had the added benefit of giving the Spanish I students something to look forward to. Many of them commented that they couldn't wait until they could run the booths in the "market" when they were in Spanish III.

With the additional practice going on in class, the teacher can not only monitor and answer questions, but also spend time with individual students not just checking comprehension, but delving deeper to help students to make connections with the material they are working with. Comprehension is just the tip of the iceberg. Can your students take what they understand and apply it to prior knowledge? Can they make the cultural connections? Students work on their own for comprehension, and I focus my time on these higher-level thinking questions such as "What changes do you think could take place in Venezuela now that Chavez has died?" or "How do you think Michelle Bachelet being elected the first female president of Chile will change the perceptions and roles of women in Chilean society?" I love asking my students these questions because since there is no one correct answer, they have to think and not just recite something from the selection like they can do with comprehension. Since I have more time to work with students individually, I am able to help more and more students reach this level of understanding, not just of Spanish, but the culture and how it compares to our own.

FLIPPING IS MORE FUN WITH FRIENDS

As important as videos and curriculum are when you are beginning to flip your class, having a Personal Learning Network that has other teachers and administrators with goals and objectives similar to yours is equally important. Some teachers are lucky to be able to find like-minded professionals in their school, but some, like me, come from smaller schools with only a few World Language teachers. Finding teachers that are interested in using the flipped model may require looking outside of your school. Luckily, in our technological world, this is not so hard to do if you know where to begin. Join groups on Edmodo, become a part of the Edutopia community, #langchat on Twitter, or for the best interaction with other teachers interested in flipping their class, check out the #flipclass chat on Twitter. I find Twitter chats very effective because they spark new ideas and are a great tool for reflection on in my own class.

By participating in these communities and interacting with other teachers with similar goals, I have not only been able to learn how to deal with problems that arise, improve my class environment, and get some fantastic project ideas, but also mentor others that are beginning to flip their World Language classes. The best advice often comes from unexpected sources, so I keep up with English, History, Science and Math teachers and the things they are doing in their classroom. As a result of some of the ideas of these different content areas, I have been creating some very interesting cross-curricular units.

The advice and feedback that I get from my PLN helps me hash out great ideas, effectively evaluate what is going on in my classroom, and gives me a place to vent and work through problems, concerns, or new ideas with people who understand what I am going through. For example, as any World Language teacher knows, professional development at the school level often does not fill our needs. Talk to the other teachers in your building or in your PLN about projects that have worked for them and adapt them for your needs. Being able to learn more about Project-based Learning with World Language from other WL teachers or designing better thought provoking assessments by talking to math teachers makes having a large PLN invaluable.

REFLECT, EVALUATE AND REVISE

Shortly after I began flipping my Spanish classes, I also began a blog. It started just for me, my way to keep a record of the ups and downs in my classroom. It is full of things I wish I had done differently and things that were surprisingly great in my class. It has been a wonderful source of reflection, and the writing process is very cathartic. Often in the middle of writing a blog post I will come up with possible solutions, or realize how I could turn something that was going horribly wrong around. Writing the blog has been invaluable in my evaluation of how things were going in my classroom, not just how I felt after the frustrations of a bad day.

Sometimes when I am stuck trying to find a new way to practice a concept, or a better idea to keep the students in the target language, all I have to do is look back through my blog and the great ideas are there, just waiting for me to come back to them.

A couple of months after I began, I realized that other people were reading my blog, too! Maybe it sounds ridiculous, but I was truly surprised. Who cared what was going on in my classroom? Then I began to get comments on the blog, which were full of questions, answers, and great ideas. I felt like I had won the lottery. I get emails from people that have read my blog full of questions and excitement, and it helps me stay excited about what is going on in my classroom. Blogging has turned into one of my favorite things I have done when I began flipping my class.

The hard part with reflection and evaluation is the realization that so much of the curriculum that I have created could be done better. I am always reworking and tweaking my assignments, assessments, and videos.

As I walk around the classroom and am checking on student progress, they think I am writing notes about them when in reality I am writing notes for myself about what changes I can make, the great idea a student just had to do it better, or even making notes

277

about something they have learned which I did not know. I am always open to student suggestions and continually ask for their input to keep improving my class. Asking students to participate in the conversation about making improvements to their class really increases student buy-in because they know that I value their opinion and care about their ideas.

However, even though the revising is hard work and often time-consuming, I feel as though it helps me keep everything fresh and relevant to my students. Everything in my class is always changing based on my student feedback, and often, since I am working with them and not being "on stage", I am able to make these changes very quickly. Before I flipped my class, my reflection and evaluation of assignments often came too late to help my current students, and I am glad that now my class structure enables me to be more responsive to my students' needs in real time. If there is an error, or students misunderstood something, I can address it quickly and before they practice the information incorrectly.

My research and all my planning and preparation had not prepared me for how hard I would work during class when I implemented the flipped model. Although I rarely sat down in class when I taught traditionally, now I am constantly in motion. Moving from group to group while being asked questions about many different aspects of the unit of study is exhausting and exhilarating. My students discover more vocabulary, more interesting information, and are actively engaged using the target language for more time than they ever had been in the traditional classroom.

Since students have more freedom in class, I have also incorporated more choice into student assignment and assessments. Now not only are students more interested in the assignments, but there is the added benefit of incorporating a wider breadth of cultural information. These choices allow students to bring in elements of other content areas that interest them and then they learn more because they are truly interested in the topics. For example, at the end of last year a group of students did a presentation on "green energy". They used fantastic graphics and explained how solar panels and wind turbines worked in Spanish. I was blown away! Projects like these generate interest and excitement from all of the students because the quality of the presentations have improved and the effect is contagious We have been able to spend more time focusing on culture in our class discussions and presentations and since the students get to choose topics, I have the opportunity to learn from them. The students are always so surprised to realize that they taught me something new and that gives them an even greater sense of pride.

Best of all, I feel like I am meeting the needs of all of my students now. I am able to let my high achievers work to their abilities and not hold them back with boring grammar lectures when they can understand the concepts quickly and move on to the application. My lower-level students can spend more time with the lectures and have more time one-on-one with me to get the individual attention that they need to better understand the basic concepts so that they can spend more time concentrating on increasing their fluency. My middle students have changed from just "getting along" to working harder with the high achievers and as peer tutors with the lower level students.

My favorite story from my class is about a B-/C+ student named Rachel in my Spanish III class. She had been working with the same group of students for a while, and I was working with another group when all of a sudden she stood up and started yelling, "How many times do I have to tell you, when you say that, you have to use the subjunctive." Although her delivery may have needed work, watching a student become a peer tutor is further proof that they are really learning.

The change in my classroom environment and the increased success of my students since I made the move to the flipped classroom is clearly evident. Students are able to spend time working on their problem areas and can work more on their own timetable which *they* create based on *their* needs. They are no longer held back by me standing in front of the class all the time. Nor are they resigned to being lost because they have no idea what I am saying. Every student is working all class period. The students are spending more and more time in the target language and less just listening to me. That is the expectation, and that is what World Language teachers need in order to be able to help their students' become more fluent. If the students don't understand something, they do it again until they do. Students are not allowed to give up, and they are not allowed to "coast". They keep trying because they know that is the only way they will reach our mutual goal of increased fluency. The students enjoy my class because I treat them like adults. They enjoy the freedom that the class brings and even though they don't love everything that we do, they spend more time on activities that will help them in the "real world".

In the words of one of my wonderful students Ray D.-"With the flipped class, you get out of it what you put into it. It is not just teachers imparting their knowledge, but you have to work to learn for yourself."

Moving to the flipped class model was the best thing I ever did for my students. They continue to astound me with how excited they get when they can really have a great conversation, or when they can finally understand a listening selection in one or two tries instead of ten. The challenges and successes are measured differently for every student because the path to fluency is different for each one of them. As hard as it was to give up being the "star" of my classroom, being the students guide and facilitator has turned out to be much more rewarding for them and for me.

Heather Witten is an enthusiastic educator, presenter and blogger beginning her sixth year as a Spanish teacher at Elizabeth High School in Colorado. She has delivered numerous presentations and webinars about the flipped classroom, including at the Flipped Class Conference 2012 and AATSP and ACTFL. Heather is passionate about flipping foreign language classes because it enables teachers to better utilize class time and build better relationships with students. Heather shares her journey with the flipped classroom in her blog at www.spanishflippedclass.blogspot.com. She can also be reached via Twitter at @SraWitten, or email at hawitten@gmail.com.

Google Apps for Education
Troy Cockrum

Google Apps for Education (GAFE) is an excellent tool for management of a flipped classroom. Many of the different Google products could be used in any classroom. Some of the uses I will detail below aren't specific to a flipped classroom; however, their uses make managing a flipped classroom much easier.

Even if your school is not using Google Apps for Education, many of the features come with a standard Gmail account and can be utilized as an individual. I would recommend you consult your school's policy on communicating with student's outside your district email before sharing with students. However, many of the products can still be helpful in managing your class even if you can't utilize the benefits of sharing and collaboration built into Google Apps for Education.

I prefer GAFE for a several reasons.

1. If your school is a GAFE school, the products can be used with a single sign on (SSO). This feature requires the students and staff to keep track of fewer passwords and logins.
2. The user interface is very similar among the tools and is designed to be simple and intuitive. Therefore, teachers can spend less time teaching technology and more time teaching content.
3. Google products interact with each other pretty seamlessly in most cases. For example, a spreadsheet or document can be embedded into a site or blog easily.
4. Although optimized for Chrome, Google products are designed to be multi-platform and available in many web browsers. Teachers and students can access and use most Google products from most web-enabled devices. Google will leave out some more complex features in order to ensure the app is stable and reliable. For example, some users complain about the lack of design capabilities of Docs or Slides compared to some stand-

alone programs. However, this perceived lack of features ensures more stable usability across platforms.

5. Google guarantees a 99.9% uptime. Over the past three years of using Google Apps, I can't remember a time where products were unavailable for more than a few minutes. Better uptime means more productivity.
6. Google is constantly improving their apps, and their goal is simplicity. And, because it is web-based, you always have the most up-to-date version.

Many other technological products available have some similar uses, as seen in the other chapters on technology in this book. However, it is for the reasons above that I work primarily with Google Apps as well as Chrome Apps and Extensions. As we walk through each of the Google Apps in the following section, you will see examples of the power of various apps working together to give both teachers and students an effective set of tools for learning.

GOOGLE DOCS

I have to begin with the most obvious use of GAFE: Google Docs. (Not to be confused with Drive which used to be called Docs.) Docs allows users to create, edit, and share word-processing documents. For a paperless classroom, Docs is essential. Students can share documents with their teacher or other students without having to print. The teacher then has access to the most recent version of that document and the student can continue to make changes as necessary. The teacher can access a Revision History on the document to see how many edits were made and by whom.

Another great feature of Docs is the ability to comment on a document without having to revise the actual document. Using sidebar notes, this tool allows collaboration between multiple students and teachers without confusion or compromising the original document. Each document keeps a record of the ongoing conversation that collaborators have had while editing the text.

Chrome extensions, available from the Chrome Web Store, can add even more functionality to Docs. For example, VoiceComments is a third-party extension that allows users to add voice comments to a document. The user can see and hear your comments, allowing more robust feedback. I use it in my class to give writing feedback throughout a student's work. In addition, with scripts (more on those later) a teacher can share out a specific document to multiple students to ensure that formatting, sharing options, etc., are consistent among all students.

GOOGLE SITES

Sites allows GAFE users the ability to create an individual site on their domain. They have very user-friendly creation features to create a simple classroom website, while also adding many customizable features for the more advanced users. The site can have page-level permissions, allowing some pages to be public while others are protected. Sites can provide a central location for students to access homework, instructions, documents, videos, news, and more.

The simplicity of using multiple Google Apps *within* a site allows a teacher to populate the site quickly and edit it efficiently. I embed a Google Sheet with all assignments listed and links to related resources. The best feature, in my opinion, is when I add a resource or change a due date on a spreadsheet, the embedded app on the site is updated in real time. Therefore, there is no need to go to multiple locations to make small changes. Other teachers will embed a document with homework as opposed to a spreadsheet. That is a matter of personal preference as they both work in the same manner.

Sites also allows you to embed Google Forms. The ability to embed the Form for others to access makes the site a clearinghouse of information related to your classroom.

GOOGLE FORMS

Google Forms is a form creation tool that allows you to share forms with others and collect information or results into a spreadsheet in Sheets. Forms, I think, is a very underused tool that can digitize and streamline many processes in the flipped classroom. Combined with scripts, Forms are extremely powerful. In addition to the uses covered in Sheets, I also use forms for student feedback, assignment submission, video interaction, and permission slips.

Student Feedback

Not only do I use Forms as grading rubrics and for peer feedback, I also use it for student feedback. At the end of each unit, I send students a Form for them to provide me feedback from their perspective of how certain parts of the unit went. These feedback forms have given me the opportunity to have some amazing conversations with my students and help them learn better.

Assignment Submission

When I have students creating blogs, eportfolios, YouTube videos, or other online work, it can be difficult to manage where each one is located. If each student emails a link to their assignment, I then could have well over a hundred emails I have to sift through. Instead, I have a Form set up where the student pastes the URL into the form along with their name and submits it. I then have an organized spreadsheet with the link to each student's assignment and can view and assess them much more efficiently. Another bonus is that the form timestamps the submission. In addition, forms can be set up to no longer accept submissions after a certain preselected time.

Video Interaction

One criticism of the flipped classroom is that videos aren't engaging more thinking and/or students can't ask questions they may have immediately. However, videos can be paired with a form (using Sites or a blog) and students can fill in response items either while watching a video or immediately after. The teacher can gauge understanding by asking key questions and have students submit answer through a form. This data can be used by the teacher to determine what instruction needs to be covered and what questions need to be answered.

Permission Slips

Although not necessarily a flipped class issue, I use Forms to collect permission slips. This serves several purposes. First, my turn-in rate has increased dramatically when going to digital permission slips. Busy parents can fill it out immediately online, increasing the chances it won't get lost. I still print out about 2-3 forms per class to accommodate those families with limited access or are technology-challenged. In addition, once the permission slip is submitted, I have a spreadsheet listing all the students, their allergies, emergency contacts, etc. There is no longer a need for me to carry a large stack of paper permission slips with me on field trips. (I checked with a lawyer to make sure that the wording was appropriate and to ensure that digital signatures are legally binding in my state. I would recommend you do the same if that is a concern of yours.)

GOOGLE SHEETS (FORMERLY SPREADSHEETS)

Google Sheets is a spreadsheet creator with collaborative features and integration into the other Google products. As mentioned before, I create a spreadsheet in Sheets to act as a unit list and link to videos. However, the real power I find in Sheets is in the scripts. Scripts can be thought of as formulas or recipes that automate certain tasks from a trigger. These scripts will take data entered into the spreadsheet either manually or from a form and use that data to complete a process. In conjunction with Forms, Sheets can be an organizational and time-saving wonder.

The scripts I find most useful in a flipped classroom:

Autocrat is a mail-merge script that can automate the process of creating a documents and sharing them via email and GAFE. With this script, I create a simple rubric form and can then assess my students' work. Once I submit the form entries, the script automatically emails a document to the student showing them their grade.

I also use this script for peer feedback. A student assesses another's work using a form I provide and the peer review is automatically sent to the other student and to me, or anyone else I've set it up to email. You can set up the script to send as a Google Doc, a PDF, or other formats that fit your classrooms needs. Autocrat can be found at bit.ly/flipping62.

Doctopus allows the user to create one or multiple shared documents and send them out to an entire class roster. The teacher can also create/designate a folder the shared document will be sent. This allows the teacher to ensure all students use the same format on a document and share it with the appropriate people.

One great feature of this script is its ability to share different documents based on criteria set in the roster. For instance, if you have groups in your class that you want to have read a different document based on, say, a topic they are studying, the script can be setup to look for a trigger column to determine which group to send which document without the teacher having to create multiple class rosters. You may have different reading groups based on how you want to differentiate instruction. You may want one group to receive an article without annotations. Another group, you may want them to receive the same article with annotations or a different article. Doctopus allows you the ability to share those different files efficiently without having to setup multiple rosters. Doctopus can be found at bit.ly/flipping63.

Goobric is actually a Chrome extension that works in conjunction with scripts. It allows the user to attach a rubric to an existing document, spreadsheet, and presentation created with the Doctopus script. It has a pop-up, easy-to-use rubric that allows a teacher to automate parts the grading process in order to save time. Goobric can be found at bit.ly/flipping64.

FormMule is thought by many as one of the most basic scripts and great for beginning users. It is another Mail Merge script that sends custom emails drawn from entries in a spreadsheet. FormMule also has a great single entry calendar event option that is great for school communications. FormMule can be found at bit.ly/flipping65.

Flubaroo is a time-saving script that allows the teacher to set up a self-grading, multiple choice quiz. For a quick assessment or if you are using a mastery model, having a quiz or test set up to be self-graded can save a teacher significant grading time. Flubaroo scripts can be found at bit.ly/flipping66.

gClassFolders is a script that automates the folder creation process for multiple users or students. A teacher can use this script to create and manage folders quickly for each one of their classes and students. Used in conjunction with gClassHub, this script is a really powerful organizational tool. This is a great tool if you have a large number of students and you want to make sure all their documents are created, named, and shared consistently. Instead of having them create the document and/or folder, you create it for them and use gClassFolders to automate the process of sending out all those documents or folders. gClassFolders can be found at bit.ly/flipping67.

pageMeister allows a teacher to create a single Google Site template for an entire class. Once run, the script creates an identical site for each student based on teacher specifications. This would be great to use with portfolios wherein the teacher wanted uniformity amongst all sites for easy viewing and assessment. pageMeister can be found at bit.ly/flipping68.

OTHER GOOGLE PRODUCTS

YouTube

YouTube is now owned by Google. Over the years, Google has made YouTube more of a social platform. Because of those social features, YouTube is a great tool for collaborating in the classroom and an excellent way to host your own videos. (If it is blocked at your school, explore the option of YouTube EDU.) I host my videos on YouTube because it is a multi-platform viewer and has some nice analytics to help determine viewership.

Hosting videos is only a small part of YouTube's versatility, however. Another feature is YouTube's ability to organize videos by playlists. A hidden gem of playlists is being able to create a custom intro video for each playlist (in the edit playlist mode, mouse over the videos, a small +introduction button will appear, and then click it to create an introduction video). Playlists can be shared or embedded in Sites and blogs so students can access them. A teacher could create a playlist of several videos on a specific topic and give students the choice of which videos to watch. Or, they could add supplemental videos for students that need or want further information.

Under the upload menu in YouTube, there are also many features to help in video creation, especially collaborative videos. There you will find slideshows, editing features, video effects, and Creative Commons videos to add to your projects, webcam recording, and more. Also under the upload menu is the ability to launch a live Google Hangout. You will need a Google+ account for this, but with the screen sharing option, Google Hangouts are a great way to screencast from the web (allowing Chromebooks to screencast) and also hold video discussions or collaborations among students.

Blogger

There are many blogging options for students. I choose to use Blogger for a few reasons, but mainly for its integration with Google products. Since Blogger is owned by Google, it will accept your students GAFE account as a login, eliminating another possible forgotten password. In addition, embedding YouTube videos, Forms, and other documents is very simple.

I have my students blog for different reasons through Blogger. One can argue that other education specific blog sites allow teachers more control over each student's blog, and that's true in some cases. Regularly checking their blogs, I'm able to monitor for misuse. I also have a class blog that has daily work listings, instructions for any activities the class may be doing, as well as embedded videos or playlists students might need. This allows my students to begin working as soon as they walk into the classroom as opposed to waiting for verbal instructions. Absent students can also see what was covered that day in class, so they know what they might need to catch up on.

The most important feature for me to continue using Google products is efficiency. Their ease of use, consistent interface, and cross-platform integration allow teachers to do multiple projects, activities, communication, and collaboration in the flipped classroom without creating a logistical nightmare. Google Apps for Education has not only made my students and me more productive, it allows us to move into many creative endeavours we never thought possible.

Troy Cockrum is a middle school Language Arts teacher, Google Certified Teacher, and a Google Apps for Education Certified Trainer in Indianapolis, IN. He is also the host of the weekly Flipped Learning Network Podcast on the EdReach Network. He can be reached by email at mrcockrum@mrcockrum.com or on Twitter @tcockrum.

PART THREE:

Just for Teachers

Professional Development
Kristin Daniels

INTRODUCTION

The education field is facing dramatic changes. In a system that has changed its process very little, we are facing disruptive innovations due to technology that are changing what we know as education. Professional development is necessary for schools and districts to close the technology adoption gap and move *all* teachers towards implementing innovative ideas in their classrooms. Effective professional development is personalized, job-embedded and integrates technology throughout.

CHALLENGES WITH TRADITIONAL PD

When thinking about innovative ways to deliver professional development, you need to evaluate what works and what doesn't work in your existing model. Let's consider "traditional PD", typically a one-time gathering of educators to learn about one particular tool, process, or strategy. Just like a traditional classroom, traditional PD approaches learning as a one-size-fits-all model. The challenges of this setting is that content delivery is at one pace, one style, one time and there is no follow-up with the participants. Teachers bring a variety of experiences, skills, and interest levels to the group. An instructor will adjust as much as they can to meet the needs of all participants, but as any teacher knows, it is challenging to meet the needs of everyone in this type of setting. We know that this is not the best way to learn.

Another challenge to traditional PD is that teachers are provided very little time for their own learning. For students, the traditional learning cycle typically includes direct instruction, guided practice, independent practice, and assessment. Traditional teacher professional development provided by a school or district usually includes direct instruction and perhaps some guided practice. There is rarely follow up. It is a typical "sit-and-get" situation.

291

While there are many reasons for eliminating this type of top down professional development altogether, many schools and districts only have the capacity for "one-time" professional development. Creating a professional development model that provides ongoing support for teachers to move towards a school's or district's long range vision demands a team of individuals who work year round to create such a program. Recently, more and more schools are combining their teaching and learning department with the technology department to create a partnership between two vital components of a school district in order to create a thorough approach to curriculum, instruction, and the technology that inevitably will be used in each learning environment. Significant and sustainable teacher development requires a team of coaches to work with teachers; coaches that are well versed in instruction and technology integration. Information today, and for our foreseeable future, is easily accessible. Today's learners, young and not so young, require a facilitator, or a coach, to help them explore content at a deeper level.

WHY FLIPPED PROFESSIONAL DEVELOPMENT

If you consider what many call "flipped classroom 101", we know that there is much information that we can provide students before meeting with them face-to-face and much can be gained by this preparation. However, as a teacher extends themselves past a "flipped classroom 101" mentality and towards supporting a learning cycle that allows students to move at their own pace and to access content when they need it, the impact on student learning increases. This continuum from "differentiation" to "individualization" and all the way to "personalization" can also be applied to professional development and is seen in various implementations of professional learning, from creating Flipped Faculty Meetings and Flipped Professional Development days all the way to the more personalized Flipped Professional Coaching.

It is important to create, curate, and organize digital content for teachers. However, simply providing digital content for teachers and calling it Flipped Professional Development would be the same as providing video lessons to students and calling it a Flipped Classroom. Flipped Learning is about more than the videos. It is about the change that takes place during the face-to-face time. Flipped Learning happens when a teacher creates an environment that allows learners to explore content at a higher level, using higher-order thinking skills like "compare", create", and "design" instead of lower order thinking skills like "recall", "summarize", or "describe". Flipped Learning teachers use digital content with *intention*, sharing specific content with learners in their individual learning space and at the appropriate time in their learning cycle. This is why the video is important.

FLIPPED PROFESSIONAL DEVELOPMENT VARIATIONS

Currently, a number of "flipped" professional development models have emerged since "flipped learning" moved into the school environment. Each of the variations was created to enhance an existing professional development setting. Flipped Faculty Meetings provide an easy entry point into flipped learning while Flipped Workshops can provide teachers the opportunity to explore a topic in greater depth. Ultimately, Flipped Professional Coaching has the greatest impact on teachers. But like a flipped classroom, flipped professional development models require many iterations to meet the needs of individuals, schools and districts. If teachers want to change how time is spent with students, they must first begin by changing the way they spend time with colleagues. One of the easiest starting points for exploring flipped learning is to begin thinking about ways you can improve your own learning opportunities.

Flipped Faculty Meetings and Flipped Workshops

Consider faculty meetings, whether they are once a month or once a week. Coming together as a school staff should be positive; a time for collaborating, sharing and celebrating. Teachers should look forward to these meetings and should leave each meeting feeling energized and enthusiastic about the students, their colleagues and the school community. Could monthly faculty meetings look similar to a meeting of camp counselors just before the campers arrive? Can you imagine a meeting packed with energy, enthusiasm, and anticipation? Faculty meetings have traditionally been a time to deliver content. At best, leaders ask staff to follow-up in grade level groups or plan for follow-up with everyone at the next meeting. At worst, educators are expected to implement something to which they were just introduced. Moving back into their classroom and into their daily routine leads to resentment for an ever-growing list of things to tackle in isolation. Traditional faculty meetings perpetuate the idea that teachers work in isolation. Faculty meetings are "flipped" when important information is accessed before the meeting and consequently changes how colleagues spend their time together. The resulting meeting generates energy and momentum throughout the organization.

During a (typical) traditional professional development workshop, the instructor begins by introducing themselves and the topic that they will be talking about. The instructor is clear and concise, sharing information and answering questions about the topic along the way. Some participants are new to the topic, some are familiar and some may not see how it relates to their classroom. The face-to-face time is precious. It is necessary for the instructor to get participants excited and connected with the topic within this time frame. Ideas are presented in creative and impressive ways, showcasing the topic to participants. Teachers are jazzed.

Keep in mind the challenges of traditional professional development already mentioned. What are the outcomes of this type of traditional learning environment? For some, it works just fine. However, to reach all individuals, the challenges of this learning environment need to be minimized, if not removed altogether.

Re-imagine this time. There are two parts. There is the face-to-face time that is precious and sacred. This time should be spent doing things that we cannot do alone. And there is the "flipped" part of this meeting or workshop. What can we do to prepare for this time together? How can we get ourselves ready to maximize our limited time together?

Plan for face-to-face time.

This comes first. There are many reasons why you gather in a group. A typical meeting (faculty or workshop) uses face-to-face time for sharing information. But the real value of face-to-face time is that by being together you have the opportunity to *exchange* (this means two ways) ideas and information, rather than just receive information. Even better, you generate *new* ideas and innovations that would not have been created otherwise. Examine your current meeting structure. Is it necessary to gather together for the items on your agenda? Or could many of these items be shifted into the individual learning space. Can the purpose for gathering together be something more meaningful?

As you plan for this time, continue to ask yourself, "what's the benefit of being together?" And, for now, don't be anxious if you're not sure where to start. Select topics that are relevant to the teachers. Because face-to-face time will not be used for disseminating information, you can have more than one topic being discussed at the meeting. Review helpful team building, decision making and group facilitation strategies. Slowly add activities that allow teachers to engage with one another and explore content at a deeper level.

Face-to-face meetings could give staff the time, space and resources to:
- work in grade level teams to explore specific instructional strategies
- participate in a whole group team building activity
- share innovative projects happening throughout the school
- discuss school issues/policies as a whole group
- work in cross curricular groups to discuss student centered pedagogy
- brainstorm ideas for improving classroom space
- share strategies for shifting the learning culture of the classroom
- discuss best practices for formative and summative assessment
- engage in discussion about classroom management
- organize their own "unconference"

Get teachers excited by letting them PLAY! This time is perfect for modeling new technology tools or classroom strategies with teachers. Let the teachers be engaged in the process, allowing them to experience a student's perspective and then reflect with colleagues. It's important for our teachers to constantly be engaged in professional conversation about the classroom and ultimately, the students.

Don't forget to capture this time together by snapping a few photos or capturing a few minutes of video. Instant upload of the images and video from a mobile device to an online storage site makes sharing these moments at a later time extremely simple.

Prepare materials ahead of time.

The next step is to consider how you could support your face-to-face plans. Think of these three strategies as you build materials for teachers: SHARE—GATHER—CONNECT. What will staff need to do so that they are prepared to spend their time efficiently and engaged in the process? How can you connect your staff with one another before the meeting begins? Here are some common ways to flip your staff learning. Choose one strategy, combine two, or use all three for preparing "flipped" materials.

SHARE—Provide access to the meeting agenda using Google Docs. One step further: Allow staff to create the agenda and edit items, if necessary. Providing access to the agenda increases transparency among staff. Transparency increases trust. Provide links to any resources that will be discussed or referenced during a meeting. By doing this, you will be able to explore content at a deeper level. Tip: Consider the way that information is communicated to staff. Is there a consistent process? Is information archived in a way that makes it easy to retrieve? Do teachers know what is available and where to find it? Go to flippedpd.org/share for an updated list of various tools that can be used to share information with staff before a meeting.

GATHER—Conduct a survey. Collect information prior to the meeting. Use the information to create working groups, spur discussion or determine face-to-face plan. Sometimes meetings will include a brief showcase of instructional strategies or technology tools. Surveys can be helpful in revealing information about staff interest or questions regarding this content. Immediately sharing survey results is one way to connect teachers with one another before the meeting begins. Assess for understanding. If you really want to know what teachers understand about your meeting topic, give them a short assessment using a tool that they might be able to use in their classroom. This modeling is professional development on its own! Teachers will use their experience as a learner to make adjustments to the options they provide for their students. Today, there are many tools and methods for formative assessment. Let your teachers experience this as a student. Tip: Expand your ideas about surveys. Today, there are easy to use tools that allow you to collect feedback from your staff in a variety of ways (text, audio or video). How will this change what you want to ask your staff? Go to flippedpd.org/gather for updated suggestions on useful tools for gathering information as well as unique formative assessment tools.

CONNECT—Begin the conversation using asynchronous communication tools to engage in meaningful conversation on your own time. Pose a question to your staff and then give them some time to begin discussion with one another on the given topic. Track their conversation and add information and comments when needed. Kick it up a notch during the face-to-face time by providing them with a task to complete based on the topic area. Create a task that is dependent on prior knowledge, knowledge that would have been covered in early conversations online. Go to flippedpd.org/connect for an updated list of online tools that you can use with teachers to begin a discussion before meeting face-to-face.

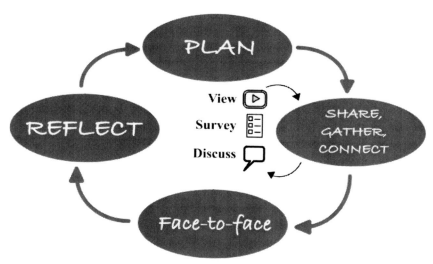

Fig. 1: The Learning Cycle in a Flipped Faculty Meeting and Flipped Workshops

With appropriate digital materials (intentional content) viewed prior to meetings, time can be used to collaborate with colleagues and explore issues at a deeper level.

Let's take a look at the following example of a Flipped PD plan. The Flipped Strategies/Materials can be used alone or in combination with one another.

Topic: Using Classroom Space to Support Student-Centered Instructional Strategies

Flipped Strategy	Flipped Materials
SHARE	Create a video that shows images of a classroom space before and after a classroom makeover. Highlight how changes made to the classroom space minimize pedagogical challenges and support student centered instruction.
GATHER	Have participants draw a map of their current classroom configuration and upload to a shared space. If participants want to share pictures, provide a tool and workflow for them to do so.
CONNECT	Allow participants to respond asynchronously to a discussion prompt: "How does your current classroom space support or hinder a student centered instructional style?"
Face-to-Face Meeting Strategy	Face-to-Face Plan
ENGAGE	If staff uploaded classroom maps, take time during the meeting to talk about 1 or 2 of the maps. Discuss possible changes that could be made to each classroom space to support student centered instructional strategies.
COLLABORATE	Working in grade level teams, have teachers redesign their classroom space to best support a student centered instructional style.

Fig. 2

Download this Flipped Professional Development worksheet from www.flippedpd.org

In the example, the face-to-face time becomes collaborative work time to address an existing issue and use collective knowledge to create a plan that will impact student learning. In a Flipped Faculty Meeting or a Flipped Workshop, the time spent together becomes time for group reflection, collaboration, conversation, discussion, and celebration. Teaching can be a very isolating profession. Do not isolate your teachers during this time. Bring them together. You are building the necessary foundation for creating a community of collaborative learners. Encourage professional discourse and help strengthen their relationships by provided an engaging, meaningful and respectful learning opportunity for them each month. In addition, this will empower teachers to take their experience and create something similar for their students.

After the face-to-face meeting time, plan to provide a "reflection" on the topic. This could be a summary of your collaborative work on the topic or an opportunity for extended exploration for those who are interested. It is important to provide a "next step" in the learning cycle, whether that is an action item or a plan to follow-up at a later time, so that this does not become a one-time event.

Flipped Professional Coaching

Research has shown that teacher quality affects student achievement. It is imperative that we plan to support the professional, lifelong learning of teachers! Therefore, effective professional is critical and cannot be undervalued. More than any other professional development model, coaching increases the implementation rates of learned skills into the classroom. Ultimately, the best professional development that you can provide for teachers is through a coaching model. Coaching is personalized from the start. By embracing the ideas of Flipped Learning and applying them towards professional development, you will be able to use digital content to convey important information and minimize large group face-to-face time, making coaching a feasible model. This is a natural progression of flipped learning. For example, in a flipped classroom, as direct instruction is shifted out of the large group space the teacher naturally moves into more of a coaching role in order to create a more personalized learning environment. But like any professional development model, Flipped Professional Coaching requires structure. Careful consideration of how you will structure face-to-face time, document teacher progress, and utilize digital content is critical to the success of Flipped Professional Coaching. But most of all, just as the flipped classroom demands that students become more responsible for their own learning, Flipped Professional Coaching requires teachers to embrace self-directed learning. This can be the greatest challenge of all and can be accomplished by establishing trusting relationships and a positive culture of lifelong learning.

Flipped Professional Coaching Learning Cycle

The Flipped Professional Coaching learning cycle has very similar components to other varieties of Flipped PD. The first step in this process is for the teacher and coach to meet so that they can explore options, interests, and strengths. Based on this information, and any school or district goals, together the teacher and coach will formulate a personal goal for the teacher. From here, it is the job of the coach to provide resources (digital content, time, technology, coaching, etc.) so that the teacher can implement projects or strategies in their classroom in order to meet their goal. Lastly, teachers should be encouraged to share their stories. Whether their goal was to create a project for students or increase student achievement in a particular area, they should be encouraged to share what they have learned. This information contributes to the common

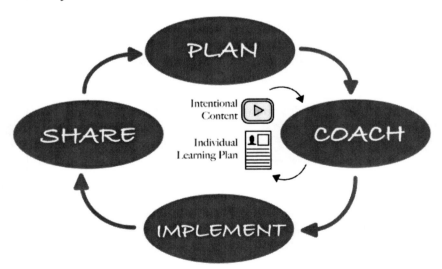

Fig. 3—The Flipped Professional Coaching learning cycle

knowledge of a school or district and can be utilized to move towards common goals and understanding.

Just as there are many teaching strategies, there are many wonderful coaching frameworks available for schools to implement. Regardless of the framework you decide upon, Flipped Professional Coaching provides the advantage of using digital content to share important and customized information with the teacher so that face-to-face time can be used for personalized coaching.

Creating Time for Teachers

Flipped Professional Coaching requires designated small group or individual meeting time for teachers and coaches. It is vital to create consistently scheduled face-to-face meetings with teachers so that teachers can begin to ask questions and have conversation that will help them to reflect on their practice and seek ways to improve their teaching. By providing time and space for natural conversation to occur between a teacher and a coach, opportunities reveal themselves. A perceptive coach will navigate these opportunities and work with the teacher to develop a reasonable goal. Scheduled time provides structure and consistency.

Working with teachers in small groups allows for exploration of personal interests.

Every school will have different opportunities for meeting time. Some common options for one-on-one or small group time include:
- non-student time (before school, after school, prep periods, lunch break, summer break)
- common planning time
- designated PLC time
- create time during the day (rotating sub model)

If you choose to create face-to-face time with teachers during the workday, consider a model that uses rotating substitute teachers to relieve groups of teachers throughout the day so that they can meet with coaches each month. Although group size can be adjusted (affecting the number of subs needed on one day), the model remains the same; bring in substitute teachers to work a rotating schedule, relieving teachers one at a time. For a workshop schedule

Grade	First Name	Last Name	Workshop Day	Workshop Time	Flipped PD ILP
	Workshop Day 1 (9/24, 10/22, 11/12, 1/14, 2/25, 3/25)				
3			1	8:00 AM	https://docs.google.com/
3			1	8:00 AM	https://docs.google.com/
3			1	8:00 AM	https://docs.google.com/
1			1	10:30 AM	https://sites.google.com/
1			1	10:30 AM	https://docs.google.com/
1			1	10:30 AM	https://docs.google.com/
2			1	1:00 PM	https://docs.google.com/
2			1	1:00 PM	https://docs.google.com/
2			1	1:00 PM	https://docs.google.com/
	Workshop Day 2 (9/25, 10/23, 11/13, 1/22, 2/26, 3/26)				
5			2	8:00 AM	https://docs.google.com/
5			2	8:00 AM	https://docs.google.com/
4			2	9:30 AM	https://docs.google.com/
4			2	9:30 AM	https://docs.google.com/
6			2	11:00 AM	https://docs.google.com/
6			2	11:00 AM	https://docs.google.com/
4.5			2	12:30 PM	https://docs.google.com/
4.5			2	12:30 PM	https://docs.google.com/
4.5			2	12:30 PM	https://docs.google.com/
6			2	2:00 PM	https://docs.google.com/
math with me			2	2:00 PM	https://docs.google.com/

Fig. 4—Flipped Professional Coaching Workshop Schedule

with groups of three teachers meeting throughout the day, a building would hire three all day subs for the day.

Figure 4 shows an example of a school that has committed two Flipped PD workshop days each month for six months (September, October, November, January, February and March). Teachers are organized into grade level teams. On Workshop Day 1, teams of three teachers meet with a coach for a two and a half hour block of time. A total of nine teachers are seen on the first day. On Workshop Day 2, the teams of two teachers meet with the coach for an hour and a half. A total of 10 teachers are seen on the second workshop day.

Figure 5 shows another example of a school that has committed two Flipped PD workshop days each month for four months (October, November, January, and March). Teachers are primarily organized into grade level teams with a few exceptions. On Workshop Day 1, two teams of three teachers each meet with a coach for a four hour block of time. The second group of teachers is relieved by the rotating subs and begins their session at 12:00pm. A total of 12 teachers are seen on the first day. Workshop Day 2 is similar to the first day.

Grade	First Name	Last Name	Workshop Day	Workshop Time	FlippedPD ILP
Workshop Day 1 - 6 subs (10/3, 11/8, 1/10, 3/19)					
0			1	8:00 AM	https://docs.google
0			1	8:00 AM	https://docs.google
0			1	8:00 AM	https://docs.google
2			1	8:00 AM	https://docs.google
2			1	8:00 AM	https://docs.google
2			1	8:00 AM	https://docs.google
1			1	12:00 PM	https://docs.google
1			1	12:00 PM	https://docs.google
1			1	12:00 PM	https://docs.google
1			1	12:00 PM	https://docs.google
5			1	12:00 PM	https://docs.google
5			1	12:00 PM	https://docs.google
Workshop Day 2 - 5 subs (10/10, 11/7, 1/15, 3/20)					
3			2	8:00 AM	https://docs.google
3			2	8:00 AM	https://docs.google
3			2	8:00 AM	https://docs.google
3			2	8:00:00	https://docs.google
2nd			2	8:00 AM	https://docs.google
6			2	12:00 PM	https://docs.google
6			2	12:00 PM	https://docs.google
6			2	12:00 PM	https://docs.google
6			2	12:00 PM	https://docs.google
PE			2	12:00 PM	https://docs.google

Fig. 5—Flipped Professional Coaching Workshop Schedule

Document Workshop Resources and Teacher Learning Goals
In the far right column of the Flipped PD schedules (*Figures 4 and 5*) you will see a link to the teachers' Individual Learning Plans. Using Google Docs, an informal Individual Learning Plan (ILP) was created for teachers participating in Flipped PD (find a template at www.flippedpd.org).

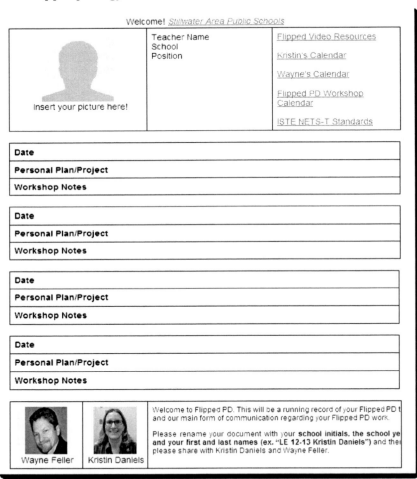

Fig. 6—A Google Doc template for an Individual Learning Plan (ILP) used with teachers in FlippedPD.

Once created, teachers can share their ILP with colleagues, coaches and mentors. The "Flipped PD" document is edited by many and used to record personal goals/plans/projects that the teacher is working on. Workshop notes are entered directly into the document and personalized digital content links are pasted directly into the document for teachers to access at any time. It is important to support teachers throughout their learning cycle by maintaining documentation, providing personalized digital resources, and establishing easy methods for communication. The individual documentation helps hold teachers accountable for the goals that they have set.

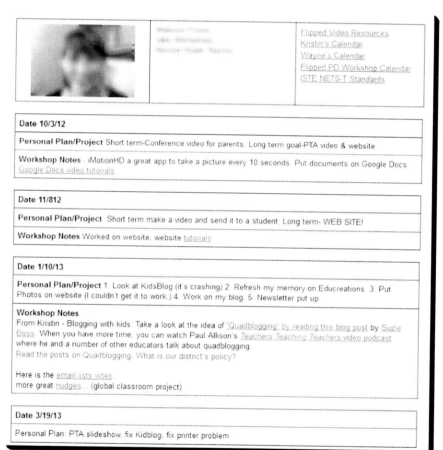

Fig. 7—An individual teacher's ILP. Note the separate workshop dates, the linked video tutorials and links in upper right-hand corner.

Fig. 8—A Coach's Perspective: Teacher Individualized Learning Plans (ILP) in Google Drive.

Creating scheduled follow-up gives them the time and support they need to implement new ideas in the classroom. Carefully prepared professional development plays a critical role at each part of the learning cycle in order to maximize personal professional growth for teachers.

Approaching Video Creation
Video is an engaging way to communicate information. It is becoming extremely easy to create video in order to communicate information; whether the purpose is to provide technical information about technology or to communicate pertinent information before a face-to-face meeting.

Depending on the breadth with which you approach creating videos for professional development, deciding on the tools, workflow, storage and delivery can be overwhelming. It is much easier to start at a personal level and figure out how you as a professional want to use video in your everyday work. Look at the grassroots work of Flipped Learning educators over the last few years. Most flipped learning educators started independently of their colleagues.

Thoughtfulness in the creation and organization of digital content is well worth the effort.

Consider the following:

1. Own your videos. You should have the flexibility to be able to move your videos from one online location to another if you need to. Be cautious about selecting video creation tools. Oftentimes applications will seem simple to use but the only way to view the videos created with their application is through their website and usually there is no way for you to download the videos that you created. Own your videos! It is also a good idea to create a backup copy of video files.
2. Invest in software that has the ability and flexibility to grow and adapt to changing needs. Think about the potential to collaborate with others on your videos and choose tools that would allow this to happen. There is a number of screen recording applications available at a low cost, or even free, (visit www.flippedpd.org for an up to date list) but as your video creation techniques grow you will want to consider tools that will allow you to do more with your videos.
3. Purchase hardware to create quality videos. This includes input tablet devices for annotating your videos and microphones to record clear audio. Audio is one of the most important factors in determining the quality of the video. Investing in dependable recording headsets is important.
4. Decide on a location to host and serve your videos. The main goal is to minimize, if not eliminate altogether, barriers to access. Remember your target audience. There is a good chance that they will be accessing these videos from a variety of locations and devices. Ensure that your videos will be easy to find, stream from a player that has simple navigation controls, and have consistent high-quality streaming capabilities.

PLAN FOR SUCCESS WITH ADULT LEARNERS

Regardless of the model, whether you choose to implement Flipped Faculty Meetings or personalized Flipped Professional Coaching, flipped learning requires intentional content. Digital content is only useful when it is accessible, relevant and timely. And, as teachers are typically very traditional learners, it is vital that you are thoughtful in your plans for utilizing digital content with adults.

Accessible

<u>Establish one location for information</u> and drive your staff there every time you interact with them. Digital content should be accessible through a web-based platform. Consider the computer hardware that teachers have available to them, as well as Internet access throughout their classrooms and schools. Many educators will access content outside of the school day. Therefore, digital content needs to be hosted on a server/platform that is accessible outside of school grounds.

<u>Minimize barriers</u> for teachers who try and access the content. Create easy to remember sub-pages or short links for the website addresses of major landing pages. These "landing pages" should be webpages where you want your teachers to begin to access content, perhaps a login page for a learning management system or a school portal. Once teachers are logged in, it should be very clear where they need to go to access content. Consider the pros and cons of making content public. On one hand, public content requires no password and would be easily accessible by all of your staff. On the other hand, public content limits what you might be able to share. Many schools and districts create content that is specific to district applications, hardware and workflow. These are things you might not want to be made public.

<u>Show your teachers how</u> they can learn through video. Many teachers can benefit from technical tips on how to view a tutorial video, from using the spacebar to start and stop the video (on many video players) to using the full-screen option when viewing the video. Do not underestimate the value of simple instruction.

Relevant

The use of digital content in the learning cycle is one of the most unique aspects of Flipped Learning. Digital content can take many forms and will vary based on the professional development model you choose to implement in your school or district. Over time, your video creation techniques will expand to include different styles and formats. Each video should be created around a specific audience and purpose. Consider the following approach to video creation.

<u>Anticipate a need</u>. Create videos on topic areas that you know your teachers will need. Along with tutorials, showcase real classroom

examples or implementations relating to the topic. Cover the "how to" basics of a variety of topic areas, from curriculum and classroom management to technology tools available in the district. These videos will be the foundation of your video library but you will continually add more videos as new strategies, tools or processes are adopted.

React to a need. Create videos for a specific purpose or need that arises in your conversations with teachers. For example, a teacher needs help getting students the necessary information on technology tools or processes in order to ensure success for a specific project. Step up and make that video. These videos can ensure the success of a project. Perhaps another teacher is interested in a specific instructional strategy to implement in the classroom. By reacting to that teacher's immediate need, you are able to provide intentional content for the teacher. The timing of the instruction, as well as a follow-up visit with a coach or mentor can increase the likelihood of successful transfer of the learned skill into the classroom.

Celebrate success. Do not be afraid to capture a moment that you think could impact others. You probably have between 2-4 cameras on you at any one time (phone, iPad, computer, etc.). Document important information and classroom moments that are shared by your teachers. Turn these source files into inspirational videos for sharing best practices and for celebrating both teacher and student success. Celebration videos can include interviews, classroom projects, student work, and teacher conversations.

Be specific. It doesn't cost anything to capture and view digital film, and images can easily be deleted. So expand your reasons for creating a video to include short and simple directions or guidance for an audience of one. That's right. In the past, the cost of capturing and editing video prohibited us from even considering a video for just one person. We would aim to create videos that could be seen by anyone. Individual videos are created for one person in order to share information. This is especially helpful for individual professional coaching. Use simple, non-editable screen capture tools for quick and easy video creation that you can upload to a server and share with a link.

Timely

Teachers are busy, busy, busy. Unless they intentionally set time aside for self-directed professional development, you have another challenge of providing them with digestible morsels of meaningful information at the right time. When implementing Flipped Professional Development, you are asking teachers to extend the traditional experience to include self-directed learning. This is an area where teachers will need to be encouraged.

No matter what variety of Flipped PD that you choose to implement, consistency is important when it comes to content delivery. Since your flipped materials are important to the success of your face-to-face time, you must establish a method that is effective. This means that your content will not get lost in an email shuffle and teachers know how to access your materials. Decide upon a reasonable timeline for viewing the flipped materials, whether you send an email with the link to digital content, establish a web location that is updated on a regular basis, or both!

THE IMPORTANCE OF TRUSTING RELATIONSHIPS

The more you get to know your teachers, the more you will understand what they need.

Flipped Learning is about the relationships between the coaches and the staff. Flipped learning requires this because the relationship between teacher and student is so important to both roles. As a coach, it's my obligation to listen to the teacher. Not only to gather clues for skill level, but also interests which lead to opportunity. In workshop settings in the Flipped Professional Coaching model, much time is spent in conversation, negotiating plans and planning for timely delivery of resources, whether the resources are for inspiration, learning, sharing or brainstorming. This is valuable time. Sharing stories of both success and failure will help teachers embrace a culture of learning, leading them to take risks and push towards innovation.

Teachers Are Courageous.

Model courageousness for students and teachers.

- **Raise your expectations for the culture of learning that you deserve as a professional.** If you are traditional in your own learning, you will most likely create a classroom culture of traditional learning. Do not be afraid of a non-traditional approach to learning.
- **Create your own professional learning network.** Connect with others around the world, making sure to follow individuals who have opinions different from yours. Engage in professional conversation. Expand your ideas.
- **Be courageous in improving your own professional practice.** Participate in innovative teaching and learning practices for your own learning. Seek out new ideas from colleagues in your personal learning network. Be open to constructive feedback.

Years from now, educators will look back at this time and acknowledge the transition we were in when it comes to realizing the impact that video content could have in the school system. One of the most important parts of learning is the relationships between students and teachers, or teachers and professional colleagues or coaches. When we are a part of trusting relationships we become more invested and dedicate ourselves to our professional work and commit to growing for the good of the organization. The relationships that are created in a Flipped Learning environment are one of the biggest benefits of Flipped Learning.

Kristin Daniels is a former middle school science teacher who transitioned into a technology integration role after eight years in the classroom. Her passions are collaboration and innovation in the hopes of helping teachers to shift their thinking towards creating more student-centered classrooms and schools. She is currently a board member of the Flipped Learning Network, a non-profit organization created to provide educators with the resources they need to implement a flipped learning environment in their classroom. Find her on Twitter @kadaniels or email her at kadaniels@gmail.com.

Technology for Teachers
Cory Peppler

Even the most tech-savvy among us knows how easily technology can frustrate us, turning a lesson with great potential into a migraine-inducing waste of time. Sadly, some will use this possibility as the excuse to avoid using technology altogether in their class and practice. We all know of colleagues who are so hesitant to use the available tools that they insist technology has a personal grudge against them.

As a classroom teacher and again as a technology coach, I've have seen far more teachers successfully infuse technology into their classroom and improve their students' learning than I have seen it blow up in a teacher's face. To be sure, transforming a lesson or unit—or an entire year—with technology is risky. However, by taking some of the following steps, you can minimize risk and increase your comfort level as you continue to transform your classroom.

USE THE TOOL YOURSELF

Before launching a tool in class, sign up and use it the way it's supposed to be used. (Don't worry; you'll push it past its limits when you bring it into the classroom. Right now, you are just getting familiar.) This is primarily why I signed up for Facebook so many years ago. I knew students were starting to use it, and I wanted to know why. I also wanted to know if it was presenting any potential problems/risks for my students. It also gives me a little more credibility when I do have to caution them about something ("Hey, kids, did you notice that Facebook just changed their privacy settings...again. You might want to turn off blah, blah, blah...")

Don't limit yourself to using the tool in an "educational" way, either. Many of the tools Flipping teachers and other tech-infusers use were not specifically designed for the classroom. When I first heard about VoiceThread and thought I might try it in my class one day, I created an account, created my first VoiceThread with some current pictures

313

of my own children, and some voiceover stories about them, and sent it to our parents. I gave them some basic instructions for logging in and commenting. Not only did I learn about where I needed to be explicit in my instructions (there were a number of emails back and forth), but I have a cool little video with all our family's voices on it from when my kids were younger. (Good thing, considering how little I've actually used that video camera Mom bought me...)

More recently, I've had gone through a similar process with Google Hangout. Though I immediately saw the potential as a teaching and connection tool, I wasn't going to set up a Hangout with an author and an entire library full of students just yet. My first Hangouts were with my sister and nieces. After that, I tried with a couple of colleagues, where our awkward trial runs often turned into goofy sessions with pirate hats and snorkels.

Besides just being fun, and increasing your own confidence with a tool (before pretending to be the expert in front of a class...more on that error later), this kind of personal experimentation allows you to see the power of the tool and the way it transforms your own communication or learning. It creates a sense of buy-in that will later keep you moving through minor glitches during implementation. A sense of stick-to-it-iveness that will remind you *"yes, this is not going perfectly yet, but it is worth it because I know how powerful this is going to be for my students."*

CREATE A STUDENT ACCOUNT

Does this sound at all familiar? You have worked with a tool, particularly a nice one for education (Edmodo, Schoology, Moodle, for example), and you are ready to start using it to deliver content and get feedback from students. You feel comfortable with the tool and have spent many hours learning its ins-and-outs, and really trying to leverage all its features. You are a pro at this. The day after you get all your kids signed up and signed in, and the first video or online activity is assigned, you are met at the door the next morning by thirty panicky kids saying they couldn't access/download/ upload/view/take the quiz/click on the links/see the assignment/... well, you've been there.

After a few of these gaffs, I started making it a habit of creating a student account right away. (My eldest son has more accounts online than he has a clue about.) I make sure to make this a *completely separate* account, even creating a separate Gmail account to use, if it asks me for an email. After creating content, I log in as him, and pay special attention to what he *can't* do. What doesn't a student have access to? How does the main menu look different? Do they have to download a file by clicking in a different spot? The point here is to prevent all assumptions by asking how students are going to see and interact with the tool *differently* than I will as a teacher.

CREATE A TESTING TEAM

One of the struggles that many flipping teachers quickly run into is creating video content that all students can view on any device in any setting. The answer to this problem is simple: You can't. Until video and video players and plug-ins and codecs (whatever the heck those are) are all the same (like .jpeg for photos?), the best we can do is test it out.

This is a similar challenge that we faced for a while with some students having Macs and not being able to open our Word docs, for example. First, we figured out that everything had to be saved into a PDF to create a consistent accessibility. Then, the software began catching up, recognizing a variety of other formats and often eliminating this problem altogether.

To minimize this compatibility issue with our video content, one suggestion is to create a testing "team" of people (including students) who are savvy enough to know their own systems and to know how to troubleshoot a little. If you are using a PC, for example, you can determine if the video runs in Chrome, Internet Explorer, and Firefox. But that's when you are logged in as you, on your machine, in your environment (your classroom, on your school's wireless, perhaps?)

To test this as fully as possible, you'll need to consider the following:

- Student vs. Teacher log in (in your building)
- PC vs. Mac
- Different browsers
- In the building vs. out of the building (public Wi-Fi or home)
- Mobile devices (Chromebooks, iOS vs. Android, even iPads vs. iPhones)

This may sound like a lot of work, but there are fortunately two things in your favor. First, many have already done this. So, if you know you are creating your video content with Camtasia, saving it locally, then uploading it to a YouTube channel, most likely someone else has done that and done some of the troubleshooting/glitch-finding already. Do a Google search for your specific tools and situations to see what's been done.

Secondly, you likely only have to do this for the first one. Once you've decided you'd like to create all your videos in iMovie, upload them all to Vimeo, and embed them in Edmodo, test a video with your test team, and you should be good to go for a while.

SHOOT QUALITY VIDEO LIKE A PRO

As you've read in previous chapters, no one expects a teacher's original video content (a demonstration, a mini-lecture, a lab experiment) to be professional-quality. Most of us don't have access to much more than the very basics of video equipment and software. However, you can achieve much better results by keeping just a few things in mind as you prepare and shoot your video.

Camera Movement

Obvious as it may sound, mounting the camera on a tripod or bracing it carefully creates a much easier-on-the-eyes video. If you have to move during the 'shoot', move slowly and steadily in a straight line (whether vertically or horizontally). Remember that this high-quality video may be compressed, which makes jerky original footage into *really* jerky thumbnail-size mobile device viewing.

Lighting Placement

Unless you are going for a dramatic silhouette, avoid backlit situations and pay attention to where the bright windows are when setting up the camera. While you don't need expensive studio lighting, you should try to create a "three-point" lighting setup. This consists of a "key light" (the strongest one) off to the side and hitting you at a roughly 45 degree angle. The "fill light" is a weaker light or reflector (or even a window with a translucent drape) coming from the other side. Often a "backlight" is used to separate the subject from the background. If you want to see a demonstration of this, search *three-point lighting* on Wikipedia.

Light Quality

With lighting, also consider the harshness or softness of the light. A bare bulb cast a lot of light, but it's pretty harsh, casting distinct shadow (and highlighting wrinkles!) A light with a shade, or a diffuser (a piece of fabric hanging in front of the bulb) or a light bounced off a white wall all create a softer, more pleasing light.

Background

A plain white brick wall might not provide any distracting elements while students are watching you, but it's also pretty boring. Depending on what you are teaching and your setting, a bookshelf, an equipment cabinet, or some furniture all provide a more natural setting. You want to strike a balance here between bland and distracting.

As a photographer, I've also learned the value of paying attention to the background. While shooting some shots of my friend and her family, I had turned all my attention to my subjects and their poses while snapping away. Only later did I realize that one of my best shots, which was taken in front of a large oak, created the impression of a significant branch growing directly out of her husband's head.

Sound

While you don't need to invest a small fortune in lighting, you may want to pick up a decent microphone that plugs into the camera (wireless lapel mics are even better, but get your credit cards ready.) Even a decent "shotgun" mic attached to the camcorder will improve the sound greatly. Of course, if all you have is a Flip camera, or your phone, you can get some very decent sound if you control your environment.

If you are at school, watch the clock for bells or regular announcements. If you are home, wait until the kids are asleep, or the evening train has gone by, or they dryer buzzer has buzzed. Be aware of all the sounds *you* make when you are shooting, too. Rustling clothes or jewelry, adjusting things on the table that also holds your laptop, or moving the microphone all create unwanted, distracting sounds. One of the sounds that I try to minimize the most (because it bugs me the most) is keyboard clicking when I'm screencasting a tutorial. I try to use the keyboard as little and as quietly as I can. You find out just how LOUDLY you type when you do your first screencast.

One last thought about shooting like a pro, don't be intimidated by all this. You are not creating a studio-quality production and no one is expecting you to. As a matter of fact, students often comment that they like seeing the teacher's home office in the background or having the teacher's four-year-old run in to say good night to daddy. You don't need perfect, you just need to make sure the students can see you and hear you clearly. The rest, especially at first, can be rough around the edges.

TAKE IT EASY

If you've never flipped your class before, start by taking the pressure off. It's not going to be perfect. Listen to the advice many flipping teachers received (from Bergmann and Sams) when they started: *"Do you want it perfect, or do you want it Tuesday?"* If it's easier, start by simply recording your lesson/lecture/discussion in class and posting an unedited clip. If you don't want to try filming yourself, then start with just a screencast of you annotating a PowerPoint slideshow for your students. Eventually, you'll want to create a more polished blend of you talking to the camera and you demonstrating what you are explaining. Isn't this how most cooking shows are put together?

Also, don't over-rehearse. Really. How many times do you rehearse your lectures before you walk into class at 7:45 and deliver it to your 1st period class? Exactly. Students will generally receive it better if it seems more like you are just talking to them. Sure, use notes or a teleprompter app for your iPad sitting nearby, but don't let the student lose your personality as a teacher.

The best advice I've ever heard regarding the infusion of any technology into your classroom? Start small—advice that is just as applicable to the flipped classroom. Don't try to create 30-minute lessons (will students watch these anyway?) Shoot for five-minute mini-lessons, or very specific demonstrations, or one clear and succinct definition each in a series of one-minute videos. Try flipping with just one class for a quarter or semester. Take notes, be reflective, adjust and improve as you go.

In this book, you've heard the stories of many successful flipped class teachers. Most of them began in small ways transforming their instruction. They all hit snags, and struggled with some of the technology. They ignored naysayers, convinced administrators, and encouraged students because they knew that this shift would transform their classroom into a more student-centered, personalized, relevant learning experience. They connected, reflected, and perfected as they went. They quickly passed the point where the flipped classroom went from being a "technology" thing to a "learning" thing. They charted a course, launched the ships, and flipped their class.

And so will you.

Cory Peppler taught high school English and history before becoming the technology integrator and library media specialist at Muskego High School in Muskego, WI. A presenter at numerous conferences, and a freelance writer and photographer, he also served as the copy and layout editor for this book. He can be contacted at mrpeppler@gmail.com or found on Twitter @pepteach.

Explanatory

These chapters include many, *many* references to websites, tools, mobile apps, and their associated companies. While most of them are trademarked names, we did not wish to plague our readers with a plethora of ™ symbols throughout. All such names are the sole property of their respective companies, and are referenced here only because they have been of value to the teacher-authors who mention them.

Though we have included many links, it is the nature of the Internet to change. We have made every effort to ensure that all links are correct and active. In addition, educational technology companies are always updating and improving their services (and/or going out of business), so please realize that while all information is accurate at the time of publication, what you actually experience may change from its original description.

CPSIA information can be obtained at www.ICGtesting.com
Printed in the USA
BVOW04s2210230414

351573BV00011B/109/P